Tourism for Sustainable Economic Development

S. B. Agarwal

Reference Press

4831/24, Ansari Road
Darya Ganj
New Delhi-110 002
Phone: 3260807
Fax: 3274173
E-mail: essess@del3.vsnl.net.in

First Published 2003

ISBN: 81-88583-00-6

Price: Rs.675/-

Published by:
Reference Press
4831/24, Ansari Road,
Darya Ganj,
New Delhi-110 002.
Phone: 3260807
Fax: 3274173
E-mail: essess@del3.vsnl.net.in

Printed in India by:
Mehra Offset Press

Contents

Preface

As expressed by the World Tourism Organisation, tourism is ambivalent. It can contribute positively to socioeconomic and cultural achievements, while at the same time it may cause the degradation of environment and the loss of local identity. Tourism growth coincides with the destination's prevailing value system and cultural integrity, and satisfy the needs of its local population. It has been argued by some authors that tourism should lend itself to the concept of sustainable development because, in so many cases, tourism growth is dependent upon maintenance of the natural environment and natural processes for its own survival.

Tourism's multifaceted function, as a socioeconomic and politico-cultural phenomenon, as a complex industry, and as a profession having its own rules and code of ethics, requires a broad intellectual background and specialized education and/or training to enable its policy makers and professionals to keep abreast of the scientific and technological changes. If we just think of the various organizational, marketing planning and technical aspects of tourism, we must realize how complex round tourism development is.

As all socioeconomic, cultural, political and environmental factors and subject to change in time and space, sustainability is therefore a relative term and not an absolute fact. Markets, fashions, tastes, motivations, images, trends and destinations are all likely to change, at least in the long term. Thus tourism has to be humane and adaptive to the needs of the tourists, responsive to the needs of local communities, socioeconomically and culturally well planned, and environmentally sound. The difficulty is to determine how tourism can protect and enhance opportunities for future generations of tourists and host communities while change continues to prevail. This is the challenge that tourism sustainability has to face and surmount. Such challenge manifests itself in evolving tourist behavioural patterns and forms, progress in host community attitudes towards tourism, and change in technology and marketing opportunities.

This book focuses on all aspects of tourism development viz., economic, social, cultural and overall recreational. It has been prepared with the aim that it could provide in detail the possible ways and means for sustainable development of tourism and addresses itself to a much wider audience, particularly those involved in the planning and management of tourism industry at different levels.

1 Introduction

As expressed by the World Tourism Organisation, tourism is ambivalent. It can contribute positively to socioeconomic and cultural achievements, while at the same time it may cause the degradation of environment and the loss of local identity. Tourism growth coincides with the destination's prevailing value system and cultural integrity, and satisfy the needs of its local population. It has been argued by some authors that tourism should lend itself to the concept of sustainable development because, in so many cases, tourism growth is dependent upon maintenance of the natural environment and natural processes for its own survival.

Tourism is no longer a soft option. On the contrary, due to multiple variables intervening, it is becoming a rather complicated developmental sector which requires expertise and professionalism. Tourism's multifaceted function, as a socioeconomic and politico-cultural phenomenon, as a complex industry, and as a profession having its own rules and code of ethics, requires a broad intellectual background and specialized education and/or training to enable its policy makers and professionals to keep abreast of the scientific and technological changes. If we just think of the various organizational, marketing planning and technical aspects of tourism, we must realize how complex round tourism development is.

The old classical approach to tourism problem-solving through day-to-day tactics can no longer hold good in the face of a rapidly growing and swiftly changing world tourism industry. While tourism has become increasingly appreciated as a contributor to he national economics of some leading tourist destinations, lack of sufficient information about the scope and essence of that activity as well as of the processes linked to it are still widespread. It is important, however, to ask what alternative forms of tourism prove to be sustainable and which do not. Some forms of tourism are considered by some writers as sustainable, such as ecotourism and special interest tourism, although as yet no empirical research has proved such claims.

The crucial question in this connection is whether tourism sustainability, at least within the narrow confines of some alternative tourism forms, could be a reality. The answer to the above question is positive. Yes, tourism sustainability could be a reality. It is the by-product of a multitude of factors that contribute to the successful present integration and future continuity of tourism it the macro and micro levels in destinations.

As all socioeconomic, cultural, political and environmental factors and subject to change in time and space, sustainability is therefore a relative term and not an absolute fact. Markets, fashions, tastes, motivations, images, trends and destinations are all likely to change, at least in the long term. Thus tourism has to be humane and adaptive to the needs of the tourists, responsive to the needs of local communities, socioeconomically and culturally well planned, and environmentally sound. The difficulty is to determine how tourism can protect and enhance opportunities for future generations of tourists and host communities while change continues to prevail. This is the challenge that tourism sustainability has to face and surmount. Such challenge manifests itself in evolving tourist behavioural patterns and forms, progress in host community attitudes towards tourism, and change in technology and marketing opportunities.

Tourism must offer products that are operated in harmony with the local environment, community attitudes and cultures, so that these become the permanent beneficiaries and not the victims of tourism development. Sustainability here does not necessarily mean that tourism maintains its viability in an area for an indefinite length of time, but that it continues to be viable for future generations for a reasonably long time. The term 'sustainability', which has gained prominence in tourism jargon, is seen by many writers as an important part of the philosophy permeating all levels of tourism policy issues and practice from national to local. Others understand sustainability as a deep-rooted concept that relates to the fundamentals of life which sometimes are obscured by the ongoing public/private debate, regulation and rationalized government intervention.

Needless to say sustainable development and management of tourism resources should coincide with economic, sociocultural, health, safety and environmental objectives at national, regional and local levels. The United Nations Environmental Programme (UNEP) adopted a definition of sustainable development as follows:

> Sustainable development is improving the quality of human life while living within the carrying capacity of supporting ecosystems... If an activity is sustainable, for all practical purposes it can continue forever.

The World Tourism Organisation (WTO) defined sustainable tourism development as that which meets the needs of present tourists and host regions while protecting and enhancing opportunity for the future. It is envisaged as leading to the management of all resources in such a way that economic, social and aesthetic needs can be fulfilled while maintaining cultural integrity, essential ecological processes, biological diversity and life support systems.

Tourism in the twenty-first century must anticipate a future marked by changing global relationships and societal structures, technological innovations, and growing spatial awareness and environmental concern. Major shifts in the nature and scale of tourism are already in evidence as the industry struggles to respond to a range of forces at work. Change and the change agents involved are powerful and positive forces if harnessed constructively. Rather than opposing change, or merely accepting and accommodating change, the tourism industry must manage change to its advantage and that of the environment which nurtures it.

Endorsement and application of the concept of sustainability and of best practice environmental management offer compelling evidence of how change can be harnessed to contribute towards the achievement of environmental excellence. Although tourism flourishes best in conditions of peace, prosperity, freedom and security, disturbance to these conditions is to be expected. The industry response must be sufficiently resilient to generate opportunities for the growth of tourism in keeping with the dynamics of a changing world and increasing concern for ecologically sustainable development.

Since the Earth Summit held in Rio de Janeiro in 1992, pressure has grown for the tourism industry to lift its environmental performance in common with other economic sectors, and to work towards ecologically sustainable forms of tourism development. At the same time, planners and developers seeking to create satisfying settings for tourists into the next century must anticipate a world influenced by a new and bewildering array of forces, many of which are difficult to predict. Given such uncertainty, the challenge is to pursue tourism growth in a manner resilient enough to respond positively to a changing global environment and societal structure, while remaining compatible with the principles and practice of ecologically sustainable development.

The era of environmental concern ushered in by the World Conservation Strategy and the Brundtland Commission in the 1980s was given renewed impetus following the Rio Summit and the adoption of Agenda 21. Most governments ground the world have now committed themselves to ecologically sustainable development in a wide range of Policy areas.

The concept of sustainability expresses the idea that humankind must live within the capacity of the environment to support it. Sustainable development is that which meets the needs of the present without compromising the ability of future generations to meet their own needs. It is difficult to argue with such a desirable, if somewhat fuzzy approach. However, it becomes more meaningful when supplemented by more specific objectives and guiding principles. These have been articulated by any number of national and international agencies and organizations, and typically embrace components of

— conservation and enhancement of ecological processes
— protection of biological diversity
— equity within and between generations
— integration of environmental, social and economic considerations.

If this all sounds familiar, it is not surprising. Indeed, the concept of ecologically sustainable development has been challenged as merely a reworking of long-standing philosophies about conservation and stewardship of resources for the future. What is new is the widespread endorsement of the concept and the incorporation of a proactive environmental dimension into corporate planning and management. Sustainability implies a fresh approach to planning and a renewed commitment to use resources within the capacity of the environment to sustain such use. Support for ecologically sustainable development is now emerging strongly in the tourism sector, as the logical way of balancing environmental concern with growth and development of the industry.

Tourism is reputed to be the world's largest economic sector, and one with a vested interest in the environment and the resource base on which it depends. The environment considered here in the broad sense as encompassing socioeconomic and cultural phenomena as well as biophysical elements, represents both a resource and an opportunity for tourism, as well as a potential constraint on the manner of its development.

Ideal tourism settings grow out of complementary natural features and 18 compatible social processes. More often than not, however, tourism in today's world finds it necessary to manipulate and modify the environment to suit its purpose. The consequences are not always predictable. Tourism certainly can contribute to environmental degradation and be self-destructive; it also has potential to bring about significant enhancement of the environment. With tourism-induced change, an Important issue, for example, is irreversibility, which in part is a function of the resilience of the resource base, along with the spatial and temporal pattern of impacts, and the scope for compensatory managerial response.

An influential conference held in Canada on 'Global opportunities for business and the environment' concluded that sustainable development holds considerable promise as a vehicle for addressing the problems of modern tourism. Clearly, what seems to be occur ring is recognition of the interdependence between environmental and economic issues and policies, and ultimately, acceptance of the notion that sound environmental management in tourism does not merely cost, it pays.

Of course, convincing decision makers of the good sense, both environmentally and commercially, of the merits of a sustainable approach to tourism may not be easy. It can be difficult to demonstrate conclusively the costs over time of environmental degradation, especially when set against the more immediate returns forgone by adopting a more restrained pattern of development. However, some significant initiatives are being pursued, and several of these are detailed in a 'Casebook of best environmental practice in tourism'.

The tourism industry of the 1990s is showing commendable preparedness to apply the principles of best practice environmental management to its activities, especially at the largerscale, corporate level.

If the process of achieving sustainable forms of development in a growing tourism industry is a formidable challenge, the task takes on additional dimensions when set against the many forces for change facing the industry as it moves into the next century. New spatial forms and settings must be anticipated as tourist developers seek to service a diverse and expanding array of interests and opportunities. Tourism can be a very volatile industry, sensitive to changes in perception and taste, and to altered biophysical, economic or political circumstances. Thus the theme of change is constant on the tourism scene. In a business sense, the professional component of tourism is constrained to keep abreast of change, and be aware of, and respond to (if not articulate) changes in travel preferences, in technology, and in the many factors which help fashion 19 the travel market. A danger is that in these circumstances, sustainability may only be pursued in a financial or business management context. Ecologically sustainable tourism development may be seen as too expensive and irrelevant to business success. Much research interest focuses on the responses of tourists and tourism to changing socioeconomic circumstances, to political., cultural and attitudinal changes to improvements in spatial awareness and communication, and to growing environmental concern for sustainability.

The potential implications for tourism of these influences, in particular, the way they appear to have intensified in the 1990s, have been stressed by Ritchie:

> the dramatic political changes that have occurred in recent years are only manifestations of more deep-seated social and cultural transformations which reflect changes in human priorities concerning the way the populations of the world wish to live. Tourism, as a phenomenon, is clearly affected as much and perhaps more by these changes as any other sector.

Tourism certainly is a highly sensitive and vulnerable activity and it is not without reason that tourists have been described as 'shy birds', who can be scared off by any number of real or perceived threats to safety, health and property, or financial wellbeing. Tourism shares with recreation generally, attributes of voluntary, discretionary behaviour. People are free to choose to become tourists and to decide location, timing, duration, mode of travel, activities and costs to be incurred. Any one of these attributes may be modified or dispensed with by unforeseen or uncontrollable factors. Moreover, the process of choice is imperceptibly influenced by pervasive adjustments to life-style, social mores, traditions and culture. The more environmentally aware tourist of the future may well opt for,

and even demand, evidence of a commitment to sustainable forms of tourism. Changes impinging upon the nature and scale of tourism in the modern world may be categorized as geopolitical, socioeconomic, technological and environmental. Some comments follow on each of these categories and how their influence may lead to fluctuations in the patterns and characteristics of world tourism. In a world marked by multiplicity of change agents, the challenge of achieving tourism growth in a sustainable manner becomes an even greater concern.

Some of the most dramatic events to impact on tourism have occurred in the political geography of the planet. The 1990s have seen great changes in Europe, the Middle East, Africa and Asia. Strong efforts will be necessary to ensure that the opportunities for tourism created by these changes are not ephemeral, but long-term and sustainable. The freeing-up of access to the countries of Central and Eastern Europe following the collapse of the Soviet Union, the removal of the Berlin Wall and the reunification of Germany is a case in point. Moreover, the process of change is multifaceted and ongoing. For example, internecine conflict in Chechnya and other enclaves continues to threaten what internal stability remains in the former Soviet Union. At the same time, evolving political and economical philosophies are altering the character and cohesiveness of Russian society, Meanwhile, civil strife following the breakup of Yugoslavia continues to overshadow tourism in the Balkans and along the Adriatic Coast.

Outcomes for this region as a tourist destination must remain speculative, with the balance tending towards a more positive and sustained trend in tourism flows in the future. In the process, opportunistic exploitation of speculative tourism ventures should be avoided in the interests of longer term programmes of sustainable development. Further west, the

European Community is pushing steadily towards a common currency and relaxation of controls on visitors between member states. Again, these moves should provide a boost to tourism, which should become more pronounced following the opening of the Channel Tunnel.

The changed geopolitical situation in the Middle East offers some of the most convincing evidence of how tourism can react to perceived threats to security and safety and yet subsequently recover. Beirut and Lebanon, now relatively free from hostilities, are reemerging as prime tourist destinations in the Eastern Mediterranean. Fine hotels, once pockmarked or reduced to rubble, are being rebuilt as foreign investment sees an opportunity to restore this area to its former importance for tourism. Similarly, the prospects of peace between Israel and neighbouring states present further opportunities to boost tourism in the region. As the horror of the Gulf War and repression in Iraq and Iran fade, these nations too should share in this resurgence. Situations can change rapidly but the peace momentum promises new freedom of travel within the Middle East, and with it an upsurge in tourist flows. This new beginning brings with it not only the promise of financial recovery, but also the opportunity to develop the region's tourist potential in a more sustainable manner.

One of the most striking examples of geopolitical influence on a country's fluctuating tourism fortunes is Egypt. The much publicized attacks on tourists by militant groups of Islamic fundamentalists led to a catastrophic drop in numbers of western tourists in the 1990s. Even visitors from Britain, traditionally the largest group from the West, showed a 17 per cent decline in arrivals in Egypt in 1994. It is estimated that the country has lost some US$2 billion in tourist earnings since the attacks began, although these were largely confined to Upper Egypt. Whereas tourist reaction to safety concerns is a matter of perception, the threat should not be overstated. It should be emphasized that since 1992, over seven million tourists have visited Egypt and only seven have been killed in terrorist attacks.

Much of the loss to Egyptian tourism has been at the lower end of' the market in package tours. One of the most important groups financially, Arab tourists from the Gulf States, has scarcely been affected. Egyptian tourism also stands to gain further from the 'outbreak of peace' in the Middle East. With the opening of international borders, tourism is now being promoted in the 'Red Sea Riviera' embracing Sinai (Egypt), Eilat (Israel) and Aqaba (Jordan) in close proximity. Egypt is making strenuous efforts to counter recent setbacks and broaden its appeal to tourists beyond the archaeological heritage of the Nile Valley, while at the same time pursuing the goal of sustainability in a demanding environment. Sub-Saharan Africa too has seen far-reaching changes to political circumstances which are reflected in fluctuations in tourism activity. Rwanda, once known as the 'Switzerland of Africa', has been effectively removed from the tourist scene by civil strife, while instability in several other nation states is hardly conducive to attracting tourists. In many instances fears over personal safety are heightened by health risks and exposure to disease.

On the positive side, Zimbabwe, Botswana and Namibia are being rediscovered as destinations for ecotourism. Further south, the ending of apartheid and the emergence of majority rule in South Africa promise a new era for tourism in that region, and an opportunity to learn from the mistakes and successes elsewhere in implementing sustainable development. South and East Asia complete the picture of significant restructuring of the tourism scene in a large part of the globe. Geopolitical change is again in evidence. The opening-up of

China to the world is reflected in impressive flows of tourists. From the openly commercial ports of Hong Kong and southeast China to the Silk Road of the interior, China is promoting new tourism destinations and experiences.

For the period 1985-92, China recorded the fastest annual growth in arrivals worldwide of almost 13 per cent. Outbound tourism from China must await further relaxation of travel restrictions, and the cessation of British rule in Hong Kong in 1997, which may act as a catalyst in the transition. Reports suggest, however, that environmental concerns may come second to economic gains in the expansion of tourism.

The countries of South-East Asia are generating substantially increased tourist flows. In 1993, East Asia and the Pacific was the fastest growing tourist region, with Australia emerging as the destination of choice. Australia expects to see more than two million visitors from South East Asian countries by the year 2000, with another half-million from japan. South Koreans have rapidly become one of the leading tourist groups in the Pacific, along with Taiwan and Singapore.

The remarkable turnaround in attitudes towards Vietnam is also symptomatic of the changes occurring in the region. Whereas some twenty years ago the only visitors to Vietnam 22 were military, the country is now actively encouraging and catering for an influx of tourists. Global geopolitics can work negatively and positively for the develop merit of tourism. Changed geopolitical circumstances can present an opportunity to redirect the growth of tourism down the path towards sustainability, while at the same time contributing to reconstruction of devascated economics, shattered societies and degraded environments.

It is not necessary to go further than the most recent global recession to trace the impact which an economic downturn can have on tourism. Tourist flows worldwide experienced severe decline in the early 1990s as discretionary incomes fell and unemployment rose. Economic recovery has been slow and patchy, matched by a positive, if hesitant, response in tourist activity, and regional contrasts in a return to previous levels. The shock of economic recession and subsequent restructuring of national economics helped focus renewed attention on the longer-term potential of tourism for boosting economic activity and employment. Butler remarks that reductions in public sector expenditure which have accompanied widespread economic restructuring, have prompted governments to encourage private sector investment in tourism projects, either separately or as joint ventures.

Construction and operation of casinos in several Australian states are examples. Societal changes normally do not exhibit the same cyclical characteristics as those of an economic nature. Rather, they are evolutionary and cumulative, and sometimes almost imperceptible. Ageing of western populations has been accompanied by a measure of affluence, increased unobligated time, and the desire to remain active, among older age groups. It is no longer unusual to find 'elderly' people undertaking strenuous tours, uninhibited by the misperceptions, restrictions and taboos of a time past.

At the other end of the demographic spectrum it is becoming common place for younger, unaccompanied people to enter the tourist flows. Youth tourism, stimulated by a range of motives and underpinned again by 'free' time, energy, a spirit of adventure, and perhaps restrained expectations, is a growing segment of the tourism market. Changes in attitudes to marriage and family, to gender, sex and racial discrimination, are additional forces helping to fashion the tourism of the 1990s. Whereas socioeconomic fluctuations can create difficulties for the tourism sector, those same societal changes and economic adjustments can lead to a more discerning tourism clientele. A greater role for communities in tourism developments and more searching scrutiny of tourism proposals should help achieve the objective of sustainability.

Technology is a powerful influence on modern tourism. Technological break throughs can change the sustainability status of a tourism business or destination overnight, but they can also offer effective means towards long term sustainability in an ecological sense. Tourism, as with many other sectors of the economy, has experienced the shock of technological change. Improvements in transport and communications have decreased the friction of distance and made the greater part of the globe accessible.

The advent of long-distance, large-capacity aircraft, has made mass tourism a reality at the international scale, and with it the capacity to make or break intermediate points oil air routes. Airlines crossing the Pacific now routinely overfly Nadi Airport in Fiji with detrimental effects on the economy of the Islands. Honolulu is frequently bypassed by long-range aircraft flying directly point-to-point. Even on the North American mainland, an airline's choice of hub can have repercussions for regional economies based in part on servicing aircraft, equipment, crews and passengers. High speed, computer-based communication and reservation facilities are now an integral part of the global tourism network. Not only do these facilities enable instantaneous links across the world, they also have added immeasurably to levels of awareness, both of tourists and those serving the travelling public.

With awareness and exposure can come stimulated demand for hitherto little known destinations. This, coupled with the ability to move vast numbers of people great distances in relatively short periods of time, means that few parts of the planet can any longer be regarded as out of the reach of tourists. This is a somewhat disturbing prospect, given the shrinking availability of sites to cater for the growing interest and involvement in ecotourism, nature-based tourism and unspoiled destinations. The natural environment is a growing magnet for tourists and great care will be needed in managing access to and use of natural sites so that technological advances do not threaten ecological sustainability. Perhaps the most exciting and powerful tool of technology has yet to impact fully on the tourism scene by way of the Internet's World Wide Web. The potential of the rapidly expanding Internet to create and disseminate knowledge relevant to tourism marketing is receiving increasing attention.

Accessed through the Internet, interactive media can create new sales opportunities for tourism enterprises and services. Hawkins stresses the importance for the tourism industry of understanding how to use the Internet, the on-line services, and interactive electronic media, to market and sell travel products. Already, travel companies have established itinerary planning systems, and tour operators, travel suppliers and destination management groups have pages on the World Wide Web. It is estimated that more than 100 million people will be connected to the Internet by the year 2000, with instant access to relevant, in-depth, up-to-date information about any country or destination.

Used interactively, the Internet offers the facility to select tourism sites and activities based on complete product information, and the promise of a fulfilling tourism experience, yet in a sustainable environmental context. As with many of the technological innovations being introduced into the tourism industry, reliance on the 'information superhighway' needs qualification. To some, the technology is seen as dehumanizing, with 'on-line' images poor substitutes for reality and authentic experiences. Hawkins points also to user confusion and dissatisfaction, as well as the lack of trained specialists, cost, and questions of security on the Internet, as issues to be addressed in harnessing these technological tools for the benefit of tourists and an ecologically sustainable tourism industry.

One of the most fundamental challenges facing tourism is adjusting to changes in the environment, both biophysical and human. Change in nature is the norm, but natural changes are typically slow and amenable to human adjustment. Changes brought about by human intervention, no matter how well intentioned, are often sharp and harsh, and likely to evoke a negative response. The fact that a site has been selected as a destination for tourists will inevitably lead to changes in the ambient environment.

The features which attracted tourists in the first place can lose their appeal with intensification of use. Alien structures, introduced to the environment ostensibly to support or protect the resource base, do not always sit comfortably with the natural environmental structures, nor will they necessarily have a positive impact in attracting or retaining tourists. This is the very antithesis of sustainable development. Typically, the initial force motivating tourists is the landscape, encompassing attributes of both the physical and social environment. As a tourist destination matures, these attributes undergo change and the landscape of tourism reflects the imprint of increasing numbers of visitors.

The transformation of the Palm Springs area of California from a desert spa and vacation site to 'the golf capital of the world' is a case in point. Created attractions are added, facilities are provided, and infrastructure is expanded to present a new blend of structures, activities and functions to service a different clientele. Not all such amendments are ill advised, and change does not necessarily equate with degradation. If carried out sensitively, tourist development can contribute to substantial upgrading of the environment and enhance visitor enjoyment and ecological sustainability. At the same time, the makeup, if not the volume, of tourist flows is likely to alter as the destination takes on a different character. However, it could well be that there would be as many tourists attracted as are repelled by the metamorphosis. Palm Springs and surrounding resorts, for example, now attract over two million visitors each year.

Several observers have alluded to what they see as a cycle of tourist area development. In an earlier paper, Plog expressed concern about what he appeared to see as the inevitable sequence of decline of resort areas: Destination areas carry with them potential seeds of their own destruction, as they allow themselves to become more commercialized and lose their qualities which originally attracted tourists. However, it is important to note that decline is not inevitable, and with sound planning and management it is possible for the downturn to be checked, rejuvenation achieved, and viability sustained. Advances made in water management in the arid region of Palm Springs are part of the success story of sustainable tourism in a desert setting.

There appear to be several modes of expression of tourism-environment interaction and the simplistic view of resisting change and isolating the environment in order to protect it *from* tourism may not be the preferred option. A more positive alternative could be to sustain and enhance the environment *for* tourism. According to Gunn, tourism and protection of the resource base are more alike than contradictory. Gunn maintains that the demands of tourism, rather than conflicting with conservation, actually require it. Otherwise the very appeal which attracts visitors to a destination will be eroded and with reduced satisfaction will go any chance of sustained viability. Ideally, tourism development and ecological sustainability should be complementary and mutually reinforcing.

The forces categorized above geopolitical, socioeconomic, technological and environmental are already highly visible and instrumental in fashioning the turbulent world of today's tourism. These same forces are also exercising the minds of decision makers charged with anticipating the future face of tourism. At the tenth General Assembly of the World Tourism Organisation, in Ball in October 1993, a round table was held on 'Trends and challenges in tourism beyond the year 2000'. Discussions were summarized under a number of headings, e.g. growth, technology, industry structures, social impacts, role of government, etc. and have much in common with those identified earlier in this chapter.

This reflects strong endorsement by the tourism sector of the drive in industry generally for more responsible and socially compatible forms of development. Environmental issues and social impacts are prompting a growing level of community concern over the types of tourism to be tolerated. This will create the need for new alliances, greater consultation, and even power sharing, in forging new tourism products to fit community values and environmental constraints. Industry representatives at the round table addressed a number of concerns regarding the future shape of world tourism, especially in regard to emerging tourism markets and destinations, and the increasing importance to environmental issues, environmentally compatible tourism developments and nature-based tourism.

A representative of Inter-Continental Hotels echoed these concerns for the global hotel industry. However, as with the issues raised earlier in this chapter, they were identified as opportunities and challenges, not necessarily problems. Among the concerns were:

— *Technology* Adapting to and exploiting technology more quickly especially in routine tasks to give an ever more expensive employee more time face to face with an ever more difficult to get customer.

— *Environment* Making sure the new hotels we build are compatible with the cultural, social and economic environment within which we operate.

Clearly, there is recognition on the part of various components of the tourism industry that the future has already arrived, and that they must respond to a range of strategic signals pointing towards a tourism scene of markedly different dimensions. Among key indicators, the following stand out:

— Socioeconomic and demographic change

— A revolution in information/communication technology

— More knowledgeable and demanding customers

— Deregulation of the market and emergence, of mega-operators

— Public sector—private sector alliances

— Need for human resources training

— Community pressure for sustainable forms of tourism.

A key element of tourism success in the future will be the ability and willingness of the industry to recognize change and use it to its advantage for longer-term sustainable growth. More and more, community and public sector support for tourism development is likely to be conditional on the industry entering into a partnership to pursue ecologically sustainable forms of tourism.

The changes and change agents reviewed in this chapter should not be perceived in negative terms, or as threats to well established modes of practice. Indeed, tourism, perhaps more than most other human activities, should welcome change and take up the opportunities that change offers change is a powerful and positive force which, when harnessed constructively, challenges individuals, groups and organizations to perform to their optimum capability. Encouraging people not to dwell on change itself, but to accept it as natural arid inevitable, is a key part of creating the willingness and mindset to not only cope with, but to thrive on the challenge. The view that change represents an opportunity and not necessarily a problem for tourism underpins the strengthening moves in many part of the tourism industry to manage change in a positive manner towards environmental enhancement and sustainability.

Enough is now known to require any tourist development, new of existing, to abide by the principles of sustainability. Industry is thoroughly receptive to sensible controls on development and properly considered management schemes to protect and enhance tourist destinations. When linked to quality assurance, the broader concept of best practice environmental management is of direct relevance to tourism in a competitive and changing world. Best practice environmental management calls for radically different organizational structures and attitudes to bring about continuous improve merit in a firm's environmental performance, in response to changing physical and economic circumstances, market forces, technological break throughs and government policies.

Translated to the tourism industry, best practice environmental management becomes a vehicle for facilitating and harnessing change. Environmental excellence is fostered through enlightened management practices incorporating new, cleaner technologies, and an emphasis on resource conservation, recycling, recovery and reuse, and attitudinal change, in pursuing progress towards sustainability. On the international scene a number of large hotel corporations, for example Canadian Pacific, Inter-Continental, Ramada, etc., have implemented a range of effective environmental measures. Environmental codes of ethics for tourism operations are also being introduced.

The expectation that tourism establishments will be developed and managed at the highest standards of environmental excellence needs to be tempered by knowledge that significant impediments stand in the way of rapid and widespread enhancement of environmental standards. The expertise, expense and long-term commitment of resources involved in lifting environmental performance inevitably means that the adoption of best practice environmental management is 'currently, a minority activity, confined, in the main, to a few large firms'. The challenge is to raise concern for the environment among the smaller and more numerous establishments, and achieve something of a 'trickledown' effect in the spread of environmental best practice to all levels of tourism activity.

2

Strategic Planning

Over the last two decades, policy makers, planners, industrialists and economists have become increasingly aware of the imperative need to consider both the environmental implications of proposed developments and also the aspirations of future generations to have the opportunities to make their own use of scarce resources. Since 1980s there has been a growing number of international reports, and accords concerning the wellbeing of Planet Earth. Notable among these international initiatives are the 1980 World Conservation Strategy, which stressed the need for sustainability in the use of natural resources; the Brandt Commission which emphasized the need for development to include 'care for the environment'; the Manila Declaration which inter alia pointed out that natural resources are of common heritage; the UNEP/WTO Accord 1982, which stressed the need for tourism development to be environmentally sound; and the Brundtland Report 1987, which indicated a path towards sustainable development with economic growth.

International concern for the environmental effects of development in its various modes and also for the effects of development on the socio-cultural choices about the life of the affected communities has stimulated a plethora of papers by academics and practitioners alike indeed it could be argued that in many cases these papers have helped in creating public awareness and concern. There is a long-established literature in many relevant fields. Unfortunately not all of the recent literary Outpourings have been helpful in clarifying the issues. In particular the introduction of some new terminologies and definitions has helped to cloud understanding and make agreements more difficult to reach.

The concept of sustainability is inherent in many papers on alternative tourism, ecotourism, green tourism, soft tourism, nature tourism, etc., but the term itself gained more common usage and acceptance with the publication of the Brundtland Report, *Our Common Future*. The Brundtland Commission defined 'sustainable development' process of change in which the exploitation of resources, the direction of investments, the orientation of technological development, and institutional changes are made consistent with future as well as present needs', and as 'meeting the needs of the present without compromising the ability of future generations to meet their own needs'.

Whereas the concepts of the Brundtland Report are probably acceptable to all but the most purblind and self-interested developers and politicians, major problems arise in defining methods of implementation and in reconciling all of the interests involved. In this context an interesting-Action Strategy for Sustainable Development' was prepared by the. Tourism Stream Action Strategy Commission of the Globe '90 Conference, on sustainable development held ill April 1990 ill Vancouver, Canada. A reproduction of the draft is provided in Inskeep. Also in Canada, D'Amore gives an interesting account of the progress made in that country towards achieving guidelines, codes of ethics and practical means of responding to the Brundtland Report.

De Kadt recognizes that whereas there is a need for future growth in some countries and regions in order to improve the material well being of the resident population, 'policy-makers can... promote sustain ability by constantly striving to make the conventional more sustainable' and that many 'alternative forms of tourism' will continue to evolve but, for economic reasons, will 'almost inevitably... [ride]... piggyback on the more cost-effective forms of the conventional, integrated international tour ism industry'. His final sentence 'how to coax that behemoth into less destructive behaviour is surely the main task ahead' could well form the theme of a major conference.

Since the Zakopane and Tamransett conferences, academics have continued to publish and the new Journal of Alternative Tourism has been launched. In addition, a spasmodic but very valuable correspondence on sustain ability in tourism is being conducted by trinetters on E-mail. This correspondence reflects the thoughts and ideas of the participants and hence is in an unpublished form. It is very much to be hoped that the trinetters will eventually use their correspondence to form the basis of a publication. So far economists have contributed relatively little to the debate on sustain able tourism and have emerged with little kudos for their part in the development of tourism. Indeed, it is easy to cast them together with developers as the villains of the act in that they have provided theoretical, conceptual and mathematical justifications for past growth and development without adequate regard to the environmental and sociocultural consequences of their recommendations.

There may be an element of truth in this viewpoint. Economists are concerned with the allocation of scarce which have alternative uses, but it should be remembered that economists *per se* do not lay down the policy prescriptions for the use of these, resources. Policy guidelines and objectives are laid down by the relevant governmental or international bodies and these stated aims govern economists recommendations regarding the allocation of resources. If, for example, a government wishes to maximize the income levels or employment opportunities for its resident population, an economist's task is to recommend optimum allocation or redistribution of resources to achieve those objectives. Also it should be remembered that an economist is not equipped to measure or evaluate ill money terms factors such as environmental effects.

Herein lies one of the major difficulties faced by economists. It is cost-benefit analysis. Economic models and techniques exist to evaluate most impact situations, but economists working in isolation are not in a position to express many of the factors involved in money terms. Perhaps the best known, but one of the least understood, economic models is social cost benefit analysis. This term is often confused by non-economists with financial analysis which, in the context of development, describes a detailed study of the revenue and costs which accrue to a developer if a new project or set of projects is to be undertaken.

Financial analysis places the emphasis oil the financial revenue and costs accruing to the developers not to the affected community or to the country as a whole. All other benefits and costs are external to the analysis and accrue elsewhere. On the other hand social cost-benefit analysis takes a wider and deeper view of the benefits and costs, being concerned with the community as a whole, including future generations. It is not concerned with the profitability of the development to the company or consortium, but with the net benefit to the host community.

The theoretical and conceptual basis of social cost-benefit analysis and the methodologies for assessing and measuring data have been the subject of much debate and investigation by, economists throughout the second half of this century. The literature is extensive, but a flavour of tile concept and its usefulness and limitations can be gleaned from Prest and Turvey, Layard and Little and Mirrlees. The technique hits been used widely and can investigate simultaneously a large number of alternative uses of the same resources, continuance of the status quo. Indeed the greater the number of alternative uses that are investigated, the more meaningful and helpful are the results. The principle weakness of the approach, as previously mentioned, is the inability of economists to recognize, assess and measure factors such as ecological and socio-cultural implications which do not have readily apparent monetary values.

In essence, social cost-benefit analysis involves assessing and measuring the consequences of proposed forms of development. All of the identified and measured benefits and costs are discounted back to their present value to provide a common yardstick of measurement. For islands and small states, one of the measures recommended is the foreign exchange equivalent value of the money in the hands of the government. The discount rate used in social cost-benefit analysis is quite different from that used by private sector developers, Whereas the latter use a discount rate which reflects both the rate of borrowing money and the risk factors involved, social cost-benefit analysts use a rate which is intended to reflect society's valuation of net benefits the present time rather than in the future. Thus, for example, in the case of a proposed airport development in Cyprus, the principal monetary benefits were identified as the net foreign currency likely to be obtained from the expenditure of additional tourists, the foreign currency likely to be obtained by exporting additional fruit as a consequence of siting the new airport close to the major fruit-producing regions, and the other net benefits accruing to some of the domestic population from the development.

The principal cost factors were the opportunity costs of using the necessary factors of production (land, labour and capital) and other resources to construct and then to operate an airport rather than in their best possible alternative uses. Among the alternative uses explored was the retention of these factors in their existing uses the land was under occasional pastoral usage, the majority of the labour force concerned was either unemployed or only seasonally employed, and the available capital was a mixture of overseas investment funds and domestic savings. The most productive alternative use was identified as irrigated agriculture.

The discount rate was selected after consultation with the Cyprus government and lay within the guidelines recommended by UNDP. In this particular study no major externalities or spill-over effects were identified. Indeed, the identification and measurement of externalities are for economists the most difficult aspect of social cost-benefit analysis. Pollution of beaches is a common occurrence in tourism development and economists can assign a monetary value to such occurrences and to the costs of taking preventative or remedial actions. Indeed it is possible to 'internalize' this type of cost to the developers themselves by legally enforcing them to take measures to prevent the occurrence of such situations. Nevertheless, many externalities, notably ecological effects, are much harder for economists and others to identify or evaluate. Unless such effects can be anticipated and the costs of preventative action evaluated, it is impossible to include them within the numerical analysis. It may be, for example, that a proposed development involves the destruction of a specific habitat and in consequence the possible eradication of a particular species of fauna or flora.

If, in such cases, some ecologists place an infinite monetary value on the preservation in situ of this threatened species, then it could be argued that the environmental costs of the proposed development would be greater than the net economic benefits, however great these may, be. On the basis of this premise, the development should riot be allowed to proceed. In such a situation, however, an economist would riot accept the premise that preserving the habitat had an infinite value. Instead, he would wish to calculate and include in the analysis the total costs of recreating the threatened habitat in another suitable location and of preserving the threatened species.

Similarly, an investigation of proposed mining developments in a National Park in the UK considered the net benefits accruing to the region over a long time span. During the period of active mining considerable environmental and other costs would be incurred, especially the impact on the aesthetic appearance of the area. If, however, at the end of the active mining period, the area were to be completely restored at the expense of the developer, then after a few years there would be few if any traces of the development. In this case the magnitude of the net present value of the benefits depended partly upon the value attached by the affected population to the environmental damage incurred over the period of mining operations rather than over an indefinitely prolonged period of time. Long-lasting environmental damage is a different consideration.

Advances in technology have made it possible for most forms of pollution and many other violations of the environment to be avoided, ameliorated or rectified at a subsequent date. As previously mentioned, such damage can be minimized by imposing legal restrictions and/or financial penalties to the cost to the developer. Admittedly, in some cases, long-term damage may occur and it is essential that a monetary valuation of such damage should be included as a cost in the cost-benefit analysis. Similarly, social scientists in other disciplines must be prepared to identify and to place a valuation on any expected changes in sociocultural patterns which might result from a proposed development. As a minimum social scientists should endeavour to produce a ranking order of such changes there appears to be little merit in undertaking still more ex-post studies, which describe outcomes as being 'good' or 'bad'.

What is needed is the degree of acceptability of any anticipated changes and their perceived costs and benefits to the residents and to the government, in order to assist economists in assessing the social benefits and costs involved. Again, the most adverse aspects of some expected changes can be, offset by forethought and planning, and the costs involved can be 'internalized'' within the Costs of development. In Mauritius, for example, in order to prevent the disruption by tourists of sega dances organized by local communities, tourist satisfaction is achieved by arranging visits by sega dance troupes to the major hotels. Examples of such ersatz provisions for visitors exist in other tourist destinations, for example, among the Indians of North America.

A second difficulty to be resolved in undertaking a social cost-benefit analysis is to define the beneficiaries, i.e. is the study concerned with the benefits and costs to the whole resident population of the country or to some subset of this population, e.g. a defined local area or region? It may well be the case that the balance of benefits and costs of a proposed development will be quite different for people living in the area most affected compared with the population of the country as a whole. Thus, for example, a major tourist development in a given region of a country may generate considerable net economic advantages to the country as a whole but may have several deleterious environmental and sociocultural effects in the region most affected.

Quite different results can be obtained if the social cost-benefit study is carried out from a national rather than regional or local perspective. In cases where local communities are worse off while the country as a whole gains net benefits, the costs of compensating the local community should be included in the social cost-benefit calculations.' In an island or small-state economy, however, because of the scale factor, the differences probably would be negligible and it might ell prove impractical in any case, because of data deficiencies, to undertake social cost-benefit studies on a local or regional basis.

Social cost-benefit analysis is not the only economic tool that can be used or adapted for assessing the overall impact of tourism. Economists frequently se input-output analysis to measure the direct and secondary economic effects of additional tourism expenditure on an area or for measuring the overall economic impact of total tourism expenditure. Traditionally, the approach involves constructing a matrix of the purchases and sales made by all economic sectors over a given time period and then by the use of matrix algebıa analysing the effects of injections of export earnings, such as tourism expenditure, on business revenue, incomes, government revenue, imports and employment in each sector of the economy. The technique thereby measures secondary effects in addition to the primary direct ones.

An alternative development should be needed which is ecologically sound give preference, where possible, to small-scale production recognize, other needs as well as material consumption give euqal consideration to future needs, including those of feature, give adequate weighting and political power to local, self-reliant communities. This approach is people centred, with decisions made predominantly at local level. It is difficult to disagree with this conceptually, except that it does riot address nor is it intended to address the situation and problems existing in areas already receiving influxes of mass tourism.

Only through convenient strategic planning we can achive a fruitful sustanable tourism. This chapter integrates the two mutually compatible approaches of strategic planning and life cycle analysis to provide a guiding framework for the implementation of sustainable tourism at the destination. A review of both quantitative and qualitative parameters of tourism growth is provided and the implications for the management of tourism destinations outlined. In particular, the growth of demand in volume terms is placing pressures upon destinations while the changing nature of demand implies that destinations adopt sustainable principles. The process of strategic planning is described and the Tourism Area Life Cycle introduced as an explanatory framework for the adoption of sustainable principles. At each stage in the life cycle the competitive position of the destination demands a distinctive strategy and approach to management.

The success of the tourism sector in the postwar period has resulted in an industry which is characterized not only by growth but also by rapid change. Pigram and Wahab suggest that the management of this growth and change will be critical in the 1990s and into the twenty-first century if tourism is to become a mature and acceptable sector. Here, concern for sustainability is identified as central to the management of this growth. This view is echoed by De Kadt who clearly states that sustainability has become the organizing concept for policy in the 1990s; a concept which has demonstrable advantages for the tourism sector as a whole.

In tourism the adoption of sustainability has been evidenced by a changing perspective away from the short term to the long term, which in turn has seen the adoption of a strategic approach to both markets and destination planning/ management. There is a clear synergy between the adoption of sustainable tourism principles and the disciplined, longer-term perspective provided by the strategic planning of both destinations and market.

The mutually complementary approaches of sustainability, and the strategic perspective provide an organizing within which to manage both the growth of tourism and to ensure that tourism becomes able resource at each stage of the tourist area life cycle. This encourages adoption of the longer-term perspective with which to deliver control and responsibility, and thus prevent destinations exceeding capacity. This view is also supported by Bramwell and Lance in their view of sustainability as the idea of holistic planning and strategy formulation. In terms of the consequences of uncontrolled growth, Farrell justifies the holistic stance by defining sustainability as:

> essentially an exercise in the optimization and finer tuning of all elements and sub-elements of the development system so that in its operation, the system as a whole maintains direction and one or more of the elements does not surge or is not enhanced to the detriment and impairment of others.

Farrell is therefore advocating the constant review and adjustment of all elements of the destination formula with the adoption of strategies appropriate to the various stages of the tourist area life cycle aim of this chapter to illustrate the utility of both the strategic life cycle approaches in the management of growth and the implementation of sustainable tourism development at the destination.

Since 1950, destinations around the world have experienced pressures resulting from the growth of demand. In the period 1950-90 the growth of international tourism arrivals has averaged 7.2 per cent per annum, whilst in expenditure terms the annual average increase has been 12.3 per cent.

Of course these rates include the relatively rapid expansion of international tourism in the 1960s and 70s, fuelled by technology, affluence and a supply-side, response on the part of the tourism sector towards the industrialization and standardization of the delivery of tourism.

In the 1990s the rates of increase have moderated although they are still positive despite both economic and political constraints in some regions. The evolutionary growth of international tourism since 1950 also demonstrates striking regional contrasts, in particular the rise of the East Asia/Pacific region at the expense of Europe and the Americas. These regional trends have been detailed earlier in this volume by Pigram and Wahab.

The WTO forecasts for tourism suggest a continuation of positive growth, with international arrivals increasing by around 5 per cent per annum during the remainder of the 1990s, and for domestic tourism to grow by around 4 per cent annum. Of course domestic tourism represents a far greater volume of tourism in the world estimated at around four times the volume of that of international tourism. WTO states that the determinants of this growth in demand for tourism. Are both external to tourism and also influenced by the tourism sector itself. External to tourism are the general health of the economy, political influences and technology. WTO states that tourism tends to follow general economic trends growing or contracting with economic activity. Superimposed on this general observation are the influences of technology and demographics.

The main influences upon tourism growth identified by the WTO are:

— socio-demographic—especially the ageing of populations in the industrialized countries;

— electronic information/communication systems;

— a more knowledgeable and demanding customer;

— a deregulating market place;

— pressure for responsible tourism development;

— a polarization between global players and 'niche businesses;

— and constraints upon growth related to labour, capital and infrastructure.

These trends have a combined impact upon destination considering future strategies to both manage and capitalize on the growth of tourism. Whilst the structure of the generating countries of international tourism is changing, the leading industrialized countries will continue to dominate. Here, WTO identifies the ageing of the postwar baby-boom population cohort, combined with the trend to independent and knowledgeable travellers as important influences upon the development of products.

Interwoven with and supporting these factors are the developments of information technology which support the independent traveller and hasten the flexibility of supply in the sector. Combined, these trends suggest an increasingly discerning and informed consumer who will choose tourism destinations on the basis of information and experience. Clearly then, destinations must be in tune with this changing demand for tourism as consumers become more experienced, informed and discerning. Poon sees a cleat evolution here from her concept of the 'old tourism' to a new and more flexible form of tourism, in part driven by demand, but also by a supply-side response. Poon's 'new tourists' have values which are oriented towards the environment and the ethical consumption of tourism, and, have motivations which are related more to active rather than passive activities and the search for escape and for the authentic.

The approach of the tourism sector to market segmentation is therefore inadequate as traditionally simple demographic, geographical and purpose-of-visit-categories have been used. Instead, techniques such as psychographic segmentation are more appropriate to the analysis of Poon's new tourists. However, there are real problems of both measuring the defining variables of new tourists, and of the clear identification of groups. For example, provides the following list of characteristics of the new tourists. They have:

— more experience

— changing life-styles

— changing values

— more flexibility

Also, they are both more independent-minded and the products of changing demographic structures. The life-style and demographic variables can be quantified but the variables related to independence, experience, values and flexibility demand a more subtle and qualitative market-research approach. Indeed, for many destinations even simple measures of volume and visitor characteristics are elusive. On the supply side, the continued increase and changes in the nature of demand will place pressures upon destinations in particular to adopt sustain able practices. This has been fuelled by the combination of media-led concern for responsible tourism, lobbying by industry groups such as the World Travel and

Tourism Council, and the development of both international and also more locally based pressure groups such as Tourism Concern. These trends all point in one direction the imperative for the development of tourism 'in a form on a scale and to standards which are sustainable'

Whilst the ultimate result of the cycle is decline, this can be prevented with sound planning and management. In other words, by the management of growth and change, sustainable tourism can be achieved at each stage of the cycle. There is, however, a continuing debate relating to the value of the life cycle as an analytical technique for the marketing and planning of destinations.

A number of authors have emphasized the utility of the life cycle approach for strategic planning. Yet Butler's original paper makes no such claims for the tourist area life cycle, and he saw it more as an explanatory framework for the understanding of the development of tourism. However, by integrating the long-term perspective provided by the life cycle with the concept of strategic planning, it is possible to devise appropriate management and planning strategies for destinations at various stages of the life cycle.

Kotler provides a clear definition of strategic planning as the managerial process of developing and maintaining a strategic fit between the organization's goals and capabilities and its changing marketing opportunities.

The defining characteristics of the strategic planning approach are the adoption of a long-term perspective; the development of an holistic and integrated plan which controls the process of change through the formation of goals; and a formalized decision process focused on the deployment of resources which commit the destination to a future course of action. Haywood views the approach as an extension of the one-dimensional marketing and planning approaches so often adopted in the short term by destinations. Strategic planning integrates these two approaches into a higher-order, formalized planning approach.

In terms of the adoption of sustainable tourism, the benefits of the strategic planning approach to the destination are clear. The process of goal setting provides a common sense of ownership and direction for the myriad stakeholders, whilst at the same time sharpening the guiding objectives of the destination. The coherence provided by this approach provides a framework for joint initiatives between the commercial and public sectors and demands the clear identification of roles and responsibilities. Finally, the approach delivers a range of performance indicators against which the destination's performance can be judged. In other words, strategic planning offers an integrated approach to the management of the destination and provides a sense of ownership for the stakeholders.

However, the adoption of sustainable principles, and indeed a longer-term strategic planning perspective by tourist destinations, is problematic. Simply put, the adoption of strategic planning at the destination is not as straightforward as in a commercial organization where responsibilities and reporting lines are well defined. In this respect, both Haywood and Pigram identify a number of implementation gaps in the adoption of strategic planning at tourist destinations. Destinations are comprised of a constantly shifting mosaic of stakeholders. Each of these groups has a different view of the role and future of tourism at the destination, and therefore the adoption of strategies becomes a political process of conflict resolution and consensus all set within a local legislative context and where power brokers have a disproportionate influence.

In addition, the tourist sector at destinations is characterized by fragmentation and a dominance of small businesses which often trade seasonally. This has led to a lack of management expertise at destinations, a divergence of aims between the commercial and public sectors and a short-term planning horizon which in part is driven by public sector, twelve-monthly budgeting cycles, but also by the tactical operating horizon of small businesses.

At the same time, the stage of the destination in the life cycle also influences the acceptability of planning and marketing. In the early stages of the life cycle for example, success often obscures the long-term view, whilst in the later stages, particularly when a destination is in decline, opposition to long-term planning exercises may be rationalized on the basis of cost. Also, the performance indicators adopted in such exercises can be controversial, as tourist volume is the traditional, and politically acceptable measure of success in many destinations. From the point of view of a sustainable tourism planning exercise, such measures are more likely to be the less tangible ones of environmental and social impacts.

There are a number of approaches to strategic planning, ranging from the evolutionary approach of Mintzberg and Ritchie's 'destination visioning' to the more formalized 'rational model' or 'planning school' approach.

The strategic planning process can be viewed as a series of iterative stages. The sequencing of these stages varies according to the objectives of the plan, but generally the following stages are identified in the tourism literature.

Situation analysis

This stage essentially provides a set of data relating to the current situation of the destination. Here, an appraisal is made of the destination's competitive situation, often through the reconfiguration of the data into a SWOT analysis. The situation analysis considers data relating not only to the destination itself, but also to the external environment. Here, the issues identified above concerned with measuring demand for a destination can be problematic for smaller destinations.

Objectives and goals

The data base provided in the first stage allows the identification of key issues from which objectives and goals can be distilled. These objectives and goals provide a direction to the planning process. It is normal for destinations to include objectives and goals relating, to both marketing and development, and for time frames and responsibilities to be attached. At this stage, parameters to be used to judge the success or otherwise in meeting the will also be identified.

Strategy formulation

This stage involves the identification of a business portfolio for the destination through a process of decisions relating to which markets and products should receive more or less emphasis. This is in recognition of the fact that destinations can be thought of as an amalgam of different products appealing to different market segments at each stage of their development.

Marketing, positioning and mix

This stage can be broken down into a series of smaller stages, beginning with the identification of target markets followed by the development of product positioning as a means of differentiating the destination from the competition. Finally, the position in the market is communicated through manipulation of the marketing mix with objectives and targets for each market segment and product.

Implementation and Monitoring

It is this final stage where many of the problems of adopting strategic planning at tourist destinations are seen. The implementation process involves 'unbundling' the plan, assigning roles add responsibilities and putting into place a monitoring system. Finally, there is a need for measurement, feed back and control systems to ensure continued implementation of the plan.

Integration of Strategic Planning

The approach adopted for strategic planning will be dependent upon the destination's stage in the TALC. In particular the destination's point in the evolution of its development, combined with its competitive position, will determine the strategic options available. This is known as life cycle analysis and is a development of the product portfolio approach.

Jain has developed a matrix which summarizes the key dimensions of this approach an evolutionary element of life cycle stages from to ageing, and a market competitive position from dominant to weak. Within the matrix appropriate strategies can therefore be identified, dependent upon a destination's stage in the life cycle and competitive position.

However, whilst many destinations may know intuitively their position within the life cycle, this is more difficult to quantify. Here, Knowles identifies eight factors which can assist in identifying the life cycle stage:

— market growth rate
— growth potential
— range of product lines
— number of competitors
— distribution of market share amongst competitors
— customer loyalty
— entry barriers
— technology

Another approach is to consider instead growth indicators such as

— rates of volume growth
— ratio of repeat to first-time visitors
— length of stay
— visitor profiles expenditure per head
— visit arrangement.

For the competitive dimension on the matrix, Porter's classic analysis of competitive forces assists in the identification of a destination's competitive position:

— the entry of new competitors
— the threat of substitutes
— bargaining power of suppliers
— marketing power of suppliers
— rivalry amongst existing competitors

Quite simply, at each stage of the life cycle the mix of evolutionary and competitive forces differs, and thus strategies to deliver a sustainable tourism industry at the destination should be distinctive at each life cycle stage.

Strategic options

By adopting Jain's approach to life cycle analysis, it is possible to define the strategic options available for destinations and outline the destination's characteristics and possible responses to be taken.

Exploration and involvement

Here the resort is visited by a small volume of explorer-type tourists who tend to shun institutionalised travel. The natural attractions, scale and culture of the resort are the main draw, but volumes are constrained by lack of access and facilities. At this stage the attraction of the resort is that it remains as yet unchanged by tourism, and contact with local people will be high.

At the involvement stage, local communities, have to decide upon whether they wish to encourage tourism, and if so, the type and scale of tourism they prefer. Local initiatives will begin to provide for visitors and advertise the resort, which may lead to an increased and regular volume of visitors.

A tourist season and market area emerge and unforeseen pressures may be placed on the public sector to provide infrastructure and institute controls. At this point it is important to establish appropriate organizational and decision making processes for tourism to involve the local community to ensure that locally determined capacity limits are adhered to and that sustainable principles are introduced in these early stages.

Communities who decide to enter the tourism sector will find that, in the stages of exploration and involvement, growth of tourist volume is slow; gaining awareness takes time, and indeed many resorts may not progress beyond this stage. At involvement, destinations which decide to attract tourists will need to promote their products and access distribution channels in order to build a strong market position before competitors enter.

Traditional marketing thinking at this stage is outlined by Kotler who identified the early stages of the cycle as where intensive growth opportunities occur, before the destination has exploited its current opportunities in products and markets.

There are three major possibilities here: market penetration involves attracting more visitors from its existing markets to the resort without changing the product; market development involves seeking new markets as a source of visitors; and product development involves increased visits through developing closely related, new or improved products.

Development

By the development stage, large numbers of visitors are attracted and the organization of tourism may change as control passes out of local hands, and companies from outside the area move in to provide products and facilities. These enterprises may have differing aims and time-scales from those of the local community in terms of sustainable development. It is therefore at this stage that problems can occur if local decision taking structures are weak.

Control in the public sector can also be affected as regional and national planning may become necessary in part to ameliorate problems, but also to market to the international tourist generating areas, as visitors become more dependent upon travel arrangements booked through the trade. This is a critical stage, as these facilities, and the changing nature of tourism, can alter the very nature of the resort and quality may decline through problems of overuse and deterioration of facilities.

Clearly then, it is in these early stages of the cycle that community initiatives for tourism and sustainable development strategies are most appropriate in order to guide the resort's future development.

In the development stage emphasis changes to the management of market expansion through the careful matching of appropriate tourism market segments to particular products and destinations to provide a truly sustainable destination.

The detailed marketing actions include building market share through increased visitor numbers and preempting competitors' customers, as well as relying on word early 'adopters' spread the word. It is important at this of-mouth promotion as, stage to look to diversifying distribution channels, maintaining the quality of the resort's products, continuing promotion to keep awareness high and adding new facilities. Kotler summarizes this stage as when integrative growth opportunities occur. This involves gaining control of distribution systems. This is only really applicable to destinations where computer reservations systems can be developed and used as a competitive tool; or where regional alliances of destinations/resorts can occur.

Consolidation and stagnation

In the later stages of the cycle, the rate of increase of visitors declines though total numbers are still increasing. The resort is now a fully fledged part of the tourism industry with an identifiable recreational business district.

At stagnation, peak tourist volumes have now been reached and repeat visits from more conservative travellers dominate. Business use of the resort's extensive facilities is also sought, but generally major promotional and development efforts are needed to maintain the number of visits. Resorts in this stage often have environmental, social and economic problems.

As consolidation and stagnation approach, defence of market share against competitors becomes important, as does maintaining margins and cashflow by cost control and avoiding price wars. By this stage the competition for visits is fierce and comes from a number of well entrenched, mature resorts; but a good strategy is to test market with new segments and to consolidate use amongst current visitors, to modify the product through improvements in quality, features and style, and to modify elements of the marketing mix. In other words, once visitor numbers stabilize, management should not await decline as inevitable but should seek to revitalize visits by seeking new markets, repositioning the resort, or looking at new uses for facilities.

Decline

Visitors are now being lost to newer resorts and a smaller geographical catchment for day trips and weekend visits is common. From the point of view of sustainable principles, the decline stage is very problematic. The destination has been adapted and designed to handle large numbers of visitors, and once they cease to visit, the very economic, social and environmental viability of the destination is threatened. Destination managers may recognize this stage and decide to 'rejuvenate' or 'relaunch' the destination by looking at new markets or developing the product. Introduction of new types of facility such as a casino, as at Sclieveningen in The Netherlands and Atlantic City, USA is a common response.

As at stagnation, a destination should seek to protect its traditional markets whilst also seeking new markets and products such as business, conference, or special-interest tourism. This helps to stabilize visitation, may combat seasonality, and reduces dependence on declining market segments.

Strategies for the decline stage are much more difficult when managers are dealing with the built fabric of tourist destinations rather than with a consumer product. Indeed, it is at this stage that the analogy of a product life cycle and the tourist area life cycle breaks down, simply because tourism is so closely woven into the very way of life of the town and supports jobs, services and carriers. Here, the longer-term view on the scale of the life cycle can provide managers with an historical perspective and prompt a new scale of strategic thinking which will include the option of leaving the tourism industry completely.

The nature of destinations and their markets means that many of the opportunities identified above are led by product development initiatives. At each stage in the life cycle new product development is essential if sustainability is to be achieved. New product development spreads the risk of depending upon a small range of traditional destination formulae by allowing diversification.

New product development therefore enhances the competitive position of a destination. Of course, if the process is flawed then the product will fail. This may be through poor assessment of demand and market needs, or through poor product design and positioning and/or made quate communication of the benefits. In tourism in particular, the fragmentation of supply can also act as a significant constraint on the development of new products at the destination level. New product development has received considerable attention in the marketing literature. Tellis and Crawford for example see new product development as closely linked to the evolution of a market. They suggest that products are in a constant state of evolution, influenced by market dynamics, managerial creativity and government intervention. Here, five basic stages can be identified:

— *divergence:* the start of a new product type, which may be completely new or a modification of an existing product type

— *development*: sales increase and the product is adapted to suit better consumer needs

— *differentiation*: here, a successful product is differentiated to suit varying consumer interests

— *stabilization:* the product changes little, but the packaging, accessories, etc constantly varied

— demise: the product fails to meet consumer expectations and may be discontinued

The new product development literature envisages a series of sequential stages of development representing a continuing, ongoing process. Of course, the development of new products in tourism must be guided by the overall strategic objectives of the destination. From this point of view, Moutinho identifies a number of possibilities:

— a completely new product offered to the market;

— repositioning of an existing product; or

— modifications of an existing product.

These options must he related to jain's matrix of life cycle stage and competitive position. For example, a destination at the later stages of its life cycle and in a weak competitive position may look to repositioning and modifications rather than launching completely new products. Consideration of new product development highlights one of the major handicaps to the operationalization of the TALC approach to strategic options; that of the level of generalization. At the level of the destination a TALC is often identifiable, yet in terms o f new product development it is more likely that the destination will identify product types within the destinations suchas business tourism, adventure tourism or ecotourism. Each of these product types will also exhibit life cycles, but these may not conform to that of their parent destination. At a lower level of generalization, individual enterprises within these product types will also exhibit life cycles.

Tourism Development Policy

Coherent policy conception, formulation and implementation are not yet well structured in most developing countries. This is particularly true in tourism which is a multifaceted industry requiring a good deal of coordination, organization, planning, motivation, sound utilization of resources and proper implementation.

Whereas legitimate demands on government are usually large in developing countries the capacity for sound public management of available and potential resources is not usually well developed. This results in an *ad hoc* reactive approach to solving problems that impose them selves on the community, instead of a systematic policy that typifies proactive approaches.

General tourism policies are those policies which serve as a framework specifying the national tourism goals, objectives, priorities and actions that will provide the basis for future development of tourism in the destination area. In other words, tourism policy determines the climate in which the country functions economically, socially, culturally, politically and environmentally. As Sessa observed, tourism policy, 'as an integral part of a nation's overall economic policy, must be coordinated with the policies of all other sectors directly or indirectly related to tourism'.

Despite the indispensability of tourism policy as a precursor for future tourism planning and development, many developing countries have yet to develop statements of their tourism policies. Typical tourism goals are:

— *economic goals*, meaning optimization of the contribution of tourism and recreation to economic prosperity: full employment, regional economic development and improved international balance of payments;

— *sociocultural goals*, represented by (1) the personal growth and education of the population and the boosting of their appreciation of the history, geography, and ethnic diversity of the country; (2) avoidance of any activities that may undermine or denigrate the social and cultural values and resources in the country or area as well as negatively affecting its traditions and/or life-styles; (3) maximizing the chances for a more beneficial enjoyment of travel and recreation for foreign visitors and residents;

— *environmental goals*, oriented towards (1) judicious use of natural resources; (2) avoidance of all possible causes of pollution; (3) utilization of new and renewable sources of energy. (4) safeguarding the physical environment through strict adherence to carrying capacities and clearance of solid waste; and (5) preservation of national heritage resources and urban revitalization.

— *market development goals*, represented by (1) frontier facilitation procedures; (2) increasing the chances of a better tourist image of the destination in generating markets, and (3) enhancing the opportunities for a broader market for the national tourist products; and

— *government operations goals*, which include (1) maximum harmonization of all government activities supporting or relating to tourism and recreation; (2) supporting the need to educate all policy makers on tourism; (3) legislation for necessary tourism activities; (4) regulation of the various facets of tourist action at the national, regional and local levels; (5) the raising of tourism-consciousness amongst the general public; (6) encouraging the private sector to increase its activities in tourism development through various incentives; (7) ascertaining the limits of tourism growth; and (8) safeguarding internal and external security in tourism operations.

Tourism programmes

Having established the tourism policy, various tourism strategies and programmes are needed to achieve the policy's goals and objectives. Examples of such strategies include specifics of the tourism facilitation strategies, investment incentives, development research, marketing research, priority tourism development areas and zones, marketing and promotional strategies in various niche markets including domestic tourism, air transport and cruise strategies, and a tourism education and training strategy.

The question of quality versus quantity appears at the forefront of tourism development strategies. Besides the prominence given to quality as a major tourist destination attraction at the macro and microlevels, the logical inclination may well be to wish to attract the visitor with the highest daily expenditure who accordingly adds most to the national income (unless the additional expenditure is outweighed by a greater volume of imports), the visitor with special interest in culture, or the incentive visitor.

Carrying capacity is a central principle in any strategy for sustainable tourism development. It determines the maximum use of any place without causing negative effects on the resources, on the community, economy, culture and environment, or reducing visitor satisfaction. It is virtually a limitation on ill-conceived tourism growth.

The respective roles of the public and private sectors as entrepreneurs in tourism are matters of a political decision in the light of a country's economic and social system, forming an integral part of the tourism development policy.

Community participation

Community participation in the decision-making process of tourism development is a key issue in ensuring the acceptability of tourism, thus contributing to its sustainability. This derives not only from fair and just rules of democracy, but also from the fact that tourism should not expand at a rate beyond which citizens in a given community actually desire and can control. Acceptance by consensus would not be required. However, suffice to say that in order to channel the social impact of tourism in its proper path, tourism should not cause disillusionment to the host society.

A model that was based on research in Barbados developed an irritation index of five stages, starting with initial euphoria, then apathy, increasing irritation, outright antagonism, and finally a stage when cherished values are forgotten and the environment destroyed by mass tourism.

Community participation in the tourism development process differs in developing countries from developed countries. By and large, such difference manifests itself in three ways.

First, local communities in some developing countries devote minor attention to issues of tourism development and planning as they are much more troubled by the lack of clean and hygienic food and drink and suitable shelter in the short time frame.

Second, lack of democracy in many developing nations dictates that the will of the ruling class expresses the *pro bono publico*.

Third, there is no system that would allow social outputs to be determined by the people most immediately affected by them, even in the presence of local government, as tourism is usually looked upon as an industry of national concern.

Community attitudes towards tourism might change in time, e.g. from enthusiasm to euphoria or apathy when tourism fails to live up to its promise over a reasonable period of time. This may also happen when the community leadership changes over time.

A typical example of such change in community attitudes is the case of Luxor's visitor centre in Egypt. In 1983, a 'Study on visitor management and associated investments on the West Bank of the Nile at Luxor' recommended *inter alia* the creation of a visitor centre to meet visitors' needs for tourist information and for services and amenities. The primary function of the visitor centre was to serve as the central focus of an information interpretation programme. Another equally important function was to house priority tourist amenities specifically a restaurant, theatre and shops. The Luxor West Bank of the Nile encompasses the Valley of Kings and the Valley of the Queens and Nobles, in addition to some important temples and monuments. Other organizational and management recommenda-tions were intended to reduce pressure on the most-visited tombs, which were in danger of deterioration.

Consultations with the Government Archaeology Department and the Luxor Community represented by the City Council resulted in unanimous endorsement of the project in 1986. When the visitor centre was constructed seven years later, an opposite front soon appeared: the Luxor Business Community became antagonistic to the visitor centre and the whole of the proposed Luxor West Bank organization and management system came to a halt. This was due to the change in leadership of the Luxor Business Community, which considered that the plan was against the local population's recognized interests.

Tourism, as a vehicle for development in developing countries, should be an evolutionary process of change to a better future. It should create a structure that aims to create a steady and balanced rate of change. Such rate of change has to be consistent with the prevailing socioeconomic, politico-cultural, educational, organizational and environmental conditions in the destination, because development starts with people and not with goods. As rightly raised by Schumacher, every country, no matter how devastated, which had a high level of education, organization and discipline, produced an 'economic miracle'.

Demands for a growing volume of tourist traffic can affect a country's resources sustainability potential. Nevertheless, sustainability is still a new concept and a costly notion to implement in developing countries. These countries cannot normally shoulder the costs of environmental management and therefore they have to approach it in a gradual manner. The only blessing they enjoy is that their physical environments are still comparatively natural, and therefore the pertinent cost should not be excessive.

While this is true in many cases, some writers consider that as most tourists arriving in developing countries are unfamiliar with local conditions and unaware of finely balanced ecological systems, they are potentially, if unintentionally, dislocative and destructive. Even the ecotourists' motto, 'Leave nothing but your footsteps, take nothing but your memories', needs to be amended in the face of, for example, the rainless desert of southern Namibia. There, 'footsteps in the sand, and 4-wheel drive vehicle tracks, can scar the landscape for years'.

This is an exaggerated view on the part of conservation biologists, which if taken into consideration in sustainable tourism development, would mean that no tourism activity would be warranted in developing countries.

Competitive tourism strategies are becoming critically important for developing countries because tourism, by its nature, is a sensitive and highly competitive industry. White natural attributes form distinctive advantages for developing nations, and there is a growing trend towards nature-based tourism, the use of human intelligence and creativity, and the application of scientific knowledge and technology can make the difference.

Cost-effectiveness in tourism investments is a must and not a luxury in developing countries, Total quality management has become another limitation that conditions sound development planning from which sustainability can ensue. The quality of services delivered by the tourism inner circle staff is of prime importance. Equally important is the protection and conservation of natural and cultural assets, the cleanliness of the whole destination, necessary hygiene in food and drinks, friendliness of the people, innovation in product development, creativity in marketing strategies, access to the proper distribution channels in the market place, suitable use of technologically advanced information systems, and the capability to anticipate and accommodate change. All this could make tourism a lead sector in a country's developmental strategy.

But tourism cannot and should not be developed in isolation from other productive and service industries in the destination. It is an industry that interacts with many sectors and a multitude of government functions, and should therefore be developed with a view to such multidimensional characteristics.

Adoption and implementation of new development and marketing strategies, activation of the main sector-related issues, development of an environmental focus, encouragement of the private sector through various incentives to become a dynamic sector, guaranteeing adequate accessibility, human resources development, and transformation of the role of national tourist administrations in the market place to become active and effective image builders, are some of the main tools with which to build a sustainable tourism development programme.

Needless to say, a shortsighted approach in order to achieve maximum economic returns from tourism in the short term, may cause detrimental repercussions in developing countries. This approach manifests itself in prices that are disproportionate with service quality, and results in tourists, dissatisfaction and a potential decrease in tourist traffic.

The charter of sustainable development adopted at the World Conference on Sustainable Tourism, which met at Lanzarote on 278 April 1995, is significant in providing guidelines for the various governments seeking to ensure the creation of a sustainable tourism industry.

Tourism in the economy

Egypt is one of the oldest civilizations in the world and is mentioned in Biblical and Quoranic texts. Being endowed with historical monuments, sites and landmarks covering several millennia of civilization as well as extensive beautiful beaches, it has considerable potential for developing its tourism sector. Besides its diversified topographical and cultural attractions, Egypt's tourist endowments are further enhanced by mild weather for at least eight months of the year.

The Egyptian sector initially received substantial attention. However, this support softened as the development emphasis shifted to the industrial sector. Deterioration of the tourism industry was further aggravated by the war of 1967 and continued hostilities for about ten years until the Peace Agreement.

During this period the influx of tourists to Egypt was substantially impaired. A change in economic philosophy, coupled with the signing of the Peace Agreement in the mid-seventies, brought with it increased emphasis on tourism. The number of hotels increased, facilities for servicing the tourism sector improved, and as a result the number of arrivals rose substantially relative to previous decades. This was further assisted by a liberalized civil aviation policy and the diversification of Egyptian tourism from a cultural destination to a combined leisure and cultural attraction.

Between 1985 and 1989, tourism in Egypt, as measured by the number of international arrivals, grew on average by about 13.6 pet cent pet annum, much higher than world tourism, which grew at an average annual rate of about 5.9 per cent in the same period. From being a modest contributor to foreign exchange earnings of about US$700 million in 1986, tourism, receipts reached $1.5 billion in 1990 and $2.8 billion in 1995, putting the industry in second place after workers' remittances, but ahead of Suez Canal revenues and revenues from oil exports.

In addition, Egypt has considerably more domestic control over the generation of foreign exchange through tourism, which has shown a greater responsiveness to favourable domestic policies than other sources of foreign exchange. As an illustration, the 37 pet cent exchange rate depreciation in May 1987 coincided with a 28 pet cent increase in tourist arrivals, a 34 pet cent increase in nights spent in Egypt and a 133 pet cent increase in recorded tourist receipts in 1987-8 over the previous year.

Apart from being an important foreign exchange earner, tourism development also has a substantial impact on employment in other sectors such as transport, food industry, textiles, the air-conditioning industry, the furniture industry, cottage industries and the informal, small-scale sectors of manufacturing and services. This is especially relevant in view of the current problem of growing unemployment and the need to redeploy redundant labour from government and publicly owned enterprises.

Direct and indirect employment in the tourism sector is estimated at 350,000. This is based on estimates of 110,000 employed in the hotel sector, 25,000 in travel agencies, 10,000 in restaurants, 50,000 in tourism-related retail trade, and some 4,500 tour guides, the remaining 150,000 or so being indirectly employed. About 20 pet cent of the workforce in tourism are women. Although tourism still contributes less than 3 per cent of GDP, it has been since 1987 the fastest growing sector in the economy, in response to favourable economic reforms at both macro and sectoral levels. The opportunities for increasing its contribution to the economy are excellent, given the country's unique but under exploited tcurist potential.

The tourism market

Tourism to Egypt consists of two separate markets: Arab and foreign. The Arab market comprises visitors from Saudi

Arabia, Kuwait, Libya and other Arab countries, who account for about 38 pet cent of Egypt's tourism market. The foreign market is dominated by visitors from Germany, France, the United Kingdom and Italy. Only in three long-haul markets has Egypt built up a significant market share: the USA, Japan and Australia, Egypt attracts insignificant numbers of tourists from Canada, Latin America and sub-Saharan Africa. Tourism arrivals are evenly spaced between the summer months and winter months.

The majority of foreign tourists are on leisure trips rather than business, and an estimated 60 pet cent are attracted to the country by the historical attractions of the Nile Valley. In general, most visitors take one of a variety of trips along the Nile valley between Cairo, Luxor, Aswan and Abu Simbel. The traditional 'cultural' visits, however, do not bring about much repeat tourism.

Recent government policy has been oriented towards spreading tourism more evenly throughout the country rather than continuing to concentrate heavily on the traditional historic sites of the Nile Valley. Implicit in the policy is diversification, by providing new tourism products which would allow Egypt to appeal to a much wider overseas market than was possible to the past. The coastline along the Red Sea and the Gulf of Aqaba are being promoted for beach tourism. In recent years there has been a rapid expansion in hotels and tourism facilities along the Red Sea coast south of Hurghada and along the coast of the Gulf of Aqaba. This has begun to attract a number of visitors for sea coast tourism as well as those whose main pursuit is diving. This is a relatively specialized though potentially lucrative market, and rapid rates of growth have been achieved. There are assurances that the beach market in these areas will be able to compete with comparable Mediterranean destinations such as Morocco, Tunisia, Greece and Turkey.

Like other tourism destinations, Egypt is vulnerable to political instability in the region and has suffered setbacks following the Achille, Lauro affair in 1985, the police riots in 1986 and the US bombing of Libya shortly afterwards, However, Egypt has shown resilience, and after the Gulf Crisis and a number of terrorist events, signs of recovery are apparent with tourist arrivals during 1995 reaching more than 3.1 million.

Institutional setting

The Ministry of Tourism (MOT) is the main authority dealing with tourism in Egypt. The Ministry is organized into four major functional parts dealing with planning and development regulation of touristic services, administration, and financial and legal affairs. Like most other ministries, MOT suffers from overstaffing and inadequate technical capability. The Ministry is being streamlined to strengthen its technical expertise in support of a private sector-led tourism development strategy, to be competitive with neighbouring countries and to protect the country's unique cultural and natural resources. The first step has been the creation of the Tourism Development Authority (TDA) in September 1991, which draws principally on private sector expertise to assist MOT in guiding and promoting increased private sector investments in the sector. These changes are expected to provide the sector with a stronger institutional framework for coherent, private sector oriented and environmentally sound tourism development.

The Ministry also oversees the following public sector organizations: (a) Egyptian General Authority for Promotion of Tourism; (b) Public Authority for Conference Centres; and (c) Tourism Development Authority. Under Law 203, the public sector Tourism Authority, which was under the supervision of

MOT in the past, became a holding company for the sector and consists of the following affiliated companies:

1 Egyptian General Organization for Tourism and Hotels (EGOTH)

2 Misr Travel Company

3 Egyptian Hotels Company

4 Misr Hotels

5 Grand Hotels of Egypt

The cabinet and MOT have taken important steps both the at macro and sectoral levels towards the liberalization and deregulation of the tourism sector, These include the liberalization of exchange rates, which brought about an immediate response in terms of the increased number of tourists visiting Egypt; the easing of restrictions on chartered flights; and inviting private airlines to introduce international scheduled services on routes not served by Egypt Air, Egypt's flag, carrier. An institutional framework has been set up to facilitate privatesector participation. Notwithstanding these reforms, the sector still faces minor constraints which impede the implementation of a privatesector-led development strategy for the industry.

Public and private sector partnership The tourism sector has historically depend on budgetary allocation for its investments. A small share of its programme is financed from, internally generated revenues and the test is allocated under the five-year budgetary process.

These allocations have usually been either Insufficient to maintain the growth of' complementary infrastructure in the sector, or were provided in an untimely fashion which resulted in serious delays in the completion of major projects. Planned investment for the tourism sector during the second plan was about Eg.p828 million, about Eg.p408 million of which would be from the public sector, while about Eg.p420 million was assigned to the private sector.

The sector has always been, attractive to private investors, and private investments have extended to hotels, holiday villages, Nile cruises, travel agencies and tourist investment companies. Actual investments totalled more than four times the planned investments by the private sector. Since 1992 more than three billion Egyptian pounds have been invested in tourist development projects by private investors.

At present, Egypt's tourist accommodation capacity has reached 150,000 beds in about 760 hotels and a general average rate of occupancy in 1995 was 67 pet cent in rooms and 49 per cent in beds. Egypt's accommodation capacity is expected to rise to 250,000 beds (130,000 rooms) by the end of 1999. The private sector is being encouraged through various incentives to introduce area infrastructure in new tourist regions by large investment companies. An example would be the Sahl Hashish area (thirty-two square kilometres) on the Red Sea south of Hurghada, which is being developed by the newly formed 'Egyptian Resorts Development Corporation' with a subscribed capital of US$200 million. This company would qualify to benefit from a World Bank Loan to the government to build tourism infrastructure in the Red Sea region. Another private sector company was given the franchise to build Egypt's first private airport in Mersa Alam on the Red Sea. Because the tourist sector, despite its contribution to the economy, needed the database necessary for indicative planning, this has already been remedied and a computerized data system is already installed and operated through the Cabinet Centre of Information and

Despite the fact that Egypt has not yet formulated a binding national tourism policy, deliberations between the government and World Bank resulted in agreement to a number of goals, namely:

1 changing the role of the public sector from that of owner/operator to planner/regulator and promoter/facilitator;

2 deregulating the industry to allow the private sector to operate freely in competitive environment;

3 protecting and conserving the unique cultural and natural resources in the tourism areas; and

4 promoting a larger role for the private sector in the design, financing, implementation, ownership and operations of tourism facilities.

These goals are expected to sustainability increase the role of the private sector in the development of new facilities and operation of existing public sector facilities acquired through privatization and divestiture, or leasing arrangements. Private sector investments, however, have tended to concentrate on the narrow corridor of the Nile Valley and Cairo, where infrastructure is already developed and where tourism demand has been growing substantially. Attractive but remote sites, suitable for leisure tourism, have to be developed with the residual resources, resulting in unattractive facilities and inadequate infrastructure.

Tourist facilities along the Red Sea coast have evolved in response to demands and in the absence of long-term landuse plans. Today, Hurghada, the first site a few years ago to be developed for tourists and vacationers, stands as an example of unguided development, inadequate infrastructure and virtually absent environmental management.

The government's approach to stemming this undesirable process of the development of Red Sea coastal areas was to give responsibility by decree to the Ministry of Tourism for planning, developing and monitoring tourism development in the remaining coastal areas and sortie of the areas in the Nile Valley.

The Ministry's approach to development of these areas was the initiation of extensive landuse plans undertaken with the assistance of international consulting firms, and to promote private sector investments in accordance with these plans. Initially MOT's approach was to assume responsibility for infrastructure and let the private sector develop the super structure.

This approach implied that MOT would secure loans and credits and use its own resources to develop infrastructure on a large scale, with the hope that development would allow the private sector to mobilize the funds needed for superstructure. In this case, the public sector would bear all risks associated with the development of infrastructure.

Provision of publicly financed infrastructure without parallel development of superstructure would result in land speculation, allowing the private sector to capture the rent associated with the ownership of land where services were developed by the public sector. A different approach is needed if MOT's strategy for the Red Sea and Sinai areas is to succeed. There is a need for an integrated development of infrastructure and superstructure in an environmentally sound manner, and for private sector investments to be based on the principles of project finance under limited recourse, where lenders and investors assume well specified risks and rely on the project's ability to generate revenues needed for securing the loan and providing the returns.

Under this concept, the private sector would assume all the commercial risks. This approach has the advantage of subjecting projects to the scrutiny of the financial community, and avoiding need for direct intervention by MOT In project design and implementation, thus reducing the probability of resource misallocation. Furthermore, a gradual approach to infrastructure development by the private sector would allow the public sector to postpone major investments in trunk infrastructure until they were economically or environmentally justified. The Ministry of Tourism has solicited international assistance in spearheading a private sector-led strategy for the development of infrastructure in the Red Sea and Sinai areas. This is already under way. At present, Egypt is conscious of the fact that planning for sustainable tourism is the key towards a successful tourism development strategy.

3

Sustainable Tourism Systems

Sustainable is a value positive word. Simply put, it has such strong, positive connotations that it is easily and eagerly embraced by almost all members of society. Its root meaning is to nourish or prolong. Problems arise however when people begin to use the concept in an operational context. For example, assume a resort destination area has been experiencing double-digit growth rates for the last five years. For developers, sustainable could easily mean maintaining those growth rates into the foreseeable future. For members of the host community the concept may mean growth must be significantly reduced to maintain the quality of life, including off-season periods of recuperation, that the residents currently enjoy. Both groups believe in the concept of sustainable tourism systems but disagree on how it is interpreted and applied.

Even the most widely accepted definition of sustainable, which involves continued use without depletion of resources is problematic. Many argue that change is a constant. Even without human intervention natural systems change as they evolve. Therefore, embracing a concept that disallows change is contrary to natural law. Sustainable development concerns grew out of the rapid exploitation of the earth's environment for economic gain. Realization that short-term gains were coming at the expense of long-term losses for future generations began to reshape global development strategy. In spite of all the attention it has received, sustainable development is still a concept searching for a clear definition. While it is risky to paraphrase given by international experts, definitions proposed by Pearce and Turner and action strategies such as found in Inskeep deal primarily with the basic premise that all groups involved in tourism should become more aware of development's environmental and sociocultural impacts and strive to reduce undesirable by-products of tourism activity. Given that actions to accomplish this aim would result in less intrusive forms of tourism development, there is still no clear definition as to what sustainable development is, and how sustainable tourism systems change over time to accommodate population increases or increasing tourism demand.

During the last twenty years image research has been an active field. Many researchers have studied how images change over time and the stimuli behind the change, and some have attempted to model the image formation process. Destination images, regardless of how they are formed, play an important and powerful role in an individual or group's travel decision process.

Since sustainable development is a function of use and destination images can be used to increase use, there appears to be a direct link between how images are formed and the concept of sustainable tourism systems. There is indeed a link between the two but it is fat from direct and it does not follow that images used to increase visitation make achieving an operationally sustainable system more difficult. However, before delving into that line of reasoning, some background on the image formation process is necessary.

Images Formation for Sustainable Tourism Systems

The process of image formation involves not only creating awareness of place but projecting selected images to an identified audience or market segment that is deemed most receptive to the message embodied in the images. Organic images emanate from sources not directly associated with any development organization. News reports, movies other ostensibly unbiased sources of information generate organic images of difference between an induced image and an organic places. The underlying one is the control that people in the destination area have over how the image is presented. Induced images are presented by destination promoters project what the destination is offering to travellers. Organic images are not directly controlled by destination promoter idea of what exists there.

Images are formed on two levels, primary and secondary. Secondary image formation results from any information received from another source. Primary image formation results from actual visitation. In a sense Phelps has grouped both Gunn's induced and most of the organic image formation agents into one type and separated out actual visitation into a distinctly different form of image formation. To understand the relationship between the image formation process and sustainable tourism systems it is necessary to analyse further the different ways in which destination images are formed.

Using Gunn's image typology as a starting point, it is possible to view the image formation process as a continuum consisting of eight distinctly different components. The stages often operate concurrently, forming an image in the mind of the prospective traveller that is individually distinct in other words, an individual's perceptual filters will form an independent image unique to that person but with features shared by others.

Over Induced I

Beginning at the induced end of the continuum, the first image formation agent is termed Overt Induced I and consists of traditional forms of advertising. The use of television, print media, brochures, billboards, etc. by Gunn into destination promoters is a direct attempt to form particular images in the minds of prospective travellers.

The person receiving the message is not confused by who is delivering it. It is clearly a blatant attempt to construct an image of the salient attributes of the destination in the minds of the targeted audience. Depending on the type of medium chosen, the cost of reaching an individual may be very low although total cost can be quite expensive.

Overt Induced I image formation agents have the advantage of being able to achieve widespread coverage as well as targeting specific markets. But they suffer from low credibility problems. People are constantly being subjected advertisements for all types of products. It does not take too marry experiences with products that fail to meet expectations before consumers become sceptical about what they are told. Tourism advertising is no exception. People may even be more dubious about some of the projected images of destinations simply because of the cost involved crying out the product.

Most of the tourism Internet and Web technology in use today can be categorized as a form of Overt Induced I image formation. Use of home pages identifies the producer, although producing the page is much less costly than traditional forms of advertising. At the moment, however, informing a potential customer of the existence of a home page and its address is becoming more problematic, as other forms of advertising are often used to direct someone to a site on the Web.

Over Induced II

Overt Induced II image formation agents consist of information received or requested, from tour operators, wholesalers and organizations which have a vested interest in the travel decision process but which are not directly associated with any particular destination.

Tour operators act as gatekeepers of information, with the type of information distributed by them contributing to the images people hold about certain areas. A major function of tour operators is to create attractive destination images for the places to which they arrange tours.

Destination promoters will work with tour operators to select images to be presented, but since tour operators are interested in increasing their business, only certain images will be passed on to their clientele. This may lead to unrealistic portrayals of place and result in destination images not supported or desired by a destination's host society.

Destination area promoters do have some control over the images presented through tour operators, especially in countries where operators must register. When this is the case, tour operators may be subject to pressure, subtle or direct, to project specific destination images.

Most of the time there is no conflict, as national organizations are primarily interested in marketing the country and increasing visitation. Images which tour operators use to achieve this goal will most likely be supported by the national tourism organization. Because of the credibility tour operators enjoy with their clients, this source of image formation may surpass the importance of all the Over Induced I forms, especially in countries where foriegn travel is heavily dependent on package tours.

Covert Induced I

Proceeding along the image formation continuum, the next component is termed Covert Induced I. It consists of developing destination images using traditional forms of advertising, as in Overt Induced I; however, the image is now being projected through the use of a second-party spokesperson.

The use of a second party rends to mask attempts by destination promoters to influence the audience directly, hence the use of the adjective covert. Covert Induced I formation are a direct attempt to eliminate some of Induced I types of the problems of low credibility inherent in the Overt Induced I image formation process.

Second-party spokespersons are generally chosen based on and credibility. Credibility with the market is therefore name recognition a improved, but the trade-off comes in terms of increasing cost since the second-party spokesperson is usually compensated for their time and audience recognition factor.

The second-party spokesperson approach works best when specific products are advertised, but it can also be used for tourism image development if the second party has positive, high-recognition value.

A recognizable spokesperson will attract attention to the endorsed product using their attractive and likeable qualities to differentiate their advertisement from the clutter of other advertising messages.

Credibility is enhanced whenever the advertised product has high psychological or social risk, which may be the case with long-haul international travel. The use of a second-party does not affect market penetration because the same advertising strategy as that in overt Induced I is involved.

Covert Induced II

The fourth component of image formation is termed Covert Induced I. The person influenced by this agent should not be aware that destination promoters are directly involved in the development of the projected image. Covert induced II agents take the form of ostensibly unbased articles, reports and stories about a particular place delivered by someone with high credibility who apparently has no vested interest in the destination.

Familiarization trips are generally the vehicle used to achieve Covert Induced II types of image formation. Travel writers for newspapers, magazines or specific activity groups may be invited to participate in an all expenses paid trip to some area to sample the attractions. The end result is that writers facing deadline pressure will often write about their most recent travel experience.

This type of advertisement is a form of image development which may be very useful in reaching identified target markets. Familiarization trips are also held for tour brokers and operators in an attempt to develop favourable images, in their minds which will then be passed on to their clients.

Credibility rises as the image is now projected through a source chat does not appear to have any connection with the destination except through visitation, Cost is less than with other forms of induced image formation, as only expenses related to the writer's visit are covered, with production and distribution costs of the image development effort borne by the publication purchasing the writers work.

The increase incredibility and reduction in cost are somewhat offset by a decline in market penetration. For the image formation effort to be useful, the intended audience must be exposed to the report, article, etc. chat has been produced. This requires that a reader be predisposed to learn more about the area or specific activity featured. There is no captive audience with this type of image formation.

The destination area has less control over the published travel account because it has no veto power over what is written. Because of this, the type of image projected may not match the type of image with which residents of the destination area wish to be presented.

However, Covert Induced II types of image, formation provide a relatively low-cost means to develop destination images, albeit with some risk. For example, resort areas and small communities with limited advertising and promotion funds may find familiarization trips for carefully selected participants to be an effective way to develop their tourism image. It should be noted that some newspapers and magazines refuse to allow their travel writers to participate in an expenses paid *familiarization* trip, in order to avoid accusations of biased reporting which may also affect other aspects of their operation.

Autonomous

The fifth image component is termed Autonomous, It consists of independently produced reports, articles, films, documentaries, etc. about specific places. There are two subcomponents in the Autonomous category: News and Popular Culture. The most common form of autonomous image formation agents are television news stories. The destination area has no control over what appears in the story and its image is subject to someone else's interpretation. News stories, because of their apparently unbiased approach, are assumed to have major impacts on tourism image development. If the event reported is of major consequence, the, opportunity for Image change in a relatively short period of time Presents itself.

For example, Gartner and Shen studied the impact of the Tiananmen Square events on the Peoples Republic of China's (PRC) tourism image. A study assessing the mature markets' image of the PRC was conducted prior to Tiananmen Square. After the incident was reported on, sometimes with live coverage, by every major news station in the free world, the study was repeated, one year after the conflict, using essentially the same sample population and an identical survey instrument.

There were twenty-two activity and attraction attributes grouped into five categories which were analysed for change. Interestingly, even though most Of the attributes did show declines in impressiveness ratings, only seven out of twenty-two were significantly lower. The researchers also investigated image change for ten tourism services. Again, even though all ten declined in absolute value terms, only four were significantly different.

Significant differences were noted for services char were most likely to be important to tourists, such as safety and security, receptiveness of local people to tourists and pleasant attitudes of service personnel.

Survey respondents did not view services affecting the efficient movement of people as having changed as much but did consider people-to-people relationships to have suffered as a result of Tiananmen Square.

In conclusion, the autonomous image formation agents did change the PRC's tourism image in the short run, with the nature of the change more related to how the provision of touristic services were perceived rather than the country's activity or attraction base.

Another example of what can happen as a result of major news coverage is provided by Roehl. He investigated changes in travel agents' attitudes after Tiananmen Square. He found many agents advocated trade and military restrictions after the conflict. As attitudes are related to image formation, especially in the cognitive state, future travel to the PRC may depend not only on images held of touristic attitudes, but also on attitudes toward the host government.

Other studies also support the influence of autonomous image formation agents. The US Travel Service concluded from a study investigating foreigners' perceptions of the United States, that many images were based on news reports and movies that depicted violence in the country. The *Pacific Travel News* reported that US citizens' images of Korea were primarily derived from the popular television series *M.A.S.H.* and represented an image of Korea dated more than thirty years ago.

The autonomous image formation agent, because of its high credibility and high market penetration, may be the only agent capable of changing an area's image dramatically in a short period of time. One of the reasons for this may be the lack of information people have about destinations that are far removed from their home residence. If people from images based on little acquired information they are more susceptible to change when massive amounts of information are processed in a relatively short period of time.

The about studies provide evidence supporting the importance news reporting as autonomous image formation agents. It is also possible that the effect of autonomous change agents, although significant in the short-term may not be an important factor in long-term image change. Thurstone contends that, in the absence of any reinforcing information, images may revert to those field before the exogenous shock.

Although not thoroughly studied, this does appear to be the case, as in the absence of recurring events visitation figures show a rebound after the event has become part of history. The amount of time it takes to rebound does show some relationship to the event's magnitude and its cause. Natural disasters have short-term effects rarely lasting more than one season. Events instigated by people show longer periods of recovery. What does seem clear is that in the absence of reinforcing negative images there is a reversion to previously held images.

Popular culture portrays images of people and places. Increased travel to certain countries has been correlated with the success of films that use country images as a major backdrop to, the story's plot. Although the effects of popular culture on image formation have not been thoroughly studied, there is enough anecdotal evidence to suggest a strong relationship exists. Many states in the US have even organized film promotion offices to encourage companies to select locations in the state for their movies, television shows, etc.

Usolicited organic

The sixth image component is termed Unsolicited Organic. It consists of unrequested information received from individuals who have visited an area or believe they know what exists there. Information on other areas is received by people on a regular basis in conversation over coffee, at dinner with friends, during business meetings or in any place or setting where the topic shifts to world politics or just simply places recently visited. The person receiving the information has not requested it and therefore the credibility factor is only moderate. However, since it comes from an acquaintance it may carry a higher level of credibility than information received from any of the induced agents. Low market penetration counters the higher level of credibility, since only those people exposed to the message will be affected as individual communication is much less pervasive than mass media. But if the information is about a destination that has received relatively little exposure through the induced or autonomous agents, then unsolicited organic information can be a very important source of image formation. Cost of unsolicited organic image formation is nonexist unless one considers the indirect cost to the destination of an unfavourable report.

Solicited organic

The seventh component is termed Solicited Organic. It consists of requested information received from a knowledge source, generally one's friends or relatives. Because of the nature of the information flow, i.e. someone responding to a specific information request, the credibility factor is very high. The solicited organic component is very important when a person is in an information search mode.

This stage of image formation is also referred to as 'word of mouth' advertising. Market penetration is very low, however, because as more and more people are contacted for information a point is reached where most people will soon be providing information that simply reinforces what was received from others. Stutman and Newell refer to this as acquiring salient beliefs.

When the point where substantial reinforcement of previously stated beliefs is reached, the information seekers will analyse the information, evaluate it in terms of their own beliefs, assess motivations and finally make a decision as to which set to move the destination into. Although there is no direct cost to the destination area for this stage of image formation, the experience provided by the destination is of critical importance in forming positive salient beliefs about travel to the area. In the long run, in the absence of any negative autonomous image formation, the solicited organic component is the most critical determinant of an area's economic tourism health.

Organic

The final component of image formation is simply termed Organic and consists of actual visitation, after which a new destination image is formed consists of actual visitation, after which a new destination in the mind of the visitor. The visitor, holding a new image, feeds back into the image formation cycle as a distributor of information in the unsolicited and solicited organic components. Many studies of image change as a result of visitation have been conducted.

Destination Image Characteristics

Having examined the different ways in which destination images formed, there are some general image change characteristics that more or less guide those interested in developing and manipulating images. Touristic images change slowly with the larger the entity the more slowly the image changes. The rate of image change is inversely related to the complexity of the system. This is as true of complex ecosystems as this is of socially and politically structured entities. A tourism image is made up of many different parts including the natural resource base on which activities take place, the sociocultural system that governs the provisions and type of touristic services, and the created structures that serve the needs of tourists and may also provide some of the attractions. Boulding suggests that information affecting held images can produce three effects.

In the first instance, information is received that is not in conformity with held beliefs, setting up a situation of cognitive dissonance. The individual will attempt to avoid the incoming information, thereby reducing the dissonance. If enough information can be avoided the image remains essentially unaffected.

In the second instance, the information keeps coming and cannot be avoided, resulting in a gradual image change. In the third instance, enough new information is received to, result in a general reassessment of the image previously held, and leads to an entirely new image. So the key element in image change is the amount and extent of new information which is in contrast to the image currently held.

Autonomous image change agents, if constant and prolonged, will eventually be unavoidable, causing an image shift. Induced image formation agents can also have the same effect, but because of their low credibility rating will take longer to affect change.

Gartner and Hunt studied touristic image change for the State of Utah over a twelve-year period. There was evidence linking increased visitation to an improved state image, although Utah's image did not improve dramatically with respect to its nearest competitors. The image of the region in which Utah was located had also improved, leading to the conclusion that an improvement in a larger entity, the intermountain region of the United States, had benefited all states within the region.

Further evidence of the relatively long time factor involved in changing touristic images can be found in Crompton, Cumings and Kotler. In the absence of any major news event causing an individual to process massive amounts of information quickly, destination image will remain relatively constant in the short run. Consistency should not be confused with repetition of the same message. Exposure to the same advertisement can result in a diminishing marginal a 1990. Six exposures to the same commercial may be the point at which diminishing marginal rates of effectiveness.

The smaller the entity is in relation to the whole, the less of a chance to develop an independent image. This rule has its exceptions, and generally they relate to distance from market and strength of brand image. Hunt in one of the earliest tourism image studies, found that in to destination was a factor in the distance from one's permanent residence from the destination in image held of the destination.

A brand, as defined by Okoroafo is a name, design, symbol or combination of these used to identify a service of products. A state, or in the case of international tourism a country, provides brand identification for image development. Slogans such as 'I Love New York', 'Akwaaba' or 'Say Yes to Michigan' all create a point of reference and create a perception based on the images evoked from these brand identification statements.

Brand identification does not rule out the establishment of a strong independent image at the community or regional level, but the more important in localized areas and establishment of that image will bless distinct the further one is removed from the community.

There are exceptions and it is possible for a smaller entity to have such a strong image that it overpowers the larger area. This may be the case where the only opportunity for developing an image through the autonomous agents. Image change, to be effective, depends on an assessment of present images. Changing an image depends on knowing what images prospective travellers now hold and initiating efforts to reinforce existing images or move images in a new direction. Image change efforts are essentially wasted if baseline data establishing present image position are not known. Understanding images held by target markets is essential to avoid moving the image into a position held by an able and strong competitor.

To achieve a sustainable tourism system, host communities must become directly involved in identifying the appropriate images to project, and must decide which groups will be the recipients of the images. They must also decide what they mean by sustainable, and then determine if their resources are sufficient to support the images they wish to project.

The reason for this is that images build experience expectations and different touristic experiences will tax local systems in different ways. Cohen discusses four fundamental factors that affect environmental impacts. They are resiliency of the ecosystem where the activity takes place, intensity of site use, type of activities engaged in, and length of stay. In the absence of any proactive planning, the chances for achieving a sustainable system diminish.

One can look at the process as a series of steps that must be addressed concurrently. Basically, the process begins by answering questions which will provide a good idea of the current situation and the desired outcome. Some of the questions that should be asked include:

1 What type of tourist do vie now attract?

2 Is this the type of tourist we want to attract in the future?

3 What is the image we currently project?

4 How do we project our current image

5 What type of tourism development planning is currently in place?

6 Are there any indications that the type of tourism we have is civet whelming any of our local systems (e.g. environmental)

7 What indicators can we use to measure change?

8 Who is responsible for measuring change'

Once these questions are addressed then an appropriate image mix can be determined. However, if a community is tourism-dependent or the image it currently protects is not the one it wishes to project, the right image mix may contain some of the agents at the induced end of the continuum. Extensive use of these agents should be viewed with caution.

Because many of them have the ability to reach large numbers of people, the chance is present of increasing use beyond a destination's ability to cope with growth. To achieve anything resembling a sustainable system, intensive planning, including relevant research to assess and monitor systems, is required.

Destinations that rely heavily on the induced image formation agents enter into a high-risk game with respect to sustainable tourism systems. As an analogy, consider theme parks or amusement parks. Those that prosper are always introducing new attractions at periodic intervals. Whether it is a new type of roller-coaster, wide-screen cinema, aquarium or some other type of mega-attraction, each one has its own life-span with respect to increasing attendance from existing patrons or attracting new clientele.

At some point a new attraction is required to provide an attendance boost. The same can be said for destinations heavily dependent on tourism for their economic well being. Those destinations that rely less on natural attractions and more on contrived or human-built facilities will be more dependent on induced image formation agents to maintain a healthy tourism industry.

Little has been said about the impact of autonomous types of image formation. Evert though destination areas have little control over these agents, there still exist opportunities to make use of them. For example, the case of a natural disaster the resulting news coverage will portray an are in distress, with one of the outcomes an inevitable decline in visitation, at least in the short term.

'Sustainable' then takes on an entirely new meaning, and some marginal businesses needed for product diversity it become synonymous with survival. There are ways to manipulate the media and recover more quickly from the image formation effects of negative news coverage.

Understanding how the image formation process affects various groups is another important consideration. If the travel decision-making body is comprised of a family unit, induced image formation agents may be a top priority. Gitelson and Crompton found family groups were more likely to use media sources for information acquisition than singles. They also found that college-educated individuals were more likely to use Destination Specific Travel Literature.

Capella and Greco found that people over sixty years of age were more inclined to rely on solicited organic image formation agents as this group's destination selection was greatly influenced by families and friends. Some print media were also important information sources for this group. Age was also found to be a factor in determining credibility ratings of various companies and further investigation may show a relationship between age and different types of image formation agents. Timing also has to be considered. Van Raaij and Francken found Overt Induced 1 sources of image formation to be important information sources early in the decision process. Overt Induced II sources enter into the information search process at a later stage.

The type of image(s) to be projected must be addressed. If a strong brand image already exists, less money and effort will be required to develop a local area image which is consistent with the dominant brand image. On the other hand, if a strong unique image which is independent or counter to the prevailing brand image is to be projected, all image formation agents should be considered as important contributors. The amount of money required for a small entity to establish an image different from the prevailing brand image requires large numbers of tourists be hosted to justify the expense and time involved in forming a unique image.

Agenda-for for Sustainable Tourism Systems

In trying to determine the opportunities and limitations of visitor management it has to be recognized that, like many of the terms and phrases which occur in the tourism literature, visitor management lacks convenient definition. In general we might suggest that it is an approach which seeks:

1. To protect and ideally enhance the resource, be it natural or cultural, which draws visitors to a particular location.

2. To maintain and improve the economic benefits which tourism can bring.

3. To assist visitors in enjoying their visit.

In practice we may well recognize that encouraging repeat visits is perhaps an unstated objective, while improving the visitors' perception of the location and of the managing agency is understandably never far from the surface. Seen by some to be integral to the development of visitor management is the observation that similar situations vary with regard to their apparent maximal levels of numbers of visitors. This leads to an understandable interest in determining optimal numbers of visitors and explains the long-running carrying capacity debate and the interest it arouses.

Like all multivariate analyses, any values arrived at are almost inevitably case specific no that this detracts from case-specific programmes to propose and rigorously apply and refine models incorporating social, physical and perceptual components.

Nevertheless, it is unlikely that extensive expenditure of time and effort in determining universally applicable recommended visitor numbers will be helpful, although natural resource constraints, especially in terms of water and waste disposal, are of value with regard to total tourist bedspace provision.

Consequently, while total visitor numbers is understandably an attractive measure in an industry where total annual arrivals and bednights, total tourist expenditure and percentage contribution to GDP are values that appear to determine success and failure, what the visitors do and how they do it is equally if not more important. Therefore, it can be argued that visitor management has a significant role to play in ameliorating the undesirable impacts of tourism and potentially moving tourism activity towards a more sustainable approach.

In this discussion the concept of sustainability is recognized as deriving in part from the stewardship perception of the environment and as such it may be argued to be a logical extension of the ideas of the nineteenth-century advocates of the national parks of the new world'. While many authors anticipated the emergence of sustainable tourism, the Brundtland Commission produced the now widely quoted definition of sustainable development as 'development that meets the needs of the present without compromising the needs of future generations to meet their own needs', which placed the idea of sustainable development firmly on the public agenda.

The apparent diversity of tourism, which in many instances appears to prevent it from being given the socioeconomic priority it deserves, has not proved to be an obstacle in the appraisal of tourism activities in sustainable terms. Indeed, the very fact that we may regard tourism as a nonessential, freetime activity imbues the sustainable tourism debate with additional moral fervour.

This is understandable when we recognize that the perception of the environment, both natural and cultural, as a necessary component of a quality tourism product is now more widely shared than it was ten to twenty years ago. Accordingly, the sustainable tourism debate has readily accepted environmental concerns along with economic and sociopolitical realities. Most authors would agree that among the principles crucial to the concept of sustainability are:

— the importance of preserving essential ecological processes;

— the need to protect both human heritage and biodiversity.

Consequently, we face the task of trying to suggest practical ways in which tourism as an economic activity does not impair the quality of the natural and cultural environment or compromise the resource base and potential of future generations. Canada's Green Plan is a bold attempt to move an entire economy on to a more sustainable foundation. The Island of Bali has been the subject of an extensive study of sustainability. These contributions all propose sociopolitical and planning frameworks for the implementation of sustain able policies, whether for tourism or other economic activities. However, we should not lose sight of the many criticisms of sustainable tourism that suggest it to be a worthy but totally unrealistic ideal which has already largely been destroyed through almost universal adoption by the tourism industry. Nevertheless, what does seem to be agreed by both the advocates and critics of sustainable tourism is the need to identity clearly who are the decision makers and at what levels they operate.

One approach recognizes that natural/ environmental resources are characterized by system-like processes, interacting with the socioeconomic system, which, of course, includes the tourism system. This provides a valuable framework within which we can pose the more specific question as to what is the rule of visitor management in an industry, the product is consumed at the point of origin, unlike most other products.

Clearly defined locations such as islands and small states, as well as national and natural parks, walled cities and holiday villages lend themselves to the application of a systems approach because their boundaries, while not closing the system, are so well defined. It is in the context of these clearly defined destinations that a range of visitor management approaches, drawn from a range of different locations, will be reviewed. Their applicability !L defined tourism locations, which are either islands or small states or which share similar locational characteristics, will be discussed.

If it is legitimate to argue that management of visitors is an integral part of the overall management of tourism, then it is also appropriate to ask what features of tourism planning and development strategies are most likely to be influenced by visitor management? An indicative but by no means exhaustive list of topics may include decisions relating to:

— minimizing impacts;

— access;

— increasing the length of stay (stay longer—spend more);

— visitor and local participation;

— raising the profile of all or part of a location.

In order to achieve any of these objectives we have to communicate with the visitors, and communication is of heart of what is today widely referred to as interpretation. From its mi outset interpretation can be seen, as all informed and conscious attempt to will support !or a philosophy that is based upon the stewardship) concept and is clearly aligned to the sustainable approach.

The skill of the interpreter is to communicate information in such a way that it both improves visitor enjoyment and sustains and protects the resource. However, not all those in direct contact with the visitors see themselves in this dual role: as a 'room steward' with the UK National Trust is reputed to have remarked when asked a question about a particular piece of furniture, 'I'm not here to give you a lesson laddie, I'm here to stop you nicking it!'

The complexity of any given visitor management strategy will be a reflection of the integrity and complexity of the resource, the range of other demands and the numbers of visitors. For example, the siege tunnel running through the Rock of Gibraltar simply comprises a tunnel hewn through the rock with side chambers at different points along its length. While the main tunnel is adequately lit, the installation of sensors triggering animated installations located in the naturally dark side chambers provides an effective and powerful evocation of former events, significantly enhancing visitor enjoyment while causing no discernible deterioration to the solid fabric (stone) of the immediate resource. Equally, in this case, there is no other competing use requirement to consider.

Potential resolution of conflict is much more apparent in the management of visitors to historic properties such as those belonging in perpetuity to the National Trust (NT) in England and the National Trust for Scotland (NTS). Many of these properties, like other tourist locations, are in some ways 'islands', being deliberately separated from everyday experience with little opportunity for there to be any impact upon contemporary society.

In the particular case of NT properties, management decisions are very much influenced by the 'conservation for all time' ethic and visitor needs are generally of secondary importance. Seen in this context, the anecdote used above is fully understandable, while not necessarily reflecting the most positive attitude to integrated management. Indeed, there are those who would challenge the validity of the fundamental ethic of 'conservation for all time', believing that it is both unattainable and undesirable as an overriding management objective.

However, in order to reconcile these current objectives, the majority of the Trust's historic properties have limited opening, being restricted daily, within the week and within the year. In some instances, particularly with ,new' properties, time-ticketing has been introduced, but this can mean that the house is sold out soon after opening, resulting in highly dissatisfied visitors who arrive, so they would argue, 'in plenty of time'. The introduction of such a measure depends in essence upon a judgement as to how long each individual requires to visit the property a virtually impossible value to determine, varying by, observation from minutes to several hours. These extremes may be a reflection of the interpretative material available, which ranges from relatively simplistic to in-depth guidebook", with little in between.

The resulting visitors therefore comprise those who have been exceptionally well informed and those who have possibly gained little apart from superficial general impressions, but who have experienced a brief encounter with the 'moment in time' that the Trust seeks to preserve. It is in this context of matching the objectives of the resource managers with the aspirations of the visitor, inevitably diverse, that visitor management has a role, not least, as Weideger has shown, in questioning the objectives of the resource managers and their assumptions as to visitor interests and requirements.

In the majority of cases there are many possible tales to tell, with the added attraction of genuine rather than simulated authenticity. The production of varied information in a variety of forms with different themes a relatively inexpensive operation offers the potential to enthuse and inform different visitor groups, while at the same time significantly increasing the level of control regarding selective resource utilization, residence times and through put.

Moreover, it encourages repeat visits. Hence, while many emerging destinations can be criticized for having an overtly product-led approach to their promotion, other locations can equally fail to make best use of the diversity of their resources by not drawing visitors' attention to the range of opportunities, concentrating only upon a few and thereby accentuating problems of overuse and associated negative effects.

Clearly while site management of dedicated attractions such as National Trust properties is restricted to the management of the visitor/ resource interface, in the case of the majority of islands and small states we are considering tourism activity and management alongside a range of other activities.

In general at National Trust properties has not been maintained beyond the first two seasons of opening as demand tends to reduce. However, there are many instances where high levels of demand are maintained and there is a constant need to achieve a balance between the needs of the visitor and the needs of the resource. The Bayeux Tapestry, dating from the eleventh century, is displayed under carefully Controlled conditions of light, and temperature and humidity in its home town of Bayeux in Normandy. Visitors file past the tapestry wearing headsets at a pace controlled to some extent by the commentary. To encourage visitor enjoyment, the approach to the Tapestry incorporates both a modern tapestry version of the full story and a short film. This combination of preliminary preparation results in minimal queuing, adequate time to inspect the original and optimal conservation.The introduction of deliberate introductory experiences, developed to a high degree for example at Futuroscope near Poitiers, undoubtedly, allows a significant degree of visitor management while avoiding the inevitable frustration of queuing. Such introductory programmes clearly lend themselves to the management of what are in some senses educational attractions, rather than to the queues of people waiting for rides at a theme or leisure park.

The requirement to address visitor management and cultural resources within Europe is arguably at its most acute and complex in the Italian cities of art, especially Venice. The Venice case has attracted much attention and has been well documented and analysed, particularly from an economic perspective. In reviewing the patterns and types of visitors in relation to the socioeconomic disruption, there is again an understandable tendency to consider the total numbers as the primary quantifiable variable representing the visitor. This occurs despite the fact that many visitors to Venice arrive with considerable expectations and little knowledge of the city beyond the Rialto Bridge, St Mark's Square and the Cathedral. While an additional bridge across the Grand Canal may be seen as too extreme a management measure, clear signposting and widely available timetables in several languages for the water buses (vaporetti) are among the relatively simple steps that could be taken to ease the physical congestion which is one of the more conspicuous undesirable impacts.

There are, however, far more complex tourist management issues relating not simply to the cultural and environmental resources but more to changes in the type of tourist. Particular concern relates to a decrease in the numbers staying in high-class hotel accommodation in Venice. This decline has coincided with a rapid rise in visitors choosing to stay in the mainland environs of Venice and daytrippers from other parts of the Veneto and other regions of Italy.

The debate has to consider whether these changes are a response to price sensitivity Venice hotel prices are very high by European standards and/ or a reflection, at least in part, of a reduction, in the quality of the visitor experience. Equally confined locations have to decide they wish to encourage the development of an accommodation.

The experience in Venice has been an overall reduction in the economic benefits, as day visitors and those not staying tend to contribute, little. Additionally, the demands they do make have increase the numbers of souvenir shops and fast-food outlets, with the loss of grocery and other shops of a day-to-day functional nature serving residents needs. This in turn is related to the very high property prices which have forced many would-be residents off the islands, on to the mainland periphery.

Venice provides us with a microcosm of the management issues that characterize many small discrete locations such as islands. Determining the future of islands as tourist destinations requires a series of interrelated decisions with regard to access, length of stay, accommodation provision, local participation and impact reduction. These decisions are governed by the relative significance and value of the tourism industry as opposed to possible alternatives. This is especially pertinent in the case of islands that wish to, diversify the industry towards cultural tourism, such as Malta, The visitor effectively places an economic value on the culture of an island.

Those responsible for tourism management have the objective of visitor satisfaction directly (e.g. through interpretation and information) and indirectly (e.g. through good water quality, litter disposal) in order to ensure maximum economic return. What is also very evident is that visitor management has to be implemented within a coordinated approach to the management of the tourism operation. This may be seen as one of the functions of the socioeconomic structure of an island. In cases like these the systems' view of the three overlapping fields of economics, environment and society provides a model within which we can begin to identify the processes and outcomes leading to and resulting from decision taking.

Proposals have been made to exercise control through regulation of access in order to ration the number of visitors. This type of control can be managed more easily in the case of visitors on package tours than in the case of independent visitors, but is nevertheless a feature which lies within the power of many locations. In some instances actual numbers of arrivals are limited, as in Bhutan, and in others a limit may be placed upon bed numbers, as in the Seychelles. The Galapagos Island while riot setting absolute limits, are able through the agency of its park, status to impose a management charge upon all is for international arrivals and is expected to rise to $120. Admission charges for protected areas are not idea and have been reviewed by Boo and Lindberg among others.

Both the Galapagos Islands and the islands of the Venice Lagoon are world examples of natural and cultural resources and, as such, would appear to be able to present a very strong, case, for the principle of visitors paying the cost of the necessary resource management. Once this principle has been established, it can be extended to less well-known sites, as has been the case with Ecuador's other less known national parks on the mainland of South America.

Given the range of those involved in the tourism industry, of islands, one might argue that the tour operator, as the overall provider of the tourism product, is best positioned to manage the visitors. This challenge has been accepted to varying degrees by different companies, both large and small. Examples include a specialist company based in England that offers a range of guided walking tours in various parts of southern Europe.

Group size is controlled to a maximum of fifteen or sixteen and the party is accompanied from the moment of arrival in the country to the moment of departure. Care is taken to select accommodation and restaurants of the highest quality which typify the local gastronomy. Equal effort is given to the provision of information about the location and appropriate interpretation of the natural and cultural environment. Visitors are guided in terms of local customs and practices in order that the social interaction is positive and complementary. Such holistic approaches present an attractive prospect for the future, but they come at a cost, in this particular case of around $120-$180 per day, excluding airfares. Nevertheless, this particular company has earned high praise from customers and accolades from the industry, for providing an alternative experience which values and preserves all aspects of the environment. Initially, their programmes were most successful in specific locations which have maintained a quality cache, such as Tuscany, and not so successful in less known and positively perceived destinations, reflecting the broader picture of sustainable tourism as being more readily applicable to small-scale activities occurring in cared for environments.

As tourism often involves a large private sector commitment, the various components of the product, including transport, accommodation and attractions, are frequently under separate management and decision making regimes. In these situations visitor management tends to be undertaken by individual attraction authorities, as in the case of Venice, and concentrates upon the visitor experience, principally within the

Concern is often expressed that tourism development plans and strategies are produced by the public sector and imposed upon the private sector, which sees itself as the major provider of the tourism product and recipient of the impacts. An example of this can be seen on the Portuguese Algarve, in the resort of Albufeira, which claims to have 50 per cent of the region's beds and therefore approximately 20 per cent of all the bedspace in Portugal. Here, coincident with the development of a long-awaited regional tourism plan, private sector interests in Albufeira, have formed an Albufeira Promotional Agency on behalf of the residents. This Agency will operate, so it is claimed, interests involved within a country. Given, however, that both nation states share a number of characteristics notably of less developed status and of smallness of size there are important potential pitfalls in ecotourism that are highlighted by the experience of Belize.

There is no doubt that ecotourism will continue to offer the tantalizing prospect of economic diversification and enhanced foreign-exchange earnings for such small countries, with little else to base their development prospects on other than their natural resource endowment. It is essential, to recognize that ecotourism is not automatically a sustainable Option. Without adequate understanding of tho underlying factors and careful planning and management, ecotourism may compromise prospects for sustainable development not only for tourism in particular, but also for the nation in general. The central message is one of collective responsibility and a holistic approach involving governments, tourists, tourism enterprises and destination areas alike.

4

Sustainable Tourism in Small Islands

The origins of the concept of sustainability can be traced back to the conservation movement in the mid-nineteenth century, and the economic notion of maximum sustainable yield with regard to common property resources such as ocean fisheries. Boulding anticipated more recent thinking in his perception of the spaceship earth, echoed by Schumacher, while others forecast more dramatically resource depletion and environmental degradation.

Sustainable development is a multidimensional and vague concept, there being over three hundred or more definitions, with the result that much controversy surrounds the meaning of the term and its application. This vagueness is its greatest shortcoming for different sectors in society such as natural scientists, conservationists, economists, industry, governments and planners who have each interpreted it to legitimize their own actions and objectives.A central feature of the concept and the controversy is the role of the natural environment. However, a debate has arisen as to the relationship between the natural and human-made environment in terms of the capital assets which are handed on to future generations to meet their needs. While it is largely agreed that the assets total should be maintained, or ever] increased, there is certainly no consensus that, for example, the human-made environment can be increased at the expense of the natural.

If the present generation, as a result of economic development, damages the total asset value through degradation of the natural environment, the question arises as to how future generations can offset this. The soft or weak approach, largely reflecting the view of orthodox market economists and industry, accepts that environmental considerations need to be taken into account in policy or decision making but allows for substitutability between human-made and natural environments. In the extreme soft case, development can be equated with the continued pursuit of economic growth with minimal regard, or reaction by individuals or enterprises, to the natural environment.

Conversely, the hard or strong approach, advocated by natural scientists, conservationists and economists, imposes the imperative of environmental absolutes. In general the hard view posits that in the face of uncertainty, of irreproductibility resources and possible irreversibility of decisions, what is known as the precautionary principle should prevail this simply state that is should be assumed that, unless proved otherwise, an activity might damage the environment. The hard approach to sustainable development, with which the authors identify, embraces therefore not only the issue of maintaining or even enhancing the natural physical environment but also the socio-culture composition of a community. This is not to argue that its culture and social structure should remain unchanged sustainable development recognizes that societies are dynamic. What is asserted is that these may have been or are being impoverished by the pursuit of economic growth. Thus in a sense the sociocultural issue is akin to that concerning biodiversity.

The aim of a sustainable development policy is to ensure that the detrimental impacts of economic development are minimized, or ideally, eliminated. This implies that fundamental changes in production and consumption patterns encompassing cultural and social dimensions, as well as the economically based material ones, need to be brought about. Sustainable development then is concerned with improvements in the quality of life, emphasizing conservation and acknowledging that the natural environment is of equal, or even greater, value as capital, labour or land as a productive input. This raises not only inter-temporal issues but also those concerning intragenerational distribution, suggesting the duty of stewardship by the present generation to avoid irreversible change through species destruction or in creasing risks to life in the future from, for instance, radioactive or toxic chemical wastes.

As an industry dependent on natural and human-made resources or attractions, tourism is sensitive to any degradation of the environment and hence has a vested interest in its maintenance and quality. A principal somewhat incoherent theoretical idea, involving economic, environmental concern is, understandably, to sustain its resources base but at the same time and social issues into strategies for action, which balance these competing ensuring that development takes place. As such it tends to adopt an attitude much like any other industry, focusing on its competitive position of allowing consumer demand to determined to determine whether sustainbility will be embraced. There is then a suspicion that sustainability is interpreted as viability.

It is against the background of a somewhat confused and confusing conceptual debate at both international and national levels, overlaid by statements, sometimes bordering on the hysterical, of blatant self-interest, to which land-use planners have had to respond. In general the message they have received is that the main issue is conservation of resources and protection of the environment and its quality, consistent with improving the quality of life.For example, in the UK, which does not have a specific legal framework for the implementation of environmental policies at a national level, the promotion of sustainable development has largely been devolved to the local level Considered in this way the criteria for sustainable development dictate through the land-use planning system.

A number of planning policy guidance that the needs of both present and future generations have to be redefined to notes indicate the central government's strategies, which also suggest lessen the importance of material elements. Local authorities have issued their own strategy on environmental policies, reflecting the Agenda incoherence that surrounds the concept which consequently also applies to 21 declaration at Rio de Janeiro and the European Commis the notion of sustainable tourism.

While acknowledging that sustainable Fifth Environmental Action Programme, recognizing their obligation in achieving sustainable development. They have also cooperated with central government to promote it through a local Agenda 21 process. The planner's problem is to translate this ill-defined and somewhat incoherent theoretical idea, involving economic, environmental and social issues into strategies for action, which balance these competing claims, implementing them within the existing political structure.

Planners have already taken a stance development beginning to define and delineate principles, strategies and policies within their existing framework of empowerment to this extent they are ahead of social and political awareness and commitment. In general the profession advocates national environmental agencies linking with international organisations in bodies and members of society in another. With respect to specific policies, particularly those concerning the setting of limits to acceptable environment bodies and members of society in another. For instance the UK local Agenda 21 initiative contains statements regarding the setting of limits to environmental impacts and imposing constraints on the generation of waste and pollutants.

The dilemma facing planning is not only a complex conceptual one of devising sustainability procedures and practice, there being a wide chasm between well-intentioned statements on action at an international level and implementation at the local, operational level, but also a structural one.

The pervasive transnational nature of environmental processes necessitates an integrated approach bringing together environmental protection agencies and land-use planning, a structure and process only recently recognized as essential in many countries. A more integrated approach implies the development of responsibility down to the local level, which runs counter to tile current trends towards greater central government control in individual states and within the European Union (EU) concerning the degree of subsidiarity allowed to member countries. Here, a tension can undoubtedly arise between the desire by individual countries to maintain autonomous priorities, policies and means for achieving environmental goals and the need for international cooperation and coordination.

With respect to environmental issues, there is one specific EU instrument already in place, namely environmental impact assessment (EIA) for a wide spectrum of planning. However, EIA covers only certain categories of new development and redevelopment. Moreover, EIA is not a continuous process for monitoring the operation of a development after its completion. There fore, it cannot be employed to assess the environmental impact of existing development. Thus, in endeavouring to secure environment sustainable tourism, particularly in more mature destinations, EIA is of limited benefit simply because most tourism facilities, services and infrastructure already exist.

The challenge to planning, if it is to make a meaningful contribution to environmental matters, is to move beyond mere statements of principles or state of the environment reports, and the limited powers at its disposal such as EIA, to derive operational processes and procedures of its own. Despite its espousal of actions for environmental protection at this highest level, realistically planning can only initiate sustainability on a bottom-up basis. That is, it can advocate the introduction and application of procedures by the public, private and personal (household) sectors at the lowest and most practical level.

The implementation of environmental auditing, defined below, provides such a procedure for evaluating and monitoring the relationship between existing tourism development and activities, and an island environmental quality (with EIA performing a similar role for proposed of, future development). The findings of environmental auditing may well imply a withdrawal from those current tourism activities, and certain curtailment of further tourism development, which rob or imperil sustainable development for future generations.

However, neither EIA nor environmental auditing are directly concerned with the implementation of sustainable development policies. Their purpose is to assess and evaluate performance as a prerequisite to devising appropriate strategies and instruments. For example, arising from an environmental audit of a visitor attraction, if negative environmental effects are identified, visitor impact management strategies and policies would need to be introduced or existing ones revised.

This suggests that 'the best environmental management conies with regular monitoring of how the planned and developed visitor use is affecting the environment'

Tourism products range from those which are resource based (e.g. unique attractions whether nature's endowment or society's heritage) to those which are user-oriented (e.g. human-made attractions, such as theme parks, created especially for tourist use). Such natural, cultural or created attractions or marketing-oriented resources are the resource base which draws tourists to destinations. In large measure, the quality of the tourist's experience is determined by the quality of this resource base, that is the destination environment. This dependence can be a positive force for environmental protection and enhancement by the destination tourism industry. Questions, however, arise concerning the sustainability of tourism resource bases of destinations, particularly in the case of small islands because of their limited size and insularity.

Small islands are often resource-poor environments in terms of their very limited both in quantity and variety natural attractions, Limited natural resources are very much a function of restricted area. A comparative ad vantage will exist for the development of certain resource-based tourism products, frequently using the natural environment, including climate, especially in the case of tropical and subtropical islands. This natural resource base of climate and coast (beaches, coral reefs, etc.) is a sustainable resource, even though all aspects are not naturally renewable.

Coastlines are dynamic, shaped by powerful natural forces, liable in places to flood hazard, erosion and land instability, as well as being fragile environments for example, marine shallows, dune systems. This natural resource environment is the core feature of the small island tourism product, usually supporting a variant of the sun-sea-sand holiday but including, especially in the case of Mediterranean islands, a heritage environment.

Activities undertaken by sunlust holiday-makers may be particularly damaging to the environment (e.g. water-skiing, off-road driving, golf); or may be those for which alternative production, consumption and disposal practices would be less environmentally damaging (e.g. presenting scuba diving, use of swimming pool); or be attuned to environmental protection (e.g. cycling, sunbathing, whale-watching).

Therefore, assessment of the capacity of an island's attractions to support tourists needs to consider not only numbers of tourists but also the types of activity in which those tourists engage. As noted above, each activity can have different impacts on the destination environment.

Development of an island's attractions for tourism normally requires the provision of support facilities, services and infrastructure or operationally or functionally oriented resources such as accommodation and transport termini necessary to serve tourists away from home. This leads to an extension of the built environment of the island. Thus, any environmentally based assessment of the tourism potential of the island's attractions must also be related to the provision and capacity of the support facilities and services.

Development of the latter also has an environmental impact since additional demands are placed on the island's natural resource environment, especially with regard to the supply of energy, water and building materials. Indeed, such development can degrade attractions, for example where sand and coral are extracted for construction purposes.

Tourists increase the challenge of managing sustainably an island's resources. In large numbers tourists are a threat to the island's environment, as well as increasing the dependence of the island's economy upon tourism through further export concentration. Also, because island tourism is often more reliant on air travel its tourism industry is generally more structured and less diversified than that found in mainland destinations.

For certain periods of the year tourists often double the island's population leading to:

— overcrowding, i.e. increased pressure on the natural resource environment, including demands for service provision such as water;

— overdevelopment of the built environment as the location and scale of facility, service and infrastructure development, normally favouring coastal sites, pressurizes the small land area available;

— pollution from sources within the island, i.e. degradation and overuse of the natural environment.

Eventually the quality of the tourist experience is reduced and the island's comparative advantage is lost. Combatting environmental damage after it has arisen is extremely difficult, involves high costs, and requires a long time. As a prerequisite of sustainable tourism the island's tourism industry, comprising private firms and public sector organizations, must act in an environmentally responsible manner compatible with the character and culture of the destination, at a scale which it can absorb and welcome.

The notion of stewardship of the environment must condition the island authority's tourism policy objectives: the development of environmentally friendly tourism products; compliance with environmental legislation and development of further resonable and workable environmental regulations; reduction of any negative environmental impacts of current tourism activities,' increased efficiency of resource use, including waste minimization and substitution of environmentally benign and renewable inputs; fostering of environmental awareness among the island's tourism entrepreneurs, employees, residents and tourists.

Environmental Auditing

Environmental auditing is defined as a management tool comprising a systematic, documented, periodic and objective evaluation of how well organizations, management and equipment are performing with the aim of contributing to safeguard the environment by facilitating management control of environmental practices, and assessing compliance with organisational policies, which would include regulatory requirements and standards applicable. All interactions between a private or public sector organization's business operations and its environmental surroundings, including all emissions to air, land and water, legal constraints, inputs and their sources, and effects on the neighbouring community, landscape and ecology, as well as the wider global environment, can be audited.

Environ-mental auditing procedures are applicable to all tourism businesses and all tourist destinations. Such auditing is a general methodology and not an approach which is specific to small islands. The major advantages of applying environmental auditing to an island destination are that the nature and extent of environmental problems arising from its existing tourism industry can be identified before they become a liability. For example, issues such as the landfill disposal of solid waste, the sea disposal of untreated or partially treated sewage, noise from aircraft taking off and landing, the supply of potable water and energy and the visual intrusion of quarrying for building materials can be particularly serious for islands, in, addition to problems arising from numbers of tourists and the types of activity they undertake at visitor attraction sites. Auditing allows benchmarks of good practice to be developed, and a basis to be established for evolving both destination and corporate environmental strategy. Environmental auditing is therefore emerging as one aspect of a comprehensive environmental management strategy, focusing on the operational phase of the tourism industry as part of a life-cycle analysis and quantifying the industry's environmental impacts 'from the cradle to the grave'.

The appropriate role for and principles underpinning the application of environmental auditing in tourism may be developed by analogy with integrated pollution control. Both individual tourism firms hotels, tour operators, visitor attractions, etc. and destination tourism/planning authorities need to be considered.

To control pollution, public/planning authorities set emission or environmental performance standards (EPS) for individual firms, e.g. for effluent and sewage disposal by a hotel into a natural water body, as well as establishing ambient or environmental quality standards (EQS) for the destination as a whole, e.g. for bathing and drinking water quality. Under the 'bubble' concept of emission control, EQS must relate to an environmental capacity which can be interpreted as a limit to acceptable change and can be expressed as a certain number of EPSs (in this case the island destination would be treated as a 'bubble' for water quality assessment).

Tourism firms would use environmental auditing to monitor compliance with their EPS for waste water disposal and the island tourism authority environmental auditing to monitor the destination's water EQS. Legislative standards, however, tend to define a floor or minimum environmental quality and environmental auditing goes well beyond monitoring compliance with such standards. In the case of tourism firms, it can be used on a self-assessment basis to review their overall environmental performance, adopting voluntarily a comprehensive 'duty of environmental care'. Indeed the 'duty of care' principle has been incorporated into the 1990 UK Environmental Protection Act placing the onus on those disposing of waste to ensure that the firms/ persons to whom waste is handed over are competent to deal with it properly. Likewise, environmental auditing offers public authorities a systematic approach to setting EQSs and reviewing the current state of the destination environment: it should complement the traditional 'command and control approach'.

As more tourism development is permitted in a destination, EQSs come under increasing pressure, even where new development conforms to EPSs. Existing tourism development must therefore conform to more stringent EPSs with the passage of time if further development is to be assuming that the primary tourism resource capacity has

Opportunities for improving the environmental performance of firms occur whenever equipment needs replacing, buildings refurbishing and supply contracts renewing: thus existing tourism facilities conforming to earlier standards can be upgraded. The benefits obtainable from and the procedures for environmental auditing by the individual tourism firm are presented elsewhere. The way would appear open for tour ism planning authorities to take initiatives in enhancing destination environmental quality.

Current tourism practices may not be best environmental practice and the use of environmental auditing will reveal, for both firms and destination authorities, that environmental damage can be reduced or environment, quality further enhanced. What can island tourism authorities expect or ask of their tourism firms? What is feasible, i.e., the minimum that can be expected of tourism firms voluntarily acting in an environmentally responsible way?

At the very least, the principle of best practicable means (BPM) a fundamental criterion in regulatory pollution control should apply: under this system changes in practice are evaluated in terms of what is reasonable, taking into account the costs of modification and the effect on the viability of the individual firm and the destination tourism industry.

This criterion has been refined in a European context to best available technology not entailing excessive cost. Normally BAT will apply but the presumption can be modified where the costs of applying it are excessive in relation to the environmental protection or improvement achieved. BAT is consistent with best practicable environmental option (BPEO), which introduced the idea of an audit trail in which feasible options for achieving particular objectives are systematically assessed in terms of environmental effects and the preferred solution most beneficial or least damaging to the environment as a whole is regularly reviewed.

This approach is also largely consistent with the prevention and 'polluter pays' principles but can be further extended under no-fault liability as incorporated into EU waste management legislation, whereby a producer of waste which damages the environment is liable for that damage even if not negligent.

Environmental auditing is evolving rapidly. Various types of audit are distinguishable: some limited and local in the scope of their environmental assessment, others general and global. Most audit types have been developed with the interests of private companies in mind. Such company auditing emphasizes fluxes into and out of the company, especially emissions and wastes, but many of these types of audit could equally well be applied to the operations of public sector agencies, for example national offices and tourist information centres. Of the types of audit used by companies some are applicable at the organizational level of the firm, i.e. the hotel chain, and others at the establishment or plant level, i.e. the individual hotel.

From the viewpoint of island tourism and planning authorities, environmental auditing will complement their activities and duties if it can be applied to the destination as a whole, that is, provide a means of monitoring the environmental quality of the destination which results from current levels and types of tourism. Situations involving interaction between the public and private sectors of the tourism industry can also arise where the public agencies are in a position to ask for certain types of audit to be undertaken by companies at the firm or, more likely, the establishment level.

Acquisitional audit

Where a company is taking over another firm, e.g. an international hotel chain buying a national chain, a one-off audit may be undertaken to establish the nature and extent of any environmental liabilities attaching to the activities of the firm being taken over. This type of audit relates to changing business structure and is applicable preliminary at the firm level.

Associate audit

Here a firm vets the environmental practices of its agents, subcontractors and suppliers, e.g. tour operators use only hotels having adequate waste water/sewage treatment or disposal facilities thus applicable at firm and establishment levels. An opportunity may exist at the destination level for an island tourism authority to exert similar pressure, e.g. an hotel can only be included in the official island accommodation brochure if it has a satisfactory environmental code of practice.

Compliance audit

A compliance audit involves the checks undertaken to ensure that the activities of a firm or establishment comply with any current environmental regulations affecting its operations in the tourist destination, e.g. an airline checking that its flight programme and aircraft comply with any noise limitation regulations at the destination airports it uses. Island planning and environmental health authorities may be instrumental in setting the environmental performance standards that have to be met.

Corporate audit

A corporate audit ensures that the firm's environmental policy is understood throughout the organization and that appropriate technical and advisory support on environmental matters is readily available, e.g. an hotel chain assessing the effectiveness of the environmental training programme for its staff.

Divestiture liability audit

When a firm is selling off part of its business interests, which may be a single establishment, a divestiture liability audit provides a statement of the establishment's environmental status. It could also apply to the privatization of public sector activities, e.g. the selling of state-owned hotels.

Health and safety audit

Comparable to a compliance audit but focusing on workplace risks to employees' health and safety, this audit is applied at firm and especially establishment levels but it is also relevant to such risks facing tourists visiting theatres, hotels, restaurants, and other visitor attractions. Legislative regulations are normally set by the government.

Issues audit

Auditing may be a response to a specific environmental issue, such as stratospheric ozone depletion, in a firm's or establishment's operations are, evaluated in relation to that issue, e.g. an hotel chain cheeks that it uses chloro-fluorocarbon—free (CFC) aerosols, retrieves any CFCs used in air conditioning plant for controlled disposal, uses alternatives to CK-blown plastic foams for insulation. In tourist, issues audits could be used to evaluate the contribution of the tourism industry to local ground water pollution, erosion of coral reefs, etc.

Product audit

A product audit reveals how a firm's existing product range measures up to its environmental policy criteria and suggests how products can be adapted to make them more environmentally friendly, e.g. a tour operator offering a fly—drive package using only hire cars which run on lead-free petrol or diesel. Even so much may depend on how tourists consume the holiday product and on how many visit the destination so a destination product audit could be valuable for planning purposes, as well as for marketing, e.g. Green Flag

International carried out an audit of Jersey's holiday product for the island government

Site audit

Site audits take the form of regular checks of the state of buildings and plant and are commonplace at establishment level, e.g. an hotel checking the energy efficiency of its heating and lighting systems. Where primary tourism resources are common property and access is open, e.g. beaches in many countries, the site audit would be the responsibility of a public agency.

State of the environment audit

A state of the environment audit is a destination level audit of external environment conditions undertaken by a public/ planning agency for the area under its jurisdiction. In the case of an island tourism authority, the audit may well emphasize the nature and quality of the coastal environment. Environmental auditing therefore provides a means by which island tourism authorities can monitor the environmental impacts of their current levels and types of tourism.

A comprehensive approach at the destination level would require state of the environment and product audits to be undertaken by the island authority but, if resources are scarce, efforts could be concentrated upon activity and issues audits which single out pressing environmental matters. Pressure may also be brought to bear on the private tourism sector via associate audits where such firms have formal links with island tourism authorities. In so doing the island authorities create a business environment that encourages the tourism industry, to adopt environmental auditing beyond any minimum requirement for compliance and health and safety audits. Environmental auditing undertaken by the island authorities generates a vital data base, regularly updated, which is invaluable to planning for Sustainable tourism in island destinations.

Guernsey is the second largest of the 5 major inhabited Channel Islands some 30 km from the French Brittany-Normandy coast and 120 kin south of the UK. In area it is approximately 40 sq. km with a population of just under 60,000. Its principal economic activities in terms of contribution to GNP in 1991 were financial services and rentier sector (71 per cent), manufacturing (5 per cent), tourism (19 per cent) and horticulture (5 per cent), all but the first, which has grown rapidly over twenty years (8 per cent in 1972), have been declining in importance in recent years. The island is self-governing but has close political and social ties to the UK.'

From the air the island appears to be heavily urbanized, especially in what is known as the St Peter Port—St Sampson corridor. However, it possesses a moderate but equable climate with many sunny days, an indented coastline with numerous sandy beaches, a number of heritage artefacts and good mooring facilities as a major sailing centre. Transport communications between the island and the UK by air and sea are adequate but links to continental Europe are only fair. There is a high ratio of car ownership which causes some traffic congestion at certain times in the year.

The tourism industry in Guernsey employs around 2500 people augmented in the high season by local and overseas workers. Accommodation capacity is 2.7 million bed nights. Visits peaked at 450,000 in 1989 and fell to 351,000 in 1992. In that year the majority of holiday visitors were in the professional, managerial, supervisory and skilled manual groups from the UK, numbering 225,000 (64 per cent) of which 15 per cent were day visits and 20 per cent visiting family and friends. Business visits, mostly from the UK totalled just over 69,000 (20 per cent) while the rest of Europe, the majority from France, numbered almost 39,000 (11 per cent), including 10 per cent day visits. There were 18,000 (6 per cent), visits by inhabitants of the largest channel island, Jersey. Additionally 30,000 yachts men called at the island. The occupancy of hotels and guest houses was 45 per cent representing 1.25 million bed nights.

The overall aim is to expand the visitor economy beyond its 1989 level to 500,000 and increase the bed stock. The objectives relating to the accommodation, catering, culture, entertainment, recreational facilities, staffing, and management cover the period 1.994 to 1996 with a yearly review. The policy document stresses the need for public sector investment in product development and enhancement to generate additional revenue as a means of stimulating private investment.

With respect to the environment, the emphasis is on a viable visitor economy so that the board's concerns are with the physical tourism resource base, essentially clean beaches, sea-water quality, maintenance of the landscape, and the historic built environment, shopping and transport facilities and law and order.

The framework within which Guernsey's tourism industry operates is in part a reflection of the island's land use and environmental policies and practice. The core of these policies is contained in the strategic and corporate plan, with an annual review report. The main thrust of policy is to safeguard the environment without impairing economic development. Planning in Guernsey comes under the jurisdiction of the Island Development Committee (the equivalent of a ministry in a larger state) while many environmental functions are the responsibility of the Board of Administration. The activities of these two major committees are under the ultimate control of the Advisory and Finance Committee which, being composed of the presidents of the major committees, acts very much like the cabinet in the UK parliamentary system, except that there are no political parties in the island.

The principal issues being addressed in Guernsey in which continued economic growth, especially the development of financial services and tourism constitute key elements, are energy, the environment and traffic. Like many islands the problems relating to these issues are acute. There are no energy resources, necessitating total reliance on external fossil fuel. Its small size (eleven by eight km) gives rise to severe problems of waste disposal such as sewage, solid, putrescible and toxic waste. With a relatively high GNP per head, and given its economic structure, there is a large car owning section of the population. Overall these factors exert intense pressures on the natural and human-made environment.

The Board of Administration is responsible for environmental land management policies covering also waste disposal (including gas generated from tips), landfill and reclamation of sites (such as former horticultural land use), recycling and energy management. Other committees concerned with environmental matters are the Board of Health, Water Board, Sea Fisheries and Civil Defence. The Public Thoroughfares Committee is responsible for high ways, the island's watercourses, sewage and surface water drainage, the system largely being to pump untreated effluent into the sea, although some properties still use cesspits and septic tanks.

The States have acknowledged that increasing international concern over environmental issues will necessitate the consideration of tighter policies because visitors will expect standards to match those which prevail else where. Commitment to dealing with environmental problems and the movement towards sustainable development and tourism by the States will ultimately be judged not by statements of principles, strategies and policies but by action. Accordingly an evaluation of the current position in Guernsey should reveal the extent of its progress in attaining required environmental goals. However, irrespective of whether these goals are actively being pursued, of equal importance is to establish that the requisite structures, processes and procedures already exist or can easily be put in place to attain them.

Notwithstanding that as a small island state environmental matters in Guernsey should be reasonably circumscribed, it is not possible to examine exhaustively the nature of its policies and practices. Therefore, this evaluation is only illustrative. By tracing over the recent past the policy stance, statements made and actions taken on environmental issues, it is possible to ascertain the States' attitude to and progress on sustainable development and tourism, Although much reference is made to the environment, energy, refuse and sewage disposal and traffic in the most recent Strategic and Corporate Plan (States of Guernsey, 1992a), the term sustainable development is seldom mentioned. It is also apparent that some policy statements are unchanged from those made in earlier years.

Concentrating on environmental issues, the plan posits that:

> Necessary administration procedures should be implemented to provide adequate protection to the Island's environment.... The Island should use all natural resources, but in particular finite resources, in as efficient a manner as possible.... Pollution of the Island's environment should be kept to a mini mum necessary wherever this can be done reasonably and not at excessive cost.... Within the resources available, the States should take all reasonable steps to enhance the environmental quality... Steps should be taken to make the community including States' departments aware of.. matters of environmental concern.

Such statements have been made within the context of Billet d'Etat XVI and Billet d' Etat XIII in which the States have resolved to ensure that the financial services sector should remain competitive and profitable, tourism visits of an enhanced quality should increase by 5 per cent per annum over 5 years and high priority should be given to long-term planning for economic development. Sustainable development is emphasized only in relation to this goal and as a means of safeguarding Guernsey's economic future, although it is acknowledged that it has implications for resource use and the quality of life.Thus the policy document is still very much a statement of guiding principles. Specific planning and legal constraints are still under consideration. Moreover, it is admitted that in the present economic situation environmental matters have been relegated to a lower order of priorities. Indeed, although the wise use of resources and sustainable development are perceived as desirable, the issues they raise are considered as being out of scale with what can be achieved in Guernsey. Therefore, there is little indication given of how these intentions will be implemented.

At the operational level only one instance was found of a specific environmental target, this being the programme by the States' own departments to reduce energy use by 15 per cent over a five-year period based on 1990 consumption levels. Discussion regarding the tightening of building regulations to improve insulation and reduce energy use have not yet resulted in any new legal requirements. The approach adopted to date has ben to encourage projects to effect environmental improvement, such as the Environment 2000 initiative, but these have been voluntary and small scale in nature.With regard to monitoring, as a prerequisite for instituting sustainable development policies, this is certainly being done for pollution and is likely to be stepped up. However, surprisingly, some, actions are contemplated, that are contrary to the interests of the tourism, for the proposal to extend the sewer system which is seen being environmentally friendly but will in fact increase discharges into the sea and lower water quality. In other instances environmentally damaging actions have not been curtailed, seepage from a landfill tip has polluted shellfish waters and leachate chemicals continue to be pumped into the sewage system.

No evidence was found of environmental auditing being conducted in these cases as a prerequisite for monitoring and implementing mechanisms to wards sustainability. Overall the administration in Guernsey appears to suffer difficulties similar to those prevailing elsewhere. It is unable to translate the general concept of sustainable development into action. Furthermore, it has made no provision to undertake a state of the environment audit as the basis for introducing an integrated approach. In general the States' policy statement epitomizes the soft approach to sustainability. The main thrust of the most recent review is to safeguard economic development.

Tourism policy largely echoes that of the States. Sustainability, when it is referred to, is essentially equated with the viability of the industry. Environmental considerations are of concern in so far as they preserve the tourism resource base to facilitate growth. Only isolated examples were found of explicit environmental improvement which will have external beneficial effects other than merely enhancing the market competitive position of particular enterprises. During preliminary investigations it emerged that no organization or individual had heard of the term environmental auditing or comprehended its role as a necessary first step in initiating environment sustainable tourism. Yet, given the structure of Guernsey's society, system of government and administration, it possesses the potential to introduce the requisite auditing procedures.

Island destinations will only be able to enjoy sustainable tourism if they adopt fully comprehensive environmental management systems, which em brace not only the island's public authorities but also the private sector of the island's tourism industry.

Tourism policy making and both strategic, and routine decision taking need to be firmly rooted in such in system moreover one which is fully open to public scrutiny and accountability. Interaction between the public and private sectors, however, should not be wholly based upon 'command and control' of the latter by the former. Sustainable tourism involves more than just environmental conservation but an island's tourism policy needs to highlight the objective of environment sustainable tourism because of the scarcity and, frequently also, the fragility of its primary tourism resource base. That resource base is under pressure riot only from tourist numbers but also from encroachment with the further development of support facilities, services and infrastructure as well as, perhaps, being under threat from non-touristic activities, as is particularly the case in Guernsey, given the dominance of its financial sector.

There is some evidence that the conversion and demolition of housing and other buildings to offices has occurred to service this sector. Island tourism and planning authorities need to be aware of how current tourism could have environmental impacts on the island, i.e. to be able to identify threats to environmental sustainability inherent in the current level and types of tourism activity. Working from the premise that prevention is better than cure' environmental auditing has a significant role to play in identifying these threats and encouraging pre-emptive adaptation of current tourism products and practices before irreversible environmental damage occurs. Island tourism and planning authorities should undertake environmental audits at an aggregate scale, i.e. the whole destination. This would not be difficult in Guernsey where there are very full records and procedures for the collection and storage of tourist and environmental information This entails both state of the environment and product audits: the first round of auditing would establish the environmental conditions on the island, with subsequent rounds monitoring levels of improvement.

However, to the implementation of an environment sustainable tourism policy is the interface between island tourism and planning authorities and private firms constituting the island's tourism most of whom operate the support facilities and services. Controls may be exercised most readily over these firms by public authorities on those occasions when the firms seek to intensity which require planning or other licensing approval. This is somewhat easier where businesses are locally owned, as is the position in Guernsey, as opposed to international organizations which insist on a brand design or minimum size of development.

But existing types and levels of tourism activity could be impacting negatively on the island environment, with every possibility that this may become more severe where the intensity of the activity can be raised by increasing occupancy levels and extending the season. This situation is unlikely to be a danger with more mature island destinations like Guernsey, which have declining visit rates and the emphasis on providing higher quality tourism.

Environmental auditing has the potential to shape the operational, industrial and business practices of these private sector tourism firms. Will firms voluntarily adopt environmental auditing? Can island tourism and planning authorities influence or persuade such firms to adopt environmental auditing? As suggested earlier, given the tight control that the Guernsey planning authority exercises and the structure of the political system, firms should be easily persuaded.

While net benefits accruing to the firm from adopting environmental auditing may be sufficient in some cases, others may be influenced by the example of the island tourism and planning authorities in introducing destination level auditing, while yet others, who have direct dealings with the authorities, are brought into the auditing system where the authorities practice associate audits (although opportunities for the latter course of action may be limited). Introduction of mandatory auditing is likely to be restricted to insuring compliance with EPSs, Questions remain regarding the extent to which existing tourism firms adapt their products and practices, bearing in mind that environmental auditing itself involves re source costs and that, given the BATNEEC principle, the feasibility of adopting change is not always a foregone conclusion.

Moreover, in the Guernsey case current practice frequently falls short of what is technologically possible within existing budgets, but on this score the island is little different from any other tourist destination. Indeed it has been argued in a general context that environmental auditing is unlikely to be used by firms to question impacts deriving from activities which are central to a firm's operations and where removal or significant reduction would go beyond incremental, low-cost changes to current practices.

Environmental auditing is therefore not without limitations in inducing action to alleviate or anticipate environmental damage. The structure of the destination tourism industry with its many small firms, especially in the hospitality sector, may compound those limitations since small firms are least likely to undertake comprehensive environmental auditing according to general surveys of industry. This general surveys of industry.

This certainly likely to be a problem in Guernsey, with its small, often family-run businesses lacking the requisite resources. Furthermore the most powerful firms involved may well be foreign-based hotel chains whose activities are largely beyond the influence of island tourism authorities. Again this is not a problem in Guernsey, except some ownership (if large ravel companies which are Jersey-based. Tour operators hold the strongest hand in negotiating for destination accommodation and will readily consider alternative destinations for their future package holiday programmes if adoption of environmental raises the price at which accommodation can be obtained in a particular destination. Competition could be distorted if environmental auditing is not adopted in all destinations. The challenge is therefore wider than the integration of environmental auditing into planning for sustainable tourism namely, to operationalize the environmental auditing concept throughout the tourism industry. How ever, as a first step an education process concerning environmental auditing needs to be undertaken to give impetus to more concrete proposals.

Audits of external environmental conditions resulting in state of the environment reports have been neglected in comparison to internal audits of policies, practices and procedures of organizations them selves and this is as true of tourism as of other industries. Auditing, it must be emphasized, is a process not a single event and used intelligently throughout both the public and private sectors can demonstrate the 'art of the possible', encouraging the adoption and continuous updating of best environmental practice. It is not simply a defensive response to a need for legal compliance. During the last few decades tourism has moved towards the forefront of environmental, cultural and social concerns on a global scale. The magnitude and intensity of visitors able and willing to visit all corners of the earth has resulted in tourism being regarded as a seriously destructive power. Congestion, noise, litter, environmental deterioration and cultural degradation are some examples of suggested outcomes of tourism.

Advances in technology, increases in personal disposable income and educational influences have created the opportunities for considerable numbers to travel to areas which were previously within the reach of mainly high socio-economic groups or were totally inaccessible due to the lack of development and infrastructure. This shift to large volumes of tourists and the ability to reach almost any destination have paved the way to suggestions that mass tourism creates such damage.

As a result, many government and other bodies, the tourism industry and host communities have sought to address these problems. Among these policies, the current solution to try to alleviate negative aspects is responsible tourism (although it is referred to under a variety of headings including sustainable, soft, eco, alternative, special interest, green, etc.) Thus, responsible tourism is a response or alternative to mass tourism and is not often clearly defined.

Neither are the criteria and objectives. Responsible tourism can be interpreted as: 'any kind of tourism that deviates from the now standardised forms of mass tourism'. It must be 'where the pace of development is controlled, relatively slow and capable of being absorbed into the host environment without negative repercussions'. Its aims are to maximize benefits and minimize costs and to ensure an equitable distribution. It should 'encompass those ventures that are consciously designed to enhance the socio-politic environmental milieu of the host while educating and entertaining the guest'.

In essence it is a universal term targeting a supposedly more caring and aware form of tourism. Much of this type of tourism is supposed to occur in developing countries, but the ideas are also being utilized in sensitive areas such as national parks and to update old destinations in developed nations. However, there remain doubts as to whether responsible tourism is the way forward, whether it actually mitigates the negative effects, and is, indeed, even responsible.

There is a profusion of definitions and types of tourism. These ambiguities were discussed at the World Tourism Organization Seminar on 'Alternative' Tourism in Tamanrasset, Algeria. It was suggested that, because of the ambiguous nature of the term 'alternative tourism', responsible tourism was a more acceptable nomenclature. The definition offered was 'all forms of tourism which respect the host natural, built, and cultural environments and the interest of all parties concerned'. Similarly, at the first official meeting of the International Academy for the Study of Tourism in Zakopane, opinions were voiced that sustainable tourism was a more accurate and meaningful term than alternative tour ism. The aims of alternative tourism are best summarized by Wheeler. He observes that supporters see a need for an alternative to mass tourism that both minimizes costs, maximizes benefit and simultaneously ensures an, equitable and just distribution of those and benefits. Not only is it alternative but it should be responsible, that is more caring and aware; the benefits should accrue to the at the same time there should be protection from its worse Equally, there is a strong view that sustainable/ alternative tourism deflects attention from the real problem. The contradiction of alternative tourism is that 'it stands aside from the central problem... It is time to return to the central issue: What can be done about tourism as a whole?

The problem of mass tourism is growing globally.... Citing examples at the micro level gives the erroneous impression that tourism as a mass phenomenon can similarly be successfully harnessed..... In vogue 'solutions' are further fuelling the rapid spread of tourism without offering any real, lasting answer. The real problem is the massive volume of numbers of tourists. This is not being addressed. Similar views were expressed at the first official meeting of the International Academy for the Study of Tourism held at Zakopane in 1989. Smith suggested that alternative tourism was only one element of a global industry while De Kant saw the task as not to promote alternative tourism but to make conventional tourism more sustainable.

Common ground in the debate seems to be the need to reconcile conservation and tourism in the face of rising visitor numbers. The links between tourism and the natural environment have long been acknowledged, but much of the debate on sustainable tourism has been based on two assumptions and these can equally be applied to mass tourism:

1. Tourism must be made responsible.
2. Tourism has created unique problems.

The first assumption tends to be based on a moral stance with which many may agree. Tourism destroys areas, cultures, identities, etc., and hence must be controlled. The underlying assumption is that the world is perfect and infinite. However, it is time to recognize that the world is finite and that both costs and benefits exist in tourism activity. In a finite world, environments should be protected only if people's preferences place a higher value on conservation than on development. Recognition should also be given to the fact that many of the difficulties are not unique to tourism. Similar problems in other areas of human activity have been examined and form the basis of studies on conservation. In this light perhaps tourism ought to be seen as 'good' but with problems. Such an approach has led to numerous case studies on sustainability in particular locations and how an interface has been created with the precious resources that form important parts of the tourism product. These studies are useful, but Mathieson and Wall make an important distinction that still has validity:

1. Product oriented research. This involves the use of systematic approaches for the analysis of a specific project on a particular site. The finding has local use and value but may have little applicability to other projects or

2. Building a knowledge base. This type of research tackles basic problems. facing the tourism industry and produces results which have wider implications than the previous type of research.

Further, a growing proportion of research is empirically based but there is a lack of conceptual and methodological guidelines for the assessment of tourist impacts. In terms of a body of knowledge how much progress has been made since this study? Some developments have taken place in other disciplines which, to a limited extent, have been applied to tourism studies. For example, economics may have something to offer.

Economics suggests that the fundamental problem in negative aspects of tourism is one of market failure. The reasons for market failure include the existence of public goods and the creation of externalities. In tourism, many of the market failures occur with resources that are held in common and have incomplete or no property rights. Such elements of the tourism product are freely avail able to all and cannot be easily assimilated into the market mechanism thus, the market fails. The consumption of these goods also creates externalities, including those of a negative kind, which many are now concerned about. Externalities are the result of self-interested parties lacking incentives to take into account the effects of their actions on third parties. For example, a theme park may involve the loss of a visual amenity or a resort disco may create noise pollution for which the third party is not compensated. Such externalities are untraded commodities being by-products of consumption or production. Initially, the intention was to limit such externalities with alternative tourism, but this has failed to occur.

Market failure can be tackled in three ways:

1. Through the use of agencies established, for example, by governments to provide, distribute, or control suppliers and consumers of tourism public goods.
2. By attempting to create a market in externalities.
3. By attempting to create a market in public goods.

The response in tourism tends to be agency control with particular recourse to regulation, but the tendency has also been to use regulation of the 'command and control type. What can and cannot be done is set down, often in the form of legislation and regulation in art attempt to control behaviour.Tourism development which is integrated into a national and local strategic planning framework and which undertakes environmental impact assessment increases the long-term viability of tourism. The case for command and control rests oil certainty, and compliance. Regulation requires targets to be set by regulators and compliance to be monitored. Unfortunately, uncertainty exists, the measurement of impact is subjective and the economic costs of alternatives are uncertain. Hence regulatory failure may occur.

Regulatory failure also occurs because of information asymmetries where individual firms have superior information to government regulatory bodies. This leads to the second problem known as regulatory capture, which is identified in the work of Stigler. In order to set targets the regulator requires information.

Unfortunately, asymmetric information exists. The information tends to lie with those to be regulated and to be supplied strategically, to the best advantage of the regulated. Also it is argued that regulation is not carried out in the 'public interest', but to further the concerns of special interest groups who are able to organize an effective political voice. The regulator is captured and serves the interests of those from whom he is supposed to protect the public. This is the result of the regulated having regular contact with the regulator. A process of continuous bargaining occurs. At the same time, a diffused public unable to combine and coordinate has no effective voice.

Eventually, regulator and regulated will settle for a common goal. Policy also become producer-benefit oriented if only because of this regulatory capture. According to Johnston: On the one hand, the developer works with the community to structure socially and environmentally sensitive resort development. On the other hand, he uses the permits won to structure a sellout deal to another investor, manipulating the community while making profits.

Conservation and development projects are often designed and implemented in a political context in which indigenous people have minimal voice in policy and arrangement. Often a multiplicity of power structures regulate tourism and define the level of local involvement in the marketing of culture. Choy, despite favouring planning, also recognizes the problem: 'Finally, the planning process is highly political. Gaining consensus on a rational, comprehensive, long range tourism plan may be impossible given the divergent interests of the various sectors of a community'. It may still be possible, despite these limitations, for command and control measures to have a place. However, 'control and compliance' is not a costless process. Control may be more costly than the benefits created.

The second and third methods are based on neoclassical welfare economies and draw on environmental economics and valuation techniques. Basically, the notion is that products consist of bundles of characteristics and information on the purchase of such products like tourism should be obtained from consumers. The consumers will reveal their preferences, which are then aggregated. Non-priced public goods that are not market traded can thus be valued. This valuation is undertaken within the decision criterion of a Pareto improvement somebody can be made better off and no one, in their own view, made worse off.. From this theoretical underpinning many methods have been developed based on individuals revealing their preferences. Most involve the use of shadow pricing for non-market values.

The second approach also uses shadow pricing and involves the creation of a market in externalities, based on the assumption that the environment and the economy are inextricably linked. If the environmental impacts of tourism are unacceptable then it is in indication that the price of tourism products does not fully reflect the use made by tourism of environmental assets. Full social costs and benefits of tourism are not reflected in market price. Proper account needs to be taken of the effects which are external to the private decision maker. What is needed is a policy that is based on changing the economic incentives. Environmental assets cannot be treated as having low or zero cost. Lager louts create noise, aircraft pollute the skies. As Amy Hall comments about Stonehenge:

Tourism is a pollution creating industry. The fact that the economy of the country depends on it more and more now that our productive and manufacturing industry has declined does not mean we should allow the operation of double standards. The standards applied to the old industries should apply equally to the new industry of tourism. The increased cost of roads, the pollution, caused by, the motor vehicles, the additional water supplies, sewage and communication systems, the litter generated, must be taken into account in the financial balance sheet.

Externalities are examined to see whether they create a net increase or The first comprehensive work was undertaken by Pigou which recognized that utility of third parties may be affected. The allocation of scarce resources will be more allocatively efficient when proper account of the effects external to the polluter are included. Prices will be altered to reflect the real economic costs of tourist activity and costs of environmental expenditure will become part of production costs. Externalities become internalized into market prices paid and received by tourists and suppliers. The principle is the well-known one of the user pays, the polluter pays and the benefactor receives. The market mechanism based on prices become the agent of control. Tourism is treated in the same way as pollution.However, the problem is that much of the pollution is a non-tradeable product. As a result a proxy for market price is needed in order to create a market in externalities. This takes the form of shadow pricing. A price is placed on the use of the unvalued 'environment' to correct for the external effects. Either a price (through charges) or a quota (through trade able permits) system is used. Pollution rights are sold. An agency sells through a process of bidding the rights to pollute. Those rights are limited by the desired quality of the tourism asset. The price is implemented through taxation on tourists while tradeable permits work through a system of credits. If an operator does better than its allowance, it is allowed to trade its credits to obtain permits to undertake some other activity. Such methods of selling pollution rights may be preferable to taxation, subsidies or regulation and have low administrative costs as the charge is set by firms bidding against each other. In practice, however, it is the least-tried method.

The third method is the creation of a market in non-tradeable products (i.e. public goods), In tourism, previously free public goods are becoming scarce due to an explosion of demand from tourists, for example, the crowded beaches throughout the world or the vast increase in the number of trekkers in the Himalayas. Some form of allocation mechanism may now be necessary. This involves placing a value on the non-tradeable elements of the tourism product that influences tourists' utility. It is necessary to imply a monetary measure for value in use and for non-use value. Both use and non-use values have to be included. i.e. the value derived from the actual visit, plus a premium people are willing to pay to ensure existence value for possible future visits and for future generations. If such measures of value in use could be derived then the real cost of supplying the tourism product could be identified, as indeed could the real benefits.

Charging for natural attractions is simply recognising that they should not be treated as open access resources where environments are under pressure from too many tourists or alternative developments. Pricing will Simultaneously control the number of tourists while collecting enough funds to improve the management of protected areas. Good economics is good ecology. The framework within which most methods operate is that of cost-benefit analysis. Cost-benefit and economic impact assessment analyses are still common elements in feasibility studies. In tourism and recreation, one such method, willingness to pay (WTP) based on shadow pricing, has long been used. The shadow price is based on travel costs. The cost of travel incurred by the tourist is used as a proxy tor the value placed by the tourist on that destination. Visitor numbers will vary with travel cost and from these a demand curve can be constructed. This follows from the work of Clawson and Clawson and Knetsch.

There are several objections to WTP methods, but, in any the method is limited where cost of travel cannot readily, be used as a proxy. In tourism, WTP may be possible for tangible elements of the tourism product a beach, litter, etc. However, difficulties arise for those parts of the product which have no direct demand function and which cannot have a demand function implied loss of view when, say, a EuroDisney is built. This has led to the development of contingent valuation techniques.

Contingency valuation involves direct surveys where tourists are asked to place a monetary valuation on each element in the tourism product/experience. For example, a typical question may be: How much would you be prepared to pay to preserve this site?' The widely accepted view is that only contingency valuation can measure non-use value. From this information a demand curve can be constructed. A further method in attempting to measure the importance of parts of the tourism product to consumers' utility is hedonic pricing, which derives from the utility theory work of Lancaster (1966, 1971). Hedonic pricing is especially useful in tourism studies. It is well accepted that the tourism product consists of several elements.

Some elements are tangible (aircraft seats) and others are intangible (the experience). Hence, the product has a bundle of characteristics. If prices can be imputed for these different characteristics then it may be possible to evaluate the impact of tourism. This method also relies on shadow prices. A shadow price is derived for each important element in the product by comparison with other products that do not have significant differences. These values are then summated to give a demand curve. The use of all these techniques has greatly improved the ability to value the non-priced elements of the tourism product. This to say that further developments and improvements and are not needed. Indeed problems still exist.

Can these methods be incorporated into a model for assessing the impact of tourism and can any such model be made operational? An attempt has been made by Stabler in the area of quality assessment of leisure provision that may be useful. He has attempted to construct a model that has as its initial approach a cross-sectional, disaggregated assessment of consumers' preferences. Central to this at some stage would be a survey of consumers' willingness to pay. Also, hedonic pricing would be directed at the product so that implicit prices of individual characteristics can be identified. He recognizes the use of more than one tool and does not rely solely oil cost-benefit analysis. Similarly, Dow and Radford use a multi-criteria approach in their staples impact analysis. They state: However, we do believe that the policy requirements of complex assessments may be aided by prior studies based on a different, methodology which can enlighten the remit given to the subsequent cost

> One solution to the problem is to simply devise lists of questions. This, for example, can be in the form of an' aide-memoire' such as the SWOT analysis.... After thinking about the strengths, weaknesses, opportunities, and threats in a situation the decision taker is likely to have a more rounded picture of the choice which is about to be made.

Can a similar model be constructed to assess the likely outcome of tourism developments? The message seems to be not to rely on one measure but to use cost-benefit analysis with other qualitative and quantitative techniques. Yet, even these suggestions rely on the use of the, neoclassical framework which leads to more fundamental objections.But first, much of the work on sustainable tourism misses a central issue. The notion of sustainability has not been usefully defined. The debate rests on a view of the term sustainable that is more a statement of faith than one of analytical use. Pezzy offers several definitions of sustainable development which can be summarized as:

1. Stationary or increasing consumption over time.
2. Stationary or increasing utility over time.
3. Stationary or increasing stock of assets (both natural and man-made) over time.
4. Stationary or increasing stock of natural assets over time.

Since the survival of tourism is highly dependent on maintaining and/ or improving the capital assets on which it depends, 3 and 4 are at least is important as 1 and 2; 1 and, to some extent, 2 involve the neoclassical view hat the individual only derives pleasure from produced goods and services and hence these will influence the individual's revealed preference. Any policy based on definitions 1 and 2 will not capture the importance of the tourism assets.

There is another important critique into which this latter point leads. The hole neoclassical approach is questioned on several grounds, being accused of being naive, too reliant on the sovereignty of individuals and their references, and too atomistic. The argument is that neoclassical economics naive in trying to discover one single answer the 'truth' and of placing individual preferences above the collective will of communities. Within those preferences is the assumption that value (which is different from wants) derives only from individual human consumption throughout the techniques there is a tendency to be concerned only with the use value of consumers, in this case tourists. In the neoclassical search for the 'truth', its reliance on one outcome from cost-benefit analysis calculations has received criticism. The view is that the cost-benefit outcome should be seen as no more than one piece of information and that other sources of evidence should also be taken into account. This has led to the growth of ecological economics and ecological studies in other disciplines. Yet, the tourism industry still places heavy reliance on such neoclassical techniques as cost-benefit analysis. Environmental constraints in the pursuit of this preservation may have to be imposed on tourists' behaviour. In view of the severe competition faced by island states in the tourism market, this may require some countries to take very brave action, but as Klaasen and Opschoor say, 'Environment is a "merit good", not merely to be determined by the aggregation of individual... willingness to pay at any point in time'.

Implications of Climate Change

Many small islands, particularly those in the tropics, rely heavily upon natural resources of sea, sun and sand as the attractions upon which their tourism industries are based. However, global climate change, including zone depletion, may modify these resources and how they are perceived by the potential clientele, leading to the need for such destinations to adjust to hanging circumstances. It will be argued that, with respect to climate, the past may no longer be an adequate guide to the future and that climate change may be one factor among many worthy of inclusion in tourism planning and investment decisions.

The topic of the greenhouse effect and climate change is plagued with uncertainty. In such circumstances, it would be easy to dismiss the subject as being unworthy of concern until more definitive information becomes available. It is contended that this would be an unwise approach. Rather, the attempt should be made to reduce the level of uncertainty by distinguishing at which is known from that which is not known or, in other words, fact should be separated from fiction. This is the immediate objective.

The greenhouse effect results from a natural process which is well under stood. Incoming shortwave radiation from the sun passes through the earth's atmosphere. This energy, is reradiated at longer wavelengths which are intercepted by the so-called greenhouse gases. The heat which is trapped by these gases is vital to life on earth. In the absence of these gases, the energy would he lost to space and the earth would be approximately thirty degrees centigrade colder than it is now. Thus, the Processes leading to the green house effect are well known.

Most of the gases in the atmosphere have little effect upon the earth's radiation balance: both solar and terrestrial radiation pass through them with little hindrance. On the other hand, there are a number of gases which constitute only a small proportion of the atmosphere but which have a profound effect. The major greenhouse gases are carbon dioxide, which is particularly associated with fossil fuel combustion and deforestation; methane, which is probably derived from agriculture, especially rice cultivation and animal husbandry; nitrous oxide which is possibly from the use of nitrogenous fertilizers, land clearing, biomass burning and fossil fuel combustion; and halocarbons, particularly chlorofluorocarbons, which were introduced into the atmosphere for the first time this century.

Until the industrial revolution, the levels of carbon dioxide and other greenhouse gases produced and consumed were in equilibrium, although they may have fluctuated sufficiently over long periods of time to contribute to ice ages and interglacial periods. However, since the industrial revolution, human activities have been releasing everincreasing quantities of green house gases into the atmosphere. Increasing concentrations of these gases have been measured.

Knowledge of atmospheric processes, coupled with rising concentrations of greenhouse gases, have given rise to the suggestion that the earth's climate should be warming.

Evidence for global warming is derived from three main sources: the paleo-climatological record; recent temperature observations; and general circulation models. These will now be considered in turn.

Records derived from ice cores taken from the Antarctic show a remarkable correlation between carbon dioxide concentrations and temperature over the last 160,000 years. Temperatures derived from analyses of oxygen isotopes in the ice core record indicate that two very large increases in temperature and carbon dioxide occurred at approximately 15,000 BP and 140,000 BP. Carbon dioxide levels of 280 ppm correspond to the pre industrial concentration some 100 to 300 years ago. Current concentrations ire approximately 350.

Although the correlation is striking, it does not prove cause and effect, only, hat there was a strong relationship between carbon dioxide concentrations and climate variations in the past. It is not possible to conclude with certainty hat these relationships will hold in the future. The ice core record can be viewed as providing strong, but not conclusive, circumstantial evidence of a ink between carbon dioxide concentrations and temperature.

Given that concentrations of greenhouse gases have been increasing, and the likely links between such gases and temperature, one might look to the temperature record to see if an increase in temperature can be detected. Temperature trends over the past century indicate a 0.5 degree centigrade rise in global temperature. The analyses exclude urban locations, which are likely to have experienced heat island effects, but include data from marine databases to provide both land and sea coverage. Similar studies by NASA scientists suggest 1 0.7 degree centigrade rise, but their results are acknowledged to include a 0.1 to 0.2 degree urbanization effect and do not include ocean data.

Climate is inherently and have always fluctuated and will continue to do so. The seemingly small changes in the temperature record are in line with what would be expected from greenhouse gas concentrations and, in fact, many of the warmest on record globally have been experienced in the 1980 and 1990s. However because the are small numerically it is not possible to be certain that they are real changes resulting from an enhanced greenhouse effect rather than a warm period associated with climatic variability. In the jargon, it is difficult to separate the signal from the noise. Again, the evidence is strong but not conclusive.

Implications of increasing concentrations of greenhouse gases for global climate have been investigated through the application of general circulation models (GCMs). These are complex mathematical models that simulate links between temperature, atmospheric circulation, the hydrological cycle, oceans and the cryosphere. A small number of such models is in operation and, although there are differences in model resolution and in the way certain atmospheric and oceanic processes are treated, there are a number of similarities in their projections of future climate.Thus, while the paleo-climatological record, recent temperature observations and global circulation models do not provide conclusive evidence of global warming, they are mutually reinforcing and give strong, circumstantial, grounds for believing that greenhouse warming is a reality.

All greenhouse gases are known to be increasing as a result of human and their combined future effect may be the equivalent of a doubling of the concentrations of carbon dioxide by the 2030s, i.e. in less than half a century. Such a doubling may induce global surface temperature increases of between 1.5 and 4.5 degrees centigrade. The impact of this warming is expected to be greatest in high latitudes, particularly in autumn and winter. Equatorial regions should experience a lesser but still substantial warming. Less confidence can be placed in assessments of the future distribution of precipitation. There may, however, be reduced moisture availability,, particularly in middle latitudes, because of increased evapotranspiration coupled with an increased demand for water. Sea level may rise 20 and 140 cm, chiefly because of the thermal expansion of ocean waters and, secondarily, because of glacial melting. In this complex chain of events, some projections are more reliable than others. Forecasts of changes in sea level are probably more reliable than those of the climate of land areas; estimates of air temperature are more reliable than estimates of precipitation; and forecasts of latitudinal changes are more reliable than projections of the likely changes from east to west across continents.

Although there are many uncertainties, there is sufficient evidence that climate change will occur in the coming decades and that it may produce serious consequences to suggest that it is worthwhile to seek better information than is currently available on possible impacts and the potential for' adapting to the changing circumstances.

Increased concentrations of greenhouse gases are expected to result in an increase in global temperatures which in turn, through thermal expansion of ocean water and melting of ice, will result in rising sea levels. An associated increase in flooding and erosion on oceanic shorelines is projected. Such vents would place stress on both natural and built environments on marine coasts.

The economies of many small islands, particularly those in the tropics, are dominated by tourism which is concentrated in coastal locations. The importance of beaches is illustrated by figures for Hawaii, which indicate that beaches are used by more than 80 per cent of its annual tourist population the 2.5 km long Waikiki beach had 5.1 million visits in 1983-84, which mounts to a space of two to three sq.m per person in peak periods. Anything which threatens these resources or the associated infrastructure is ominous for the economies of coastal resorts. Rising sea levels ay have far-reaching consequences for coastal resorts and in some cases, ay actually threaten the very existence of some small islands. The physical processes involved in sea-level rise are discussed thoroughly by Bird and, specifically for the Mediterranean, by Jeftic et al. However, although both works discuss implications for human activities, there is only passing mention of tourism.

Rising sea levels threaten beaches are unable to extend inland because of the existence of built structures. For example, the majority of coastal resorts in the USA would have no beach at high tide by 2025 under a scenario of sea level rise. A one foot rise in sea level would generally cause beaches to erode 50 to 100 feet from the Northeast to Maryland; 200 feet along, the Carolinas, 100 to 1000 feet along the Florida coast, 200 to 400 feet along the California coast and, perhaps, several miles in Louisiana. Expensive beach protection and restitution may be required for communities whose economic welfare.

Sanitation systems and fresh water supplies may be threatened by rising water levels and salination of coastal estuaries, and potable fresh water supplies may be reduced when sea water infiltrates subterranean water tables. Should the frequency of tropical storms increase then there may be additional threats to coastal infrastructure from storm and flood damage. Damage from tropical storms has been increasing over the last two decades but it is not clear whether this is due to increasing storm frequency or greater property at risk. What is clear, however, is that it is becoming increasingly difficult to acquire insurance for development projects in vulnerable locations.

Lindh *et al.* have reviewed the efficacy of structural measures for beach protection in a Finnish context and Coke et al. have succinctly summarized coastal policy options as do nothing, planned retreat or protect. However, the viability of these options is likely to vary with the site. A current policy dilemma is that many coastal protection schemes, and other tourism investments, have long lives and there is a need to make investments so that future options are not unduly foreclosed.

Natural areas will also be modified by climate the modifications in sea level, thus altering the potential for diversifying the tourism product. For example, rising ocean temperatures may inhibit the growth of corals and widespread reports of coral bleaching that it may be a result of higher temperatures of tropical seas. Marine wetlands are one environmental setting which has received some attention in the context of global climate change, particularly from the perspective of rising sea levels . These are environments which have been declining in area as a result of subsidence and the encroachment of other land uses. According to Titus there are three major ways by which sea-level rise can disrupt wetlands: inundation, erosion, and saltwater intrusion. In some cases, wetlands will be converted to bodies of open water; in other cases, the type of vegetation will change but a particular area will still be wetland.

However, if sea-level rises occur sufficiently slowly, the ability of wetlands to grow upwards by trapping sediment or building upon the peat the sediment creates can prevent sea-level rise from disrupting the wetlands. The factors principally responsible for determining accretion rates are sediment loads, current velocity, and flooding frequency and duration. Tidal range, tidal regularity and substrate type also influence marsh boundaries and therefore help to determine adjustments to rising sea levels. Along undeveloped coasts, rising sea levels will drown the seaward wetlands but will allow new wetlands to be created inland as formerly dry land is flooded. However, the impact of sea-level rise on coastal wetlands will depend largely on whether developed areas inland of the marsh are protected from rising sea levels by levees and bulkheads. Along developed coasts, there may not be land available for wetland creation.

Many small islands have great difficulty in providing reliable supplies of potable water and energy. Tourists are voracious consumers of both water and energy. Even small increases in temperature could raise the demands for electrical energy for air-conditioning in tropical islands and, through in creased evapotranspiration, reduce the availability of water. Furthermore, if energy and water are in short supply, recreation will come increasingly into competition with other uses of these scarce resources.

Reliable sunshine is one of the major tourism assets of tropical islands. Sunbathing is an activity that is largely confined to residents of the developed Western world who constitute a large part of the current market for island tourist destinations in the tropics. A suntan is often regarded as enhancing attractiveness and is fashionable among such groups. However, the desire to acquire a tan is a relatively recent fashion and sunbathing has only been a popular activity since the early years of this century. Prior to that time, prevailing aesthetic tastes in western societies referred a pale complexion to a tan. One wonders if positive attitudes towards sunbathing will be maintained in the face of climate change and increased exposure to UV radiation associated with ozone depletion.

Last has suggested that research is needed on attitudes towards sunbathing and the use of protective measures. Weather advisory message warning about safe exposure levels have been used routinely on Australian radio and television for some years and were introduced in Canada in 1992, but such advisories are not part of routine weather reports in the USA. Sunscreen ointments and creams require rigorous evaluation. Although there are reports of the protective effect of sunscreen against sunburn, their efficacy in preventing skin cancer and malignant melanoma remains unclear. Should health education be employed to persuade people to relinquish the notion that a suntan is desirable? If so, research is needed to identify and evaluate ways to do this. What are the implications of such attitude changes to coastal communities whose economics are based upon the sale of sea, sun and sand? The suggestion is not being made that tourists will abandon sunny climates but it may be expected that their behaviours in resort areas may be modified, with less time being spent on the beach or by the pool. Thus, the challenges to resorts associated with rising sea levels may be exacerbated by changing tastes among their clientele, precipitated by increased recognition of the health effects of diminishing ozone concentrations.

Although efforts are being made to curb the production of greenhouse gases, it is likely that we are already committed to some amount of climate modification. Both natural and human systems are adapted to an unknown extent to much of the variability in current climates and it is changes in the magnitude and frequency of extreme events through which the implications of climate change will most likely be imposed. Two main groups can be considered with respect to the potential to adapt to climate change.

Tourists have choice concerning whether or not to travel, when and where to go and activities to participate in. In fact, since the products of tourism are experiences, participants may be able to substitute activities and locations without a great deal of loss in the quality of their vacation. If mid-latitude locations become warmer, it is even possible that the desire to visit the tropics may be reduced. It is true that those wishing to observe particular species of plants and animals may find them less accessible or replaced by others, and fishermen may be required to change their quarry in particular locations, but in so far as there are still tourist resorts, wild spaces and provision of tourism opportunities, most potential tourists are likely to be able to acquire satisfactory experiences.

5

Tourism for Sustainable Economic Development

Tourism is one of the largest, if not the largest, world industry and that international financial exchanges involved in tourism are comparable to those involved in oil and armaments, the most referenced document on sustainable development. Sustainable development is a political slogan rather than an analytical tool. It may be viewed as a philosophy, a plan or strategy, or a product. This is not to denigrate its utility in fostering dialogue among groups and individuals whose interests may at first sight appear to be incompatible. Thus it may be a catalyst for discussion, compromise and the identification of appropriate trade-offs between competing interests. Sustainability has become a catchphrase which, partly because of its imprecision, has attracted widespread interest and support and also, again partly because of its imprecision, criticism from its detractors. It has attracted the interest of the tourism industry, and tourism researchers who have adopted the concept in slightly modified form and advocated 'sustainable tourism'. Such terminology implies a lack of appreciation of the full implications of the concept for its advocates a single rather than a multi-sectoral approach, the latter being a fundamental attribute of sustainable development. This is a particularly important problem in the case of tourism which is a diffuse activity with far-reaching implications for many other sectors and activities. While one can appreciate the interest of tourism industry advocates in ensuring the longevity of tourism, the goal should not be to perpetuate tourism at all costs.

Development is one which means different things to different people, and these meanings have changed over time. The term is value-laden, incorporating a mix of material and moral ideas encompassing both present and future states; what currently exists and how it came to be, as well as what might be brought into being in the future. In its early formulations it focused primarily upon economic matters. However, definitions have tended to be broadened over time and development has gradually come to be viewed as a social as well as an economic process which involves the progressive improvement of conditions and the fulfillment of potential. Now, in addition to economic issues, it encompasses social, environmental and ethical considerations and its measurement may incorporate indicators of poverty, unemployment, inequality and self-reliance. Notions of development have encompassed economic growth, structural change, autonomous industrialization and self-reliance, and have been pitched at a variety of scales from the individual to the regional, national and even international. However, growth and development are not to be regarded as the same thing, since economic growth as measured by gross national product per capita can occur with increases in poverty, unemployment and inequality. In its most basic form, development is concerned with human betterment through improvement in life-styles and life opportunities. However, it is contentious as to how this is to be done and so the term has come to have strong political underpinnings. As is the case with sustainable development, the notion has also come to be used in rather different ways: as a philosophy, as a process, as a plan and as a product.

As a philosophy, development refers to broad perspectives concerning appropriate future states and means of achieving them. As a process it emphasizes the methods which might be employed to expand or bring out the potentials or capabilities of a phenomenon. A development plan sets out specific steps through which desirable future states are to be achieved and development as a product indicates the level of achievement of an individual or society, as in developed, developing and underdeveloped countries. Clearly, these perspectives are not distinct but overlap to a considerable degree. Failure to acknowledge such differences in perspective can result in miscommunication.

The concept of development often has strong ideological underpinnings with conservative, liberal and radical traditions which have led to different perspectives on the causes of development challenges and their likely solutions. It also may have a built-in western bias as western societies are often seen as being developed in contrast to other countries which are seen as lacking in development.

As perspectives on development have changed through time, means of measuring development have evolved and broadened. Initial measures used were primarily economic, such as gross national product, or close derivatives such as energy consumption. But more recent trends have seen attempts to develop more comprehensive indices, including a variety of socioeconomic and environmental variables, even encompassing the extent of political and civil liberties and the quality of life. Thus not only has there been an evolving debate on the nature of development, there have been changing perspectives on how to measure it.

The evolution of research on tourism has paralleled the evolution of development studies as a whole, with an early emphasis on economic aspects now increasingly being complemented with a more balanced perspective incorporating environmental and sociocultural matters.

Development Theories

At the risk of oversimplification, four broad approaches to development can be identified which constitute a very rough evolution in the sequence of ideas concerning development. They are: modernization, dependency, neoclassical counterrevolution and alternative development.

Each of these perspectives will be considered in turn. In reality there is considerable overlap both in the content of ideas and their timing so that there is a real risk of over generalization. However, the ideas are presented simply in order to indicate the precursors to sustainable development. They have been informed particularly by the writing of Ingham and Goldsworthy and have benefited greatly from an unpublished synthesis by Telfer.

Modernization

Modernization theorists have tended to view societies as passing through a series of development 'stages similar to those experienced by many western countries. Development has often been equated with growth emanating from relatively developed areas, and concepts such as stages of economic growth, growth poles, spread and backwash effects, and circular and cumulative causation have been guiding ideas with great stress being placed on the roles of innovation and entrepreneurship. State involvement to promote development has been encouraged and a belief in the trickledown effect, whereby benefits diffuse to disadvantaged people and regions, has been espoused.The Mexican strategy of building a number of very large resort complexes in such places as Cancun in the hope that the benefits will also accrue to a broader area, is an example of the application of this perspective. It can also be seen more generally in the proliferation of western-style hotels in relatively remote areas in the hope that they will be catalysts of economic growth. The major criticisms of modernization theory are that it involves high levels of abstraction with limited discussion of the role of local involvement, that it suggests a unidirectional path which all must follow in order to develop, and that it smacks of western ethnocentrism as revealed in the First and Third-World labels ascribed to parts of the globe. Modernization theory has little to say about the importance of traditional values, and perhaps implies that the maintenance of tradition and modernization may not be compatible goals.

Dependency

Dependency theorists see lack of development as being attributable to external forces more than internal causations, with power at the centre exploiting a disadvantaged periphery as described in centre-periphery models. For example, lack of development in developing nations may be seen as occurring as a result of exploitation by developed countries, often in the form of colonialism. These relationships may be viewed as being perpetuated by international tourism which may be viewed as a form of neocolonialism. Dependency theorists see a dualism between the rich and poor, the powerful and the powerless, both between and within countries, and see development as being best promoted by the favouring of domestic markets, import substitution, protectionism and social reforms. Again, this is a fairly abstract and also rather pessimistic viewpoint. As already indicated, it stresses external relationships over internal problems and it tends to be somewhat vague on policy implications, tending towards protectionism and isolationism in contrast to modernization which would foster increased external economic links. Dependency theory is more a critique of prevalent approaches to development than a method of development. In tourism, devotees of dependency theory have tended to spurn the involvement of international corporations and capital and have advocated the construction of small-scale, locally owned facilities, thereby overlapping with the alternative development paradigm and alternative tourism which is discussed below.

Neoclassical counter-revolution

Following the oil crises and the international debt crises of the 1970s and 80s, a group of ideas evolved which may be termed the neoclassical counter revolution. Proponents stressed the role of privatization and the free competitive market. Development prospects were to be enhanced by welcoming foreign investors with minimum state involvement.

The World Bank was a major proponent of this perspective, advocating structural adjustments and reliance upon market forces and competitive exports. In tourism, the World Bank, the United Nations Development Programme, the Asian Development Bank and other similar international agencies have helped to fund major tourism planning exercises in many parts of the developing world. The major criticism of this approach is that the financial strategies are unlikely to help the disadvantaged who are most in need. Also, the scale of some of the projects which were supported and the lack of detailed consideration of local conditions on the part of some of their advocates were a further cause of concern.

Alternative development

Advocates of alternative development place emphasis on the satisfaction of basic needs: food, housing, water, health and education. A grassroots perspective is proposed with an emphasis on local involvement which, it is argued, will permit people to control their own destinies. Sustainable development, with frequent associated demands for public participation and community level planning as advocated by Murphy for tourism, can be viewed as an example of the alternative development paradigm.

Ecotourism, nature tourism, appropriate tourism, ethical tourism and responsible tourism are but a few of the tourism descriptors which have emerged recent years, which have overlapping and imprecise meanings, but which can all be grouped under the unenlightening heading of alternative tourism. Critics of alternative development argue that the emphasis placed on basic needs tends to detract from long-term growth, and that the stress on local involvement underestimates the magnitude of political changes that will be required to make this possible, with the paradox that political changes could lead to too much state control. As indicated above in the form of sustainable development, the approach has been criticized as being too vague to be of much value.

The ideas which have been presented above have strong political and ideological underpinnings. Thus, for example, those with conservative dispositions have tended to advocate either open-market competition with minimal state involvement or, conversely, strong links between the state and private capitalists to promote top-down development. In contrast, liberals can be divided into non-structural reformists who have urged direct assaults on poverty and satisfaction of basic needs, and structural reformists who have sought broad-based changes, including reforms in the ownership and distribution of land in some circumstances, in order to promote a wider distribution of wealth and power. Marxism and Leninism are more radical approaches, the former seeing the class struggle as the route to development, whereas the latter places power in the hands of a political elite to organize production in the name of the people. The above thumbnail sketches of development paradigms have been presented to indicate the contested and political nature of development and to show that sustainable development emerged as a concept into a field which was already fraught with contention and debate. However, before turning specifically to a consideration of sustainable development, two other sets of ideas will be presented briefly. The first is gender and development, which has evolved approximately contemporaneously with sustainable development, and the second concerns the evolution of tourism planning.

Gender Perspectives

It is appropriate to consider gender perspectives at this point for a number of reasons. First, they provide a critique from a particular angle which is relevant to all of the development paradigms discussed above. They also reflect a stance which is slowly becoming a part of the tourism development literature. The viewpoints are also potentially compatible with sustainable development, for one of the tenets of sustainable development is equity and one of the objectives of the feminist literature is to draw attention to, and thereby help to redress, inequities associated with gender. In addition, it is a theme which reflects the fragmentation of the alternative development and alternative tourism literatures, but at the same time potentially cuts across them and could inform and be incorporated as a part of them. Gender and development can be considered as a particular variant of alternative development. It is useful to make a distinction between sex and gender. Sex refers to biological attributes whereas gender refers to relationship between people of different sexes and has been defined by Henderson as a 'set of socially constructed relationships which are produced and reproduced through people's actions'. It follows that, in all but a very limited number of unusual cases, sex is fixed whereas the concept of gender is more dynamic, varying with changing interpersonal relationships. Nevertheless, there is an overlap between the two concepts if only because, one's sex results in a lifetime of relationships and expectations based on and experienced as gender. Furthermore, gender is a cultural phenomenon, modification of gender relationships requiring changes in culture. Major issues of concern in discussions of gender are access to power, and equality. However, these do not depend solely upon gender. They are also influenced by such attributes as age, race, class, status and education. Thus, in discussions of gender, one should be aware of the dangers of single-variable analyses.

There is no universal woman or universal women's experience but a variety of experiences which are influenced by many factors in addition to gender. As a concept which stresses relationships, it should not be assumed that gendered approaches are only applicable to the study of women and their circumstances, In fact, gendered approaches can also be applied to men and a full gender analysis would involve investigation of both men and women and the relationships between them.

It is useful to provide a brief sketch of the history of gender scholarship. The ideas which are presented are drawn heavily from the writing of Swain. Gender scholarship is rooted in western feminism and its evolution over approximately the past thirty years. Five phases have been recognized:

1 in which women are essentially invisible and their experiences ignored (womanless);

2 a compensatory phase in which the experiences of prominent and unusual women were recognized but their activities were judged predominantly from a masculine perspective ('add, women and stir');

3 an emphasis on dichotomous differences (sex differences). This is a useful starting point but it falls short if differences are left unexplained by reference to underlying circumstances;

4 feminist approaches which stress the experiences of women, often to the neglect or the exclusion of the experiences of men (women-centred);

5 true gender scholarship in which there is an interactional view of human expectations, behaviour and power relationships.

The above sequence broadly describes a path through which 'Women in Development' (WID) has given way to 'Gender and Development' (GAD), the latter having more explicit concern with the empowerment of women.

Tourism and the processes associated with it emanate from gendered societies and are therefore likely to exhibit gendered relationships. Women are involved differently than men in both the production and consumption of tourism and so they are likely to be impacted differently. Relationships between gender and tourism are likely to be reciprocal, with gender influencing the of tourism and tourism modifying existing gender relationships.

In addition, it is likely that gender relationships will differ between host and guest cultures and, furthermore, the behaviours of visitors and their expectations concerning gender relationships may differ when they are at home and on vacation. Thus the situation is extremely complex and in the face of such complexity, both hosts and guests may fall back on stereo types. The extent to which women and men are prepared to take up various positions, and the cultural acceptability of the employment of women and men in different aspects of tourism, will greatly influence the associated opportunities and impacts and their variation by gender, and thus the extent to which women and men participate in 'development'.

Investigators of tourism have not been in the forefront of researchers adopting a gender perspective, and in fact they have lagged behind their sisters in the broader field of leisure. Nevertheless, interest in gender and tourism is growing rapidly, as witnessed in the recent production of a number of documents on the topic, three of which will be referred to below.

Norris and Wall prepared a literature review which examined the topic under the following six headings: the tourists ; tourism employment; types of tourism; images of tourism; prostitution and tourism; and tourism and the family. Kinnaird and Hall recently published the first book on the topic. It consists predominantly of case studies but also includes a thoughtful introduction and a brief conclusion. Similarly, Swain has edited a special issue of Annals of Tourism Research on 'Gender in Tourism' which, similarly, consists of an overview paper followed by a series of case studies.

Together, these three sources provide a convenient introduction to a range of relevant topics and reflect the current status of research on gender and tourism. They reveal that much work is in the case-study mode and tends to be women-centred rather than 'true gender scholarship' as described above. However, the first tentative steps towards synthesis and conceptualization are being made. It is pertinent to make a brief comment on the status of western and non western scholarship. It appears that the feminist movement has received its primary impetus from western sources but that scholarship on gender and tourism, whether undertaken by western or non-western authors, has concentrated upon non-western settings. Thus, for example, the author is not aware of any studies of tourism undertaken in Canada which have adopted a gender focus. But there are a number of studies undertaken by Canadians in Indonesia which have a gender emphasis or component, or have been undertaken from a Canadian base.

Gender and development offer a perspective which both competes with and is potentially compatible with sustainable development. To conclude this section it is perhaps worth pointing out that sustainable development requires a sustainable labour force in appropriate numbers and with appropriate skills. Gender relationships underpin and have implications for virtually all aspects of tourism, including human resources development, product development, marketing, site and infrastructure planning, and impact assessment. Also, sustainable development requires that individuals, both women and men, be provided with opportunities to achieve their potentials and equity in access to those opportunities.

Planning and Development Perspectives

Although a strong reason for encouraging investment in tourism, particularly in developing countries, is the expectation that it will contribute to development, there have been surprisingly few links established between the tourism and the development literature. Much of the economic literature as applied to tourism has been technical in nature, for example being concerned with the applications of cost-benefit analyses, economic multi pliers and input-output analyses, and there has not been a strong proclivity to engage with the full range of debate on development perspectives as reviewed in the early part of this paper.

Similarly, Ioannides has bemoaned the fact that there is a considerable gulf between the work of economic geographers and those geographers interested in tourism, although perhaps this is now beginning to change as exemplified in the recent writing of Brohman which touches on a variety of development issues.

Getz has provided a valuable review of the evolution of tourism planning traditions, and although his perspective is derived predominantly from western experiences, it reveals much about the ways in which tourism has been viewed as an agent of development.

Getz recognizes four stages of tourism planning, followed by a fifth which is perhaps as much a goat as a stage which has been reached and superseded. Each stage is described according to basic underlying attitudes towards tourism, the problems which are addressed and the related methods and models employed by practitioners. Boosterism, which espouses an uncritical positive view of tourism and stresses exploitation of resources to attract more visitors, is replaced by view of tourism as an industry comparable to other industries.

The latter approach is predominantly economic in orientation and advocates the use of tourism to create jobs, earn foreign exchange, overcome regional disparities and modernize a society through the application of such development concepts as growth poles, and such as analysis and segmentation.

The physical /spatial approaches sees tourism as a resource user and a threat to the environment and employs concepts such as carrying capacity, visitor management and impact assessment. It, in turn, is followed by community-based tourism which reflects a recognition that tourism is not inherently good or bad and that local control is desirable to direct the forms which tourist takes in the interests of community development. The fifth stage is called an integrative approach, in which a systems perspective is advocated and it is acknowledged that planning for tourism should be integrated with other planning processes.

The evolution of tourism planning, as described by Getz, exhibits many similarities to the sequence of development paradigms described above, in that a predominantly economic perspective is gradually replaced by one which incorporates a wider array of concerns and variables.The preceding discussion has indicated that there has been considerable debate over the nature of development, how development should be measured and how it should be encouraged. This debate has strong ideological underpinnings.

There is no widespread agreement on appropriate processes to promote development, or on the extent to which people should be the objects of development stimulated by others or the subjects of development relying primarily on their own initiatives and resources. In summary, there are varying perspectives on both objectives and processes; on what should be striven for and how it should be done.

Thus sustainable development has arisen in large part because of dissatisfaction with existing perspectives; but it has come into being at a time of great uncertainty and has inherited many of the challenges of the development literature as a whole. The tourism literature and the practical application of tourism as a development tool have evolved with only a tenuous relationship to the development literature, although in spite of the lack of strong links there have been many parallels between them.

Sustainable Development

Sustainable development can be viewed as a component of the alternative development paradigm discussed above. As in development as a whole, it may be regarded as a philosophy, a plan or strategy, or a product. It has been defined by the Brundtland. Commission as 'development that meets the needs of the present without compromising the ability of future generations to meet their own needs'

According to Wood sustainable development has received widespread support because 'it appeared that sustainable development was an idea whose time had come, reflecting a convergence of scientific knowledge, economics sociopolitical activity and environmental realities that would guide human development into the twenty-first century'. He suggests that it is a concept which acknowledges the needs of the world's poor and the limitations which are imposed on development by current levels of technical ability, social organization and environmental variability.

It has received strong bureaucratic support at all levels, from local grassroots organizations to international agencies, partly because it reinforces a world view of economic growth as the engine of both development and environmental protection. Again, according to Wood it lends legitimacy to the free-market economy, belief in trickledown economics and the bene fits of technological progress.

Sustainable development has been criticized on ideological grounds as promoting maintenance of the western capitalist system, as being too ambiguous and as a concept that tries to do something for everyone by tinkering at the margin of the economic system which originally created the problems that the concept is supposed to help address. At the extreme, one might regard sustainable development as an oxymoron:

sustainable implying a state which can be maintained, is ongoing, perhaps even unchanging; whereas development implies change. Maintaining change, ongoing change or unchanging change are not clear messages! On the other hand, the ambiguity of the term potentially permits flexibility and fine-tuning to meet the needs of different places and cultures, encourages greater consideration of the environment, and more effectively integrates environmental and economic matters in decision making by encouraging dialogue between individuals with different perspectives.

The concept is also in line with the community and participatory emphasis of much tourism literature. But unfortunately, the emphasis of many Third World governments is not predominantly on the poor but on large-scale projects, both in tourism and other economic sectors, and generally provides little opportunity for local input. Thus the imprecision of the term has also been conducive to the formation of a gap between rhetoric and reality, and between policy and implementation.

Imprecision has also helped to disguise the fundamental reorientation which is required in western thinking if sustainable development is to be sought and achieved. The scientific and technical approach which has resulted in great advances in knowledge has been achieved through till adoption of a narrow focus and reductionism. In contrast, sustainable development advocates holism and an appreciation of the interconnectedness of phenomena.

Humans have often been view has being separate from nature, which is there for humans to exploit, manage and control. Sustainable development implies that ultimately, humans and environments are indivisible. Conventional economics encourages people to act against their own best interests by placing greater value on present rather than future consumption. Growth in production and consumption is often equated with progress, and economic growth is still regarded as the best if not the only way to meet society's needs. Thus a belief in the value of modernity, the power of science and technology, and the 'law of supply and demand has been promulgated by western society and exported to other parts of the world. Such ideas do not fit snugly with notions of sustainable development.

Widespread interest in sustainable development has captured the attention of tourism industry representatives and researchers and has resulted in the promulgation of sustainable tourism. Butler, who is one of the most articulate critics of sustainable tourism has defined it as follows: 'tourism which is in a form which can maintain its viability in an area for an indefinite period or time'. He contrasts this with a definition of sustainable development in the context of tourism as

> tourism which is developed and maintained in an area (community, environment) in such a manner and at such a scale that it remains viable over an indefinite period and does not degrade or alter the environment (human and physical) in which it exists to such a degree that it prohibits the successful development and wellbeing [sic] of other activities and processes.

The distinction is critical and one which is not grasped by many advocates of sustainable tourism. It is essentially the distinction between a single-sector and a multiplesector approach to development.

The first definition places the emphasis on the perpetuation of tourism to the neglect of other potential uses of scarce resources. However, tourism competes with other activities for the use of limited resources of land, water, labour and capital. The appropriation of resources may be in the narrow interests of the tourism industry, but may not be in the best interests of the broader community of interests of which tourism is only a part. In fact diversity, whether it be in economy or biology, is likely to promote rather than detract from sustainability more broadly conceived.

The second definition acknowledges that tourism is unlikely to sole user of resources and that a balance must be found between tourism and other existing and potential activities in the interests of sustainable development. In other words, trade-offs between sectors may be necessary in the interests of the greater good.

The long-term perspective which is encouraged by the sustainable development doctrine is both a strength and a weakness. The strength is that it would support the precautionary and tie-in principles. The former advocates keeping opportunities open and not foreclosing options in the interests of short-term gains. The latter encourages taking actions, such as water conservation and the requirement that structures be set back from coasts, which make sense now but which will also increase resilience to future environmental perturbations.

On the other hand, in the absence of a crystal ball, it is virtually impossible to determine which experiences will be desired by future tourists or residents, or to assess the influences of technological change for sustainability. How might one recognize a sustainable option in advance of the achievement of the associated sustainable state? And is what is sustainable now necessarily sustainable tomorrow given growing populations, emerging technologies and changing tastes?

The widespread adoption of the term sustainable tourism has been a mixed blessing. It has been adopted by the tourism industry to promote a clean and green image which is occasionally deserved, but more often little more than a marketing gimmick, However, more positively, there are examples where transportation companies, hotels and restaurants have taken steps to recycle and reduce the consumption of energy, thereby reducing costs, increasing profits, and taking small steps in the direction of sustainability.

On the other hand the interchangeable use of the terms ecotourism and sustainable tourism oil the part of some spokespersons displays an inadequate understanding of both terms for, clearly, not all forms of ecotourism, are sustainable and riot all sustainable tourism need be to natural areas.

In fact, one might wonder if the average ecotourist is more demanding environmentally than the mass tourist who may not need to visit endangered species in remote locations, and whose needs and wastes can be more readily planned for and managed in large numbers incorporating economies of scale. Such questions cannot be answered with certainty until the research is done, but unfortunately the total costing of specific recreation activities or tourism types is an area which has yet to receive the attention it deserves.

In spite of the growing number of references to sustainable tourism, and even a journal which goes under that name it is a moot question whether and in what form tourism can contribute to sustainable development. The answers to such questions will likely be found in a greater appreciation of the consequences of different types of tourism. For this to occur, understanding of the implications of tourism must be enhanced, procedures must be devised to deal with complex decision making contexts, and improved procedures for implementation of plans and regulations must be devised. Few would now argue that tourism is a pollution-free industry which is environmentally benign, although many would accept that it is in the long-term interests of the tourist industry to assure the longevity of the resources on which it depends.

But this is easier said than done, for tourism exhibits many of the attributes of common property resources, with most money being spent on transportation, accommodation and food and beverages, and relatively little being directed to the maintenance of the natural and cultural heritage resources on which tourism ultimately depends.

While most would agree that if tourism is to contribute to sustainable development it must be economically viable, environmentally sensitive and culturally appropriate, the forms which this might take are likely to vary with location. This in turn means that it will be difficult to come up with useful principles for tourism development be difficult to come up with useful principles for tourism development which are true for all places and all times.

Economic Development

The term economic development is sometimes used interchangeably with such terms as economic growth, economic progress and secular change. However, certain economists, led by Schumpeter, have made a distinction between economic development and economic growth. In their opinion, economic development is a discontinuous and spontaneous change in the stationary state which alters and displaces the equilibrium stare previously prevailing, while growth is a gradual and steady change coming about by a general increase in the rate of savings and population.

According to another economist, development requires some sort of direction, regulation and guidance to generate the forces of expansion and maintain them. This is true of' most of the developing countries, whereas spontaneous growth characterizes developed countries or advanced free enterprise economics. The simplest distinction is made by Maddison in these words: 'The raising of income levels is generally called economic growth in rich countries, and in poor countries it is called economic development'. Everyman's Dictionary of economics, while using the two terms as synonyms, considers that

> economic development is used to describe not quantitative measures of a growing economy, but the economic, social or other changes that lead to growth. Growth is then measurable and objective; it describes expansion in the labour force, in capital, in the volume of trade and consumption. And economic development can be used to describe the underlying determinants of economic growth, such as changes in techniques of production, social attitudes and institutions. Such changes may produce economic growth.

We share the opinion of those economists who see a difference between growth and development.

We define *growth* as a transformation process that aims at causing structural changes in the national economy resulting in the organized improvement of the standard of living and quality of life for the population. Such growth may happen in a developed or developing country because growth is an endless road representing people's ambition to achieve progress every aspect of life.

Development, on the contrary, expresses the programmes that aim at the realization of a continuous and balanced increase in economic resources and the rationalization of productivity. It is a complex process that is based on scientific and applied endeavours to reach an optimum utilization of the various factors of production through technological progress and manpower development.

In tourism, as in the economic sector, such distinction is tenable. Growth presupposes the existence of a system that functions on its own within a prescribed framework.

Acceleration of growth may need the intervention of public authorities and private enterprise, thus becoming assimilated with development.

Development requires the interference of the human will to plan, direct, guide and regulate progress through the utilization of available and attain able resources. If such utilization is well manipulated economically, socially, culturally and environmentally, sustainability can be realized.

The two terms, however different conceptually, would lead to the same practical conclusion, which is the fulfillment of tourist expansion, albeit rough varying ways.

Real progress toward sustainable tourism growth has to be made through the integration of the viewpoints of at least three disciplines.

1 That of the *economists* whose methods seek to maximize human welfare within the constraints of existing capital stock and technologies. Economists are currently relearning the importance of natural capital.

2 That of the ecologist, who stress preserving the integrity of ecological subsystems viewed as critical for the overall stability of the global ecosystem. Environment is part and parcel of this global ecosystem.

3 That of the *sociologists* who emphasize that the key actors are human beings whose pattern of social organization is crucial for devising viable solutions to achieving sustainable development.

For sustainable tourism growth, the viewpoints of the three disciplines have to be integrated under the guidance of tourist expertise to forecast future demand, plan effective typologies and induce values for the harmonious integration of tourism development projects into a framework that is sustainable. These considerations have to be added to design criteria and land-resource use conceptualization introduced by the architect-planner.

Tourism can be one of the effective tools for building a prosperous community economically, socially and culturally. A *sine qua non* of this is that tourism must be environmentally sound and based on sustaining the natural and cultural base rather than eroding the community's resource capital. However, tourism is not necessarily beneficial or feasible for every country or territory equally. Each destination should examine whether it has adequate attractions and facilities for tourism, and if there are potential tourist generating markets that can endorse and be responsive to those attractions and facilities. Carrying capacity is a central principle in environmental protection and sustainable tourism development. It determines the maximum use of any place without causing negative effects on the resources, on the community, economy and culture, or reducing visitor satisfaction.

The principle of tourism carrying capacity implies a limitation on tourism growth that may degrade scarce resources, and at the same time offers a criterion of sustainable tourism development. Carrying capacity, therefore, represents the point beyond which the tourism industry in any destination becomes unsustainable. In other words carrying capacity, whether national, regional or local, denotes how much tourism is sufficient to yield positive returns and avoid its blights. This level is by no means easy to ascertain, especially when it is realized that the concept of carrying capacity is composite. It encompasses several elements, namely, the physical, the ecological, the cultural, the tourist social, and the host social carrying capacities.

— *Physical carrying capacity* is the level beyond which the available space cannot provide for tourist visits without a clear deterioration of the tourist experience.

— *Ecological carrying capacity* is the level of visitation beyond which unacceptable ecological impacts will occur either from the tourists or the amenities require.

— *Cultural carrying capacity* represents the number of visitors beyond which the cultural, historical and archaeological resources start to deteriorate in time.

— *Tourist social carrying capacity* is the level beyond which visitor satisfaction declines unacceptably because of overcrowding.

— *Host social carrying capacity* is the level beyond which growth will be unacceptable in terms, of detriment to the host community in its traditions this, value system or quality of life.

It is important, however, to note that the carrying capacity principle is not always an absolute principle. It may expand to accommodate more tourist traffic through planning and management techniques as well as technological factors. This may be particularly true in beach tourism. While capacities vary according to the type of beach resort, availability of space on the beach nay be increased in capacity by zoning, rostering or reclaiming more beach from the sea without hampering the natural balance. However, if the beach is rich in underwater corals, or if water undercurrents are active, it would be prudent not to interfere with it at all.

Carrying capacity varies according to the tourist season and is affected by tourists' behavioural patterns, the dynamic character of the environment and he changing attitudes of the host community. It is, moreover, affected by tourism policy determinants. The question of whether an expansion of physical carrying capacity would e detrimental or not for the destination, its amenities or for the tourists themselves, needs thorough investigation and research to ascertain the pros and cons of increasing the capacity versus the physical, social and economic cost involved. Needless to say, achieving successful tourism growth and environmental considerations cannot be separated, Tourism has to be environmentally sustainable in both the natural and cultural environments in order to be economically and socially sustainable.

Generally speaking, sustainable tourism requires a broad vision which encompasses larger rime and space-frames than what would be traditionally required in normal tourism planning and decision making. It is not sufficient to implement such general tourism planning principles as, for example, zoning, clustering, integration between attractions and facilities, interdependence between attractions and facilities, interdependence between natural and cultural attractions, multiple ways to provide accessibility, elasticity, diversity and complementarity, cost-benefit analysis, and applications of carrying capacity. In addition, certain guidelines have to be followed to achieve sustainable tourism.

— A general tourism policy incorporating sustainable tourism objectives at the national, regional and local levels should be followed.

— Parameters established for the planning, development and operation of tourism should be cross-sectional and integrated, involving various government departments, public and private sector companies, community groups and experts, thus providing the widest possible safeguards for success.

— In planning tourism development projects, primary consideration should be giyen to the protection of natural and cultural assets with due regard to the appropriate socioeconomic uses and human impacts on the physical and built environments.

— An assurance should be forthcoming that all tourism participants will follow ethical and sound behavioural and conservative rules regarding nature, culture, economy, community value systems, political patterns, social groupings and leadership.

— The distribution of tourism development projects, while abiding by a national tourism development strategy, should be undertaken with equity in mind, spreading fairly the benefits of tourism among various regions and areas including those depressed.

— Public awareness of the benefits of tourism and how to mitigate its negative impacts should be pursued.

— Local people should be encouraged to assume leadership roles in planning and development, with the necessary assistance from government, business, financial institutions and universities.

— Throughout all stages of tourism planning, development and operation, a scientific and applied assessment, monitoring and mediation programme should be carefully followed to make it possible for all those benefiting from tourism development projects to respond to changes in markets and tourism products; this is necessary if sustainability of tourism develop merit projects is to be achieved.

Needless to say, sustainable tourism should be understood as a form of economic development that is geared to:

— ameliorating the quality of life of the host community particularly in areas in need

— assuring a better quality of tourist services

— guaranteeing a higher level of tourism development that is compatible with the environment and fulfils the aspirations of the citizens economically, culturally, socially, psychologically and politically

Agenda 21

Agenda 21 is a comprehensive programme of action adopted by governments at the 1992 United Nations Conference on Environment and Development (UNCED), known as the Earth Summit. It provides a blueprint for securing the sustainable future of the planet into the twenty first century and is the first document of its kind to achieve widespread international agreement and commitment to work harmoniously towards the conservation of the earth's natural resources.

The travel and tourism industry is considered the world's largest industry, generating in 1905 an estimated US$3.4 trillion in gross output, creating employment for more than 211 million people, producing 10.9 per cent of world gross domestic product (GDP), investing $693.9 billion in new facilities and equipment, and contributing more than $637 billion to global tax revenue.

By the year 2005 it is estimated that the industry will have expanded its global role, generating $7.2 trillion in gross output, creating employment for 305 million people, producing 11.4 per cent of world GDP, investing $1,613 billion in new facilities and equipment, and contributing more than $1,369 billion in tax revenue.

With this privileged position in the world economy, the travel and tourism industry should be recognized as a world leader in contributing to sustainable development. However, Agenda 21 did not mention travel and tourism except in a few sections. Coastal states should explore the scope for expanding recreation and tourist activities based in marine living resources; Countries should 'promote, as appropriate, environmentally sound leisure and tourism activities... making suitable use of museums, heritage sites, zoos, botanical gardens, national parks, and other protected areas'Strict adherence to the promotion of nature-oriented, specialized, humanistic and low-capacity tourism to bring about environmental quality, improvement, while sound in itself, cannot live up to the promise of realizing the industry's huge expectations for worldwide improved expansion. The real benefits lie in making all forms of travel and tourism sustainable this is the real challenge facing all travel and tourism policy makers and industry professionals.

Some key objectives to be achieved in the next ten years are as follows:

— Create socioeconomic value for primitive resources including natural beauty, wildlife, wilderness and forests as well as historical and cultural heritage, built heritage and traditional ways of life.

— Offer sufficient incentives and provide means for environmental enhancement of urban areas, especially in industrial cities.

— Provide necessary infrastructure in remote areas with tourism potential, to encourage human settlements and other economic activities to grow in harmony with tourism.

— Research and develop environmentally compatible technology that could lead to socioeconomic growth and culturally oriented advancement.

— Use international communication networks to spread messages and practices of sustainable development.

Provide examples to other industries of how to conduct business practices that actively contribute toward sustainable development.

Policy considerations

While a growing trend in policy making in many countries is to leave tourism to private enterprise, and current economic conventional thinking supports the role of market mechanisms, the pendulum shows signs of change in theory and in application. As Butler puts it, 'the nature of tourism to some degree determines the nature and pattern of growth and, unless checked and controlled, will inevitably create a set of problems'.

The free play of the market may lead to overreaching capacity limits and hence a lack of sustainability. Therefore, some authors stress the fact that more attention be paid to the imperfections of the market and to those specifically necessary interventions that can correct the tendencies to disequilibrium and monopolistic positions in both private and public sectors.

An example of this would be overdevelopment of the tourist supply in touristically most-frequented areas, such as Hurghada on the Red Sea in Egypt, which resulted in a cutthroat price war that has driven down prices of tourist services to a minimum.

Governments have long exercised controls in some countries and areas, most particularly in exchange rates and hotel services price levels. Governments can influence the development of tourism in certain areas by setting the conditions of investments and the scope of financial concessions, and regulating conditions of access to land, for example by allowing only long-term leases or rights of usufruct on land for foreign investors. Some governments still play an important role in providing infrastructure for tourism development, and also include tourism in their development strategies and land use plans. State involvement in the orientation, regulation and reasonable control of the tourism industry might be deemed necessary to attain a growth rate which is regarded by governments as desirable and sometimes necessary. Such a growth rate would be higher than the market-driven rate.

If past, present and future are connected by a time continuum, change, as previously mentioned, may separate these time dimensions, creating phases of different actions, reactions and outcomes. However, these would be inter related by the forces of cause and effect. Therefore sustainability and balanced tourism growth could be deemed as two intimately related concepts.

Selective growth and striking a balance between tourist supply and demand, between attractions, facilities and services, between quantity and quality, between number of arrivals and natural, social and cultural carrying capacities, are some safeguards against mismanagement of tourism. These safeguards, among other policy decisions, would lead to sustainability and avoidance or mitigation of various detriments to tourism.

It is noteworthy that implementation of Agenda 21 requires a major shift in priorities, involving a full integration of sustainable development considerations into economic and social policies, and a major redeployment of human and financial resources at national and international levels.

In many cases there will be significant benefits from this shift; governments will spend less on health-care and face lower cleanup costs; businesses will experience cost saving from more efficient resource use; tourism destinations will enjoy long-term success; and finally our children will be guaranteed a sustainable future.

This joint document translates the Agenda into an action programme for the travel and tourism industry which aims at helping national tourist administrations (NTAs), representative trade organizations and travel and tourism companies fulfil their potential to achieve sustainable development through tourism. Travel and tourism can transform the following key objectives into reality in the medium and long term:

— Create economic value for resources where utilization and exploitation would, in principle, yield no returns. These are natural and cultural resources such as forests, wilderness, wildlife, archaeological sites, cultural heritage and modern built heritage.

— Provide good reasons and means for environmental conservation of areas which are in need of such environmental awareness. These are mainly large cities centres and old industrial sites.

— Create employment opportunities in various regions arid localities suit able for tourism development.

— Extend necessary tourist infrastructure and superstructure to remote and depressed areas, helping to stimulate economic activities in those areas.

— Use modern communications media to transfer experiences and practices of sustainable development between nations, particularly from developed to developing countries.

— Provide examples to other industries in the adoption of business practices that contribute to sustainable development and lead ideas on sound environmental management.

Mass tourism, with the detriments it may inflict on the environment, has been severely criticized as a major environmental predator. It is therefore necessary that tourism adopts a different perspective that should be compatible, for all practical purposes, with the environment and the community in which it is active. Environmental and societal systems cannot realistically exist in an operational vacuum, but mostly coexist with judicious economic development, and address relevant needs of the host community in the same global system. Many environmentalists, however, seem to ignore or be unaware of this precondition. This is another issue that confirms the necessity to subscribe to an integrated systemic approach that resides in well conceived policy which should be properly implemented in order to guarantee sustainability.

A necessary national dialogue on sustainable tourism would result in multi various policy directives to guide appropriate action within the context of respective mandates and capabilities. These would not only prescribe the actions to be taken by NTAs which are the most relevant, but also roles to be played by tourism industry associations, accommodation managers, tour operators and other tourist services suppliers. However, in the present context it is sufficient to deal with policy determinants that relate to the government as a whole, while acknowledging other tourism industry players' share of policy.

6

Requirements of Sustainable Tourism Development

Sustainable development is that which meets the needs of the present without compromising the ability of future generations to meet their own needs is a particular challenge for small and island states. These territories generally face an intensification of the problem of the management of finite space. Such micro-territories can be considered as laboratory test-cases in the clash between often conventional development strategy and environmental preservation. Many are unwilling prime candidates of global warming; and their problems are exacerbated by higher population densities and a cultural identification with the Western world which results in near continental consumption values. This notion of cultural identification also expresses itself in a 'welcoming society' orientation ripe for commercialization into a tourist industry.

Natural beauty and exotic culture may prove to be marketable assets which certain countries possess as a comparative advantage. This holds true particularly for the world's smallest states and territories. The presence of sun, sea and sand in countries such as Antigua and Barbuda, the

Bahamas, Barbados, Fiji, Maldives and Seychelles has resulted in the development of a flourishing tourist industry which remains the largest contributor to direct and indirect employment, exceeding in significance any other economically productive activity. Small and island states have figured rather prominently in fora debating the relationship between the tourist industry and such themes as commercialization of host culture, environmental management and socioeconomic development. Yet they owe their exposure mainly to the fact that they are plentiful in number or multum in parvo. While the net foreign revenue and multiplier effects of tourism are significant and readily witnessable, the leakages and costs are less transparent. Developing economies in general are caught in a vicious circle whereby they bear many of the costs but few of the fiscal benefits accruing from the tourist industry.

A case can be made for the conceptual distinctiveness of small and island states in considering the implications of tourism in the context of economic development. Hotels are large employers in developing micro-states, rivalling factories as the largest job providers in the private sector. It should therefore prove interesting to examine whether and how the condition of small size and the consequences which it engenders are going to nuance labour relations. Furthermore, it is instructive to discuss how the resulting dynamics offer a different perspective to sustainable development in small and island states. The outcome is a resourceful, home-grown series of techniques which con front and even circumvent global, legal-rational tourism practices and standardized procedures.

Management and workers are already operating in a condition where they may not agree on what, why, when and how work should be done; but overriding this 'contested terrain' one can come across another set of tensions, those which deal with the management of the small size/scale circumstance.

Intimacy, totality and monopoly are factors ex acerbated by the smallness effect and subsequently brought to bear, unwittingly or purposely, on and by system incumbents. This analysis will be grounded in the context of interviews carried out in two luxury hotels. The hotels in question are owned by foreign, transnational capital; they are relatively large and stable employers in two developing micro-states, the Mediterranean archipelagic state of Malta and the Caribbean island state of Barbados. The countries were selected because they are likely exponents of a small-scale syndrome, since they readily manifest a potential towards intimacy totality, and monopoly. The hotels were selected as the focused milieux labour-management encounters could be investigated for insights into the effects, if ally, of operating in a small-scale environment.

The two properties will be referred to by two pseudonyms, Southern Bliss Hotel (SBH) in Malta and Tropical Dream Resort (TDR) in Barbados. Fieldwork material was collected from semi-structured interviews conducted by the author on site during 1991 (SBH) and summer 1992 (at TDR). Some 80 respondents were in all, drawn equally from managerial and nonmanagerial cadres within the hotels' functional departments.

Obviously, word-of-mouth recruitment is riot confined to small territories. People in the hospitality industry worldwide know well the value of such recommendations. Existing employees recruit newcomers without the management having to incur advertising costs. There is also a tacit recommendation process, with an existing employee recommending someone as a good employer, while the same employee recommends the applicant as a good worker.

However, such activity needs to be seen in the small territory within the wider pursuit of brokerage functions carried out routinely by individuals. People are likely to know and interact regularly with a substantial percentage of the total domestic universe of human resources, and to get to know directly and incidentally about the needs of some and those of others; this also tends to be done with a more considerable degree of detail than in larger territories.

To these characteristics can be added the phenomenon of the substantial role repertoire that one tends to come across in small developing societies, which in emulating the institutional framework of larger states may be forced to combine or widen specialisms by incorporating different tasks within a individual's competence. This increases tile number of markets in which one buys and sells services, and so widens the potential of interests or obligations that one needs to satisfy or that one has available to supply. Micro-state citizens as brokers thus maintain the market of particular products. They, mail do so distinctively because of the manner in which totality, intimacy, and monopoly reinforce each other.

Both TDR and SBH have an incorporated institutional procedure for recruitment. In both cases there are formal advertisements of posts on internal noticeboards and, failing this technique, a public call for new recruits:

> 'Normally, for front office staff, we get applicants through the Hotel school. For administrative jobs, we advertise internally first and then we go to the external market and Then to interviewing and screening (Manager TDR)

Outsiders turn up regularly to express an interest in joining the workforce:

> 'We get applications even without having advertised posts. Such are kept on file for future reference.'

But the outcome may not be quite so formal and neat. Only two respondents, one in each property, claimed to have obtained their current job by responding formally to newspaper advertisements. The other interviewed employees admitted a different recruitment strategy. In both hotel properties, the most common eventuality is that employees have been used to recruit their own relatives and friends into the hotel:

> 'Basically, recruitment depended on a request for a recommendation from someone working here. And then off they go and tell their cousins.'

Many respondents owed their jobs at SBH and TDR to the networks of relatives and acquaintances, good contacts and anonymous patrons in a position to pass a good word or authoritative recommendation on one's behalf. Both TDR and SBH, although medium sized employers in their own right, are relative giants in the micro-state world. They are the largest private employers in their respective localities. They therefore recruit heavily from what are in essence 'company towns' where they command a practical monopoly of employment possibilities in a setting of near totality.

The arrangement looks innocent enough, perhaps even cost effective. The hotel managements are assured of a ready supply of labour which manages its own employment agency:

> If I were to resign, people would get to know that.- They will start talking. And even before the advert is nut they are already phoning to apply.' (Assistant Manager, TDR)

With almost nowhere else to go and work in the vicinity the hotels are also guaranteed a turnover of staff:

> Employees will stay here for years and years; as long as one gets here, one stays here. They will not resign. (Manager TDR)

And:

> Having local labour to us is a great advantage And the employees have no other place to go.' (Manager, SBH)

The hotels save on the training costs otherwise necessitated by labour turnover thanks to this situation, nor do they need to offer staff transport:

And:

> 'Only 30 per cent or so of the employees have cars. But they all drive each other home. So there is no need for hotel transport.' (Director, TDR)

> 'We are here bringing work to people, not people to work. Avoiding the costs of transportation to and from work also means a saving on foreign exchange (fuel, cars...) (Manager, SBH)

However, there are other features of this condition about which the hotel managements have little to congratulate themselves. A total institution condition stands out immediately when one tries to get a leverage over the two hotels' human environment. First, so many of each worker's significant others relatives, friends, same village acquaintances, fellow church members, hobby society colleagues, even bedfellows are fellow workers:

> 'We have father—son combinations here; brother and sister; husband and wife teams. Marriage relationships are not so consistent and employees might have a home but have a within the TDR workforce. The acceptance of such liaisons Creates a larger set of close relationship (Director, TDR)

And

> 'Whether one likes it or not, some members of staff come from the same village, even from the same street.' (Manager, SBH)

Second, the two hotels are an integral part of the respective employees' broader social existence; they are embedded within the wider mesh of socio-political community affairs. At both SBH and TDR, employees visit the beaches at/near the two hotels in their free time to swim or talk to their friends and relatives; in the case of SBH, to take family and friends out for a meal, drink or cabaret show. There is a continuous traffic across the proper ties as employees drive their relatives and friends to and from work.

At TDR, where the property dates back more than a century, employees have a feeling of ownership that has roots in childhood practices:

> 'When I was young, my brother and I used to run to the property boundaries and look inside. It looked welcoming. I thought that, if I had come to be a man I would look for work at Tropical Dream.' (Manager, TDR)

TDR is a home away from home to most of the employees; it is looked upon with a certain feeling of possession. With almost 75 per cent of full-time employees (excluding expatriates) living within the parish where the hotel is located, it is no wonder that the hotel, though owned by a foreign multi national, may feel as local as the parish church:

> 'To the locals, this hotel is their whole life.' (Director, TDR)

The low levels of staff turnover, plus the existence of extensive family and kin relations working within the hotel, increase these feelings of owning the resort. In fact, out of 21 nonmanagerial employees interviewed, only 6 claimed not to have any close relatives employed at TDR. Typically:

> I have two brothers working here: And there is a pool attendant who is related to me ... and a waitress ... and a housekeeper as well.

And:

> 'I don't have any relatives working here, as far as I know. But if a cousin popped up, I wouldn't be surprised.'

A somewhat similar (albeit not as extreme) situation obtains at SBH. With the exclusion of the top management cadres (who are usually transferred on short assignments from one of the holding company's hotels to another) and of the housekeeping department (where the majority of the staff are female and uphold short-term, non-careerist work horizons), most employees have been at the hotel since its opening in 1982. There is very little job mobility. With relatively satisfactory conditions of work, there are few push factors to leave; and with an inelastic labour market and scant comparable employment alternatives in the area, there are few pull factors to entice movement either. Add to this the very slim chance of internal movement via promotion, because most supervisory posts are occupied by relatively young careerists, and the outcome is a quasi-closed, stagnant environment that is of managerial concern:

> 'Malta is small, its people are well known. This affects human relations. Most of us have lived for 9 years together. We get to know so much about each other: Families, hobbies, wives. ... This may have its negative consequences.'

Relationship consolidation through consistent exposure and 'rubbing shoulders' in different circumstances and different role-sets has a bonding effect. As individual A realizes that individual B knows so many different facets of his/her social and life (and vice versa), the, condition is ripe fora natural devolution into erosion of privacy and anonymity generate mutual intimacy almost automatically. In this way networks are forged, complententing those established on the basis of kin. Intimacy is and management braces itself for the consequences.

> 'The best form of recruitment is word of mouth. But it has its disadvantages. It allows individuals to recruit networks into the enterprise.'

And:

> 'I agree, there is a recruitment of allies via word of mouth. It remains the most powerful means of recruitment, as far as I'm concerned. Perhaps peculiar to TDR, there is some nepotism where you bring your family members in. I've seen it done. ... The power base and information chain is extended by this practice.'

In tourism, it is necessary to add a third dimension, one which incorporates the social aspirations of the community and host-guest relationships. The subject matter of this chapter is customer care, particularly the Wales Tourist Board's Welcome Host programme, which is aimed at changing local attitudes and behaviour towards tourists. It is about generating an awareness and under standing of tourism within the community, especially to those who may not necessarily see themselves as part of the tourist product, and about improving the quality of the visitor experience in the encounter situation, whether through a chance meeting, a polite enquiry or the service relationship.

Wales is a small country by European standards and one where tourism is becoming increasingly important as a generator of employment. As a rule, improving host-guest relationships is of greater significance for islands and small states since, in general, these tend to depend on tourism much more than larger countries. Following from this, particularly for small islands, tourists are more likely to come into contact with a considerable number of the host population by virtue of their higher propensity for employment in tourism-related activities and the smallness of the country. Smallness also benefits the spread of training when compared to large states, because it is easier to identify leaders and opinion-formers, and disseminate good practice through business and informal networks.

In Europe and North America it would be reasonable to say that quality in terms of management, systems and assurance has become the watched in the 1990s. The object is to ensure repeat purchase. This is likely to be achieved when delivered value for money is equal to or just greater than expected value for money. Unless there is some deliberate policy in terms of, say, market penetration, the costs of delivering quality have also to be traded against what the customer is willing to pay.

The British Standards Institution defines the quality concept as:

> the totality of features and characteristics of a service that bear on its ability to satisfy a given need.

This includes every aspect from raw materials through to manufacturing marketing and delivery to the customer. However, in attempting to provide quality service within the tourism industry the needs differ in that customer contact is important in providing the product, while the manufacturing of goods takes place behind the scenes, remote from the public. Tourism is an experiential product: the tourists buy the product in advance and then become part of the production line from the moment they leave home to the time they return. Total customer service is about building in quality and flexibility to meet customer requirements at every stage of the production process and afterwards when they return home.

Quality management

Quality thus becomes a synonym for meeting the wants of customers and their expectations. Quality management is not about quality control, but rather about setting in process a quality system which aims to exterminate the wastage costs of quality mismanagement by ensuring that all production and service tasks are completed correctly first time. Thus the aims is to reduce the unpredictability of the product where can often be over-exaggerated by customers because of the unfamiliar surroundings in which they find them selves. It is also about dispensing with complacency as indicated by comments such as 'We are making money' or 'Not many complain' or 'We are prepared to put things right if the customer complains'.

The British Standards Institution sets out guidelines to help determine the level and areas of activity to be covered by a quality system under the code. The guidelines are based on practices that have been found to be effective in a variety of organizations. They, set out to show how businesses can establish, document and maintain an effective quality system that will prove to its customers that the company is committed to quality and has the know-how to meet their needs. The factors that constitute quality for a product or service are left to be determined by the individual organization, based on their particular knowledge of the market.

Customer Care

The opportunities for customers to switch brands in the travel industry are relatively frequent, and given the comparative homogeneity of hotel rooms, hotel restaurants and airline seats, large corporations have learnt that customer care is an important factor in determining customer choice and generating brand awareness. Moreover, hosting guests in a manner that meets their aspirations may also compensate for any lapses in the tangible elements of the product.

Lockwood sums up this position in terms of service industries: 'the management of quality is not therefore, just a technical problem, but a behavioural one'. Operators must also consider 'customer attitudes, preferences and perceptions to be able to provide quality'.In determining service quality standards, managers or operators usually consider past performances, thus reflecting the more readily measurable attributes such as physical and technical aspects. But good operational standards are not enough: a guest who encounters a negative impression through poor staff/customer interaction may not return and is hence a lost customer. If the right image is created in the mind of the consumer then the experience will be successful and the customer will return to the sector that provides the most satisfaction.

To take this a stage further, Zeithmal *et al.* highlighted five dimensions in their evaluation of service quality: tangibles, reliability, responsiveness, assurance (meaning competence), courtesy, credibility and security, and empathy (meaning access), communications and understanding of guests.

From a management perspective, the implication of a quality system is a shift of emphasis towards monitoring the reactions of guests rather than employees, in order to maintain a competitive edge. Empowering employees through training and greater latitude in decision making is considered an essential ingredient of quality management. Experience has shown that this also has the effect of reducing staff turnover. It is unfortunate that too many tourist businesses still do not develop the behaviour and attitudes of their staff. They simply poach labour from others or allow their staff to learn on the job and take their experiences out on the customers. Management then becomes a process of long hours of personal control and 'firefighting' forever trying to put right mistakes and placating dissatisfied visitors.

Clearly, even the best organizations do not always get it right first time all of the time, particularly as evaluation is more concerned with the individual expectations and perceptions of the customer than the provider. Customers are willing to forgive mistakes, but when incidents do occur they open up what Laws calls the 'consumerist gap' the gap between the actual delivery of the service and what is expected. The whole service experience can stand or fall depending on the seriousness of the incident and how staff respond to closing the gap. Hence, there is a need to consider some means of controlling the service to instil confidence in quality and close the gap through appropriate customer care procedures. Blueprinting is one such method.

The problems of designing and managing service delivery systems been recognized by Shostack who introduced the technique blueprinting, a means to understanding how consumers experience service systems, while identifying problems or constraints them

> In a blueprint one can trace through all the components of the underlying design and see how they culminate in the various encounter points during which the customer interacts with the service... it makes the services the tangible and can provide employees with a picture of the service includes the key quality determinants.... It can model the actual [lie desired qualities of the service delivery system... it can provide training, market research and control.

The following are the five stages where the visitor ineracts with the service

Stage 1: *Arrival.* Customer impressions will commence on arrival. The means of communication, organization and flow of information at the point of entry are essential to the return of the customer a greeting and a smile will work wonders.

Stage 2: *Information.* Customers now require different forms of information. They are in unfamiliar surroundings; perhaps there is a communication barrier such as language or they seek special requirements in the case of disabled persons. Details of all available facilities are necessary: accommodation, amenities, refreshments, toilets and merchandising.

Stage 3. *Problem situations.* A variety of situations may arise that cause problems; emergencies such as a lost child, accidents requiring first aid or more serious treatment, Customer behaviour depends upon staff reaction in identifying the difficulty and offering a solution, remaining calm, patient pleasant, friendly and helpful in the face of emergencies and complaints, and being knowledgeable in what action to take.

Stage 4 *Staff-customer interaction.* Staff awareness of customer interaction is important to ensure a satisfied visitor. If staff portray a professional caring approach to their work this will contribute to the customer's enjoyment and they will see the attraction as fun, leaving them with happy memories and keen to return or prepared to give word-of-mouth recommendations to others.

Stage 5: *Assess customer behaviour.* Assessment procedures for feedback from staff, management and customers at a central point within the organization need to be undertaken to evaluate customer behaviour towards the service and product offered. These may include comment cards, guest questionnaires, market surveys, customer freephone numbers, mystery guests/ visitors and so forth. Changes may then be initiated to improve customer service and customers should be informed accordingly via thank you letters.

The application of management systems alone is insufficient to guarantee quality of service and customer satisfaction. The concept, design or blueprint and presentation of the service or product must be right before the benefits of quality assurance can be experienced. Through the establishment of Tourism Quality Services Ltd and the implementation of the Welcome Host pro gramme, the Wales Tourist Board, in hosting the guest, has taken action to match the words of its previous Chairman, Prys Edwards:

> Achieving quality is about setting standards to meet your visitors' expectations... quality will determine the future success of tourism,

The consumerist gap in customer care was recognized by the Wales Tourist Board, which developed the Welcome Host initiative in order to promote commitment to visitor care through changes in local attitudes and behaviour to ensure the quality of welcome received by all visitors to Wales. The Board recognized that the experiential nature of the tourist product in Wales is provided by many different agents. Failure of any one agent to close a gap that has been generated by its actions could have a lasting effect on consumer satisfaction and an adverse impact on repeat visits, particularly if the incident is critical. For example, airlines have long recognized that while they do not own or manage airports, any adverse incident in an airport is likely to reflect on them by virtue of the fact that the passenger holds their ticket to fly.

Welcome Host is seen as having an important role to play in the development of Welsh tourism towards the year 2000, It is based on the very successful Canadian hospitality programme Superhost which was introduced in British Columbia in 1986 to support the growth of tourism. The scheme is an ongoing comprehensive community-based programme de signed to upgrade the standards of service and hospitality provided within Wales. By involving the whole community, the scheme provides access to more formal training for the smaller operator who may also conic into contact with the visitor, for example, the local newsagent, grocer or hair dresser.

People helping people; and its objectives are: Professionalism and pride. It is promoted on the premise that if we leave a good impression with customers, the chances are that our business will grow, they will stay longer, spend more money in our communities and return to visit us again'.

Welcome Host concentrates on interpersonal communication techniques and customer service skills. Therefore the scheme aims to:

— enhance the level of service and hospitality provided to the visitor and the consumer throughout Wales;

— increase awareness of the importance of tourism to Wales and the role we all play in making tourism work for us at the local level.

Welcome Host is a one-day course and the seminars include: getting to know you; tourism in Wales; making an impression; communicating; handling complaints; and guiding the visitor. Learning is carefully controlled by providing each participant with a programmed workbook. On completion of the course each member is awarded a Welcome Host certificate and badge, to signify their affiliation with the scheme.

Welcome Host benefits participants by seeking to increase their confidence in the skills of communication, customer relations and interpersonal techniques and to heighten their job satisfaction. It recognizes that such skills are just as essential as technical ability in delivering the product or service in the host-guest encounter.

Welcome Host was launched in November 1991. Recruitment was under taken to seek community trainers and community coordinators. A total of 64 programme trainers completed the course successfully with 61 currently taking part. Their backgrounds range from commercial trainers to college lecturers and consultants from the tourism and hospitality industry. Involved in the scheme are 36 community coordinators who arrange the venues, invite participants and call on the community trainers. The coordinators include groups such as local authorities, tourist associations, enter prise agencies, colleges, training organizations and the police force.

The scheme commenced in March 1992 and proved so successful that within the first year some 6000 participants were trained in Welcome Host, exceeding the anticipated target of 4000. As the programme developed it was clear that two categories of participants could be identified for training purposes, community clients and charter corporate clients. The total number trained to date is over 20,000.

The participants cover a wide range of backgrounds, including taxi drivers, police, traffic wardens, hoteliers, accommodation operators, shop assistants, travel agents, tour operators, tour guides, caravan park workers transport workers, AA patrol men, and all Wales Tourist Board staff.

To underpin rural and peripheral communities, the Board has implemented its LEAD (local enterprise and development) programme. Rural tourism is seen as a of contributing to local income generation, thereby holding together communities in sparsely populated districts. To strengthen host-guest relationships, the Board has consciously set out to introduce Welcome Host to whole villages, alongside the usual programme of public and private sector Projects,

The majority of corporate Welcome Host organizations are in this category. Most large service sector organizations such as the National Trust, Welsh Water, Bass Brewers, high street banks and major department stores (for example, Marks and Spencer) already have customer care training courses.

Where these programmes meet the objectives of Welcome Host, the Board awards them prior learning credits towards the course and presents the company responsible with a charter certificate. Briefing sessions are arranged for the in-house company trainers to familiarize them with the tourism aspects of the programme, of which they are usually unaware. The company trainers thus deliver a modified form of Welcome Host and are restricted from organizing courses outside of their firm. Other corporate clients, for example the Midland Bank and the Countryside Commission, have taken the complete Welcome Host package and integrated it into their own in-house training.

The Board's Training Liaison Unit has now introduced Welcome Host into schools and colleges. The Unit not only recognizes the significance of strengthening relationships with the education sector in terms of promoting an understanding of tourism, but also sees great potential for spreading Welcome Host throughout the country.

Consumer reaction to Welcome Host has been very favourable. A survey was undertaken of 300 consumers within the commercial and tourism sectors, revealing that 85 per cent supported Welcome Host and its benefits to the companies. The Course was found to be very beneficial, by 50 per cent and, information, it reinforced the importance of providing, new relations and interpersonal skills.

The structure is now in place, the community trainers and coordinators meet on a regular basis to exchange views, update knowledge and discuss problems. While the programme is still in its early stages, the enthusiasm, interest and motivation of all concerned are contributing to the improvement of visitor care, making Welcome Host a success story in Wales. To extend the programme on a UK basis would have an even greater impact. Both the English and Scottish Tourist Boards are currently implementing Welcome Host and it is expected that this will lead to the scheme being delivered throughout the British Isles in the near future, and from there to an inter national host network.

7

Mass Tourism: Economic Possibilities

Mass tourism refers to the participation of large numbers of people in tourism, a general characteristic of developed countries in the twentieth century. In this sense the term is used in contrast to the limited participation of people in some specialist forms of tourist activity, such as yachting, or in contrast to the situation in developing countries or in countries with extreme inequalities of income and wealth, or, indeed, to the limited extent of tourist activity everywhere until a few decades ago. Mass tourism is essentially a quantitative notion, based on the proportion of the population participating in tourism or on the volume of tourist activity. Poon emphasizes more the large-scale packaging of standardized leisure services, and for her mass tourism exists if the following conditions hold:

— The holiday is standardized, rigidly packaged and inflexible. No part of the holiday could be altered except by paying higher prices.

— The holiday is produced through the mass replication of identical units, with economies of scale as the driving force.

— The holiday is mass-marketed to an undifferentiated clientele.

— The holiday is consumed *en masse*, with a lack of consideration by tourists for local norms, culture, people or the environments of tourist-receiving destinations.

The notion of mass tourism should be distinguished from the notion of popular and social tourism. Once again to refer to Burkart and Medlik:

> Popular tourism denotes tourist activities meeting with a wide acceptance by people, because of their attractiveness and availability. The acceptance may be due to meeting the needs or tastes of people or more particularly to being available at a low price. Popular tourism is, therefore, essentially a qualitative notion, although by its nature it may give rise to mass tourism.

As distinct from the former two examples, social tourism is concerned specifically with the participation in tourism of people of limited means and with the measures to encourage this participation and to make it possible. From these definitions two main features can be derived:

— the participation of large numbers of people in tourism, whatever the tourist activity may be;

— the holiday is mainly standardized, rigidly packaged and inflexible.

The phenomenon of mass tourism can be illustrated with the evolution of the net and gross participation rate of the residents of a number of European countries Holiday participation in a number of European countries are not fully comparable, for example, the definition of a holiday is not the same in all countries.During the last three decades there has been a substantial increase in the number of holiday-makers. However, in two of the five countries, the net participation rate seems to have reached a ceiling. For the period 1970-94 the net participation rate in Great Britain is close to sixty. The same trend for France for the period 1985-94 is noted, and The Netherlands and West Germany may also have reached a maximum or the ceiling. Tthe main growth of the holiday market can be noticed in the gross participation rate.

It is, however, wrong to believe that the accommodation sector underwent a similar increase in, demand for lodging capacity. In other words nights stayed did not increase to the same extent. On average the holidays became shorter. This can be illustrated with the night participation rate in a number of countries. The night participation rate stands for the number of nights per inhabitant.

The increase in the night participation rate is far lower than the increase in holiday participation during the period 1980-93. France has experienced a stagnation of the night participation rate. In the Netherlands the rate has still increased, from 13.0 in 1980 to 14.7 in 1994. This growth is, however, far below the evolution of the holiday participation rate. On the other hand Belgium has seen a substantial increase in night participation. Belgium is, however, the country with the highest increase in holiday participation.

The different evolution of gross holiday participation and the night participation rate has an unequal impact on the subsectors; of tourism such as transport, travel agencies, tour operators and in-going tour operators on the, one hand, and accommodation on the other.

A new aspect of the holiday market is short holidays. Indeed, besides holidays, more attention should be paid to short holidays of between one and three nights. The growth of short holidays is at least surprising and more spectacular than the expansion of second holidays. Also, here a simple comparison between countries is not valid. In certain countries (e.g. Belgium) second residences and holidays with family and friends are not considered. In other countries (e.g. The Netherlands and West Germany) only holidays with family and friends are excluded.s The short holiday market is booming, and the rates for these three countries are typical for all Western European countries.

Tourism is a mass phenomenon. For most Europeans a holiday each year is a 'must', even when the economic situation is temporarily less brilliant. Economic crisis may mean the destination is different or the stay shorter, but none the less the participation rate is more or less unaffected. So far the discussion has dealt with participation rates in generating countries. On the other side of the coin are the arrivals in receiving countries. Of course not all holidays are taken abroad; a high percentage of tourism demand is domestic. Three points seem to be evident:

1 International tourism has grown spectacularly over the last three decades. In fact the phenomenon started after the Second World War.

2 This growth is very unequally spread-over the different regions. East Asia and the Pacific have become the new receiving areas of the world.

3 There is a trend to lower growth rates in the last decade, especially during the first half of the 1990s.

In his publication *Trends in International Tourism*, Baum underlines a number of key factors for the growth of mass international tourism:

— economic growth;

— more leisure time;

— life-style and work-related changes;

— technological change; the, automobile and the aeroplane become reliable modes of travel for a large middle class;

— changes in the demographic structure of the most affluent societies, especially improved health among the retired;

— reduced international tensions; less bureaucracy involved in travel to an from many countries; and

— a growing awareness of and interest in other cultures and ways, of living, sense of belonging to 'one world'.

Today the number of international tourist arrivals is close to twenty times what it was in 1950. Can this trend be expected to continue? The last long term travel forecasts, the fifth set published by the Economist Intelligence Unit (EIU), leave no doubt, Travel is projected, in terms of trips made, from each of the world's thirty leading countries of origin to each of ten standardized major destination regions, of which the Europe/ Mediterranean region is by far the most important.

In aggregate, the EIU's forecasts expect world tourism to grow significantly more slowly in 1989-95 than in the 1980s. This is largely, but not solely, due to the impact of the 1991-92 economic recession. During 1995-2000 there should be an appreciably faster growth, but with some slowing after 2000. During 1989-2005 as a whole the forecast overall growth rate of 4.2 per cent per year in terms of trips is expected to be very to that experienced during 1980-89.

In 1995 the World Tourism Organisation (WTO) published its own eye are in line with the projections of Edwards. For the period 1990-2000 WTO predicts a worldwide growth rate of 3.8 per cent, and for the next decade, 2000-10, 3.6 per cent. This would lead to 661 million International arrivals in 2000 and 977 million in 2010. When the origin-destination flows published in the above-mentioned EIU study are analysed carefully and WTO publications confirm this almost all regions of the world are involved in the phenomenon of mass tourism. The economic impact must be great and has two different aspects: benefits and costs.

Mass tourism is not a phenomenon of the 1990s, but started in the 50s and 60s. Nevertheless it is surprising that at the first Lome conference in 1975, tourism was not considered as a sector supporting economic development of ACP countries. Lome II paid a little attention to it. It was only in 1985 on the occasion of Lome III that tourism received the interest it deserved. Why was it so long before tourism was recognized as a valuable component of economic development? In the 1970s many publications reports, books, and articles were written by authors who had never seen a developing country and/or only emphasized the negative effects of tourism due to insufficient economic knowledge. Import leakages, income transfers, foreign ownership, tourism as a factor of inflation, destruction of culture, mono industry and social impacts were keywords of this literature. It cannot be denied that all these negative factors more or less exist in many destinations. However, from an economic point of view it is not realistic to deny the positive factors.

Many benefits are mentioned in the literature. Unfortunately this is a phenomenon as chaotic as the Tower of Babel. Variables frequently mentioned are expenditure, income generation, employment creation, foreign exchange earnings, tax-receipts, social benefits, tourism multiplier, transaction multiplier and many more benefits or presumed benefits. Very often these variables are not put in their right context or relationship. In this section the benefits of mass tourism for a nation, region or local community are considered. Further, the benefits of a tourist project within the framework of a cost-benefit analysis are examined.

The two basic incentives for the tourism sector are expenditure and invest merit. Both are essential elements of final demand in an input-output table. Receipts in foreign exchange are a component of expenditures and as such the export element of final demand. Foreign exchange earnings in tourism can be of great importance in certain countries. Spain is a good example. Some developing countries can improve their international liquidity position with earnings from international tourism.

The basic elements of the final demand, tourism expenditure tourism export included and tourism investment, are the bases of two key benefits: income and employment. In other words what does tourism create in terms of income and employment generation? In this way the relationship between four key variables in the tourism sector is linked: expenditure and invest merit on the one side and income and emplcyment on the other side.

Between these four key variables there are special links. Investments depend on the expenditures in the present, the past and the future. In turn, investments can stimulate expenditures.

What is the relationship of the key variables with other above-mentioned variables. Starting with government receipts, the latter are a derivative. In principle, each economic activity can yield returns for the public sector such as direct taxes, value-added tax (VAT), company taxes, social security receipts, etc. These returns are a function of the key variables, as is the case for any other economic sector.

Tourism sector does not have an independent existence in society. Each tourism as a first phenomenon provokes social costs and social benefits. This can be illustrated by an important investment such as holiday village or a theme park, products of mass tourism. Such an investment is responsible for costs which are not paid by the investor. The same projects lead to social benefits which do not accrue to the investing company. One group of social benefits are the well known tourism multiplier effects.

A tourist product is composed of several elements, attractions, facilities, transport, entertainment, image, etc. The basic element is the attractions. These can be of very different types. Many developing countries or developing regions in Europe are rich in natural or human-made attractions. A development based on these attractions offers the tourism sector some comparative advantage *vis-a-vis* other economic sectors.

The first comparative advantage is directly related to natural attractions. These attractions are raw materials which can be made beneficial at reduced costs, and the danger of exhaustion is more or less nonexistent, Here reference is made to an old but very good contribution of Mosse: Besides, the host country may have been endowed by nature with an abundance of readily marketable assets for whose enjoyment tourists are willing to play: sandy beaches, picturesque sites (mountains and forests), a sunny climate, and the remnants of ancient civilizations. Out of the 20 dollars, the tourist may well have gladly spent 5–6 dollars to enjoy these 'free utilities', as Bastiat would have called them, on whose supply the host country did not have to spend a penny, either in local or in foreign currency

The second comparative advantage concerns the import content. There are good grounds to believe that tourism on average has a lower import content than other basic economic sectors. A number of publications support this thesis. The reason is evident. The tourists are buying services which the local population can to a large extent provide. Furthermore, it is not too difficult at least run the agricultural sector towards the needs of the hospitality industry. Mosse supports this point of view. 'As a source of foreign exchange, tourism is on a par with other export industries, but with one difference: they require costly inputs'.

The third advantage is the very high growth rate noted earlier. This growth, together with the good perspective and high income elasticity, make tourism preferential sector for economic development.

Fourth, tourism has a stabilization effect on exports, Export markets in materials are unstable, and therefore foreign earnings are uncertain. The price obtained for raw materials is governed by the world market price and is subject to terms-of-trade conditions. To avoid a deterioration of terms-of-trade, tourism development is often a solution. Mass tourism yields important amounts of foreign exchange, which allow the country to import manufactured goods. The counterpart is a limited quantity of resources To quote Mosse:

A balance of what is given and what is received should be struck not on the basis of the hours of work necessary, but in regard to the utility of the items exchanged. The utility of exports consisting of abundant wild fruit, stretches of sandy desert or trees growing by themselves in the forest, is insignificant, in contrast to the great utility of importing electrical and telephone equipment, transport facilities, etc. Unfortunately, there is no universally accepted measure of utility and use must be made of costs expressed in money or man-hours.

But the tourism sector should not be presented as too optimistic a matter. Tourism is very sensitive to internal problems, political events, diseases, bad news, etc.

A fifth comparative advantage is related to the labour-intensive nature of the sector. This high labour-intensity is notable in the accommodation sector, the subcontracting sector, services, etc. This comparative advantage finds a lot of support in economic theory.

Development of tourism on a large scale, based on mass tourism, creates external economies. Improvements in transportation networks, water quality and sanitation facilities may have been prompted by the tourist industry but benefit, other sectors of the economy. An international airport—a *conditio sine qua non* for tourism development—provides improved access to other regions for locally produced goods.

Another benefit is the generation of entrepreneurial activity. According to Mathieson and Wall, the extent to which the tourism sector can establish linkages with local entrepreneurs depends on:

—l the types of suppliers and producers with which the industry's demands are linked;

— the capacity of local suppliers to meet these demands;

— the historical development of tourism in the destination area.

— the type of tourist development.

In terms of technical polarization one can identify backward linkages. When a number of big hotels are located in a region, there is an immediate demand for large volumes of' agricultural products and different kinds of services. Local suppliers are often unable to meet this demand in quantity and quality. After a number of years, however, the imported supplies might decrease and the local supplies increase, much depending on the capacity of local suppliers to meet the new demands. Entrepreneurial activity may be further stimulated by the external economies created.

If labour or land is used for tourism its social costs ti an economy is its opportunity cost, or the lost opportunity of using it in the (presumably) next-best activity. As ions will a tourism vocation noted, in most tourist countries or regions is no full employment. The choice is seldom between industry and tourism, but between tourism and unemployment. Even when an alternative activity can be retained, a tourism region with valuable resources starts from the free raw materials as a main advantage. Is it not remarkable that many objective 1 regions of southern Europe, eligible for European Regional Development Fund support, have opted for tourism as a strategic develop merit path Overdependence on tourism can be a danger. The sensitivity of tourism demand to all kinds of external factors has been underlined above. Tourism is susceptible to changes from within (e.g. price changes and changing fashions) and without (e.g. global economic trends in the generating markets, political situations, religious confrontations and energy availability).

Mass tourism and inflation

The relationship between tourism and inflation is more complex, temporal and local. A high inflow of tourists during a season can provoke a rise in prices of many goods and services in the tourist region. Durand *et al.* assert that it is indisputable that in cities and tourist areas prices for products and services are, in general, higher than in cities or regions where there is little or no tourism, and that in holiday resorts prices for tourist services are higher in the peak season than for the rest of the year. This upswing of prices is presumably higher in poor regions than in richer ones. Tourists can afford to buy items at high prices. Retailers increase their prices on existing products and provide more expensive goods. This has a double consequence. First, local residents have to pay more for their goods. Second, retailers selling to tourists can afford to pay higher rents and taxes which are passed on to the consumer.

But how far does one notice the spatial impact? Tourist demand is very often concentrated in a limited number of streets or areas. Local residents change their buying behaviour and move to other points of sale. Furthermore, tourists in general are only interested in a narrow range of goods and services such as souvenirs, sports articles, clothes, beauty products, meals and special products (e.g. chocolates and lace in Bruges). A different aspect is the price evolution of accommodation (hotels, rented apartments) and other facilities. In the short term, supply is inelastic and an upswing of mass tourism in a region may lead to higher prices. There is not always much discipline in the tourism sector. A substantial increase in demand is followed by price increases. Regions very often forget that they are in competition with other regions. The classical movement of demand from one Mediterranean country to another is a well known phenomenon.

Mass tourism makes land prices higher. Growth of tourism creates additional demand for land, and competition from potential buyers forces the price of land to rise. The local inhabitants are forced to pay more for their homes. Are the increasing land values to be considered as negative ? All owners, land owners and local residents profit from the additional value from he macroeconomic point of view the final result is, benefit. Furthermore, this effect is quite local. All in all the impact of mass tourism on local residents should not be overemphasized. The costs are largely compensated by the benefits: more wealth, more jobs and higher land value. However, one can imagine situations when tourism demand is very high where inflationary tensions in tourism spill over into the economy at large and contribute to a rise in general inflation. In some countries tourism demand represents 10 per cent and more of GDP, and inter-sectoral linkages of tourism are intensive. Another question is: what are the factors responsible for inflationary pressure in the tourism sector? The

French authors Durand et al. make a distinction between demand and cost inflation in the tourism sector. First of all there is a demand inflation which results in a number of characteristics:

— seasonal demand;

— inelastic supply;

— insufficient market reaction (certain resorts or firms profit from an economic rent);

— imported inflation due to international arrivals (impact of hard currencies and increase of the money mass). Cost inflation is a consequence of a number of factors:

— peak management;

— high taxes on some tourist products and services.

However, one cannot increase prices without considering the consumer, given the law of supply and demand which moderates prices. Many tourists changed their destination from France to Spain, and from Spain to other destinations, because of price differentials.

Incidental costs of tourism

The costs emphasized by De Kadt, Krippendorf and many other authors are summarized in an excellent way by Frechtling and covered by the term 'incidental costs' or detrimental externalities or external diseconomies. Incidental costs, according to Frechtling, lead to quality-of-life costs and public or fiscal costs. Indeed, the local population of a region affected by, external diseconomies of tourism can choose to deal with them, in one of three ways:

1. they may or have to accept a lower quality of life than they enjoyed without tourists

2. they may redress the decline in their quality of life through public expenditure for which they pay taxes;
3. they may directly impose, monetary costs on tourists through taxes and fees.

In Table 1 Frechtling summarizes a number of important categories of incidental costs that are related to tourism import. It is not certain that a specific volume of tourists will produce costs in all categories.

Table 1: *Possible direct incidental costs of tourism*

Life-quality costs	*Fiscal costs*
Traffic congestion	Highway construction, police services, public transportation, port and terminal facilities
Crime	Police services, justice system
Fire emergencies	Fire protection
Water pollution	Water supply and sewage treatment
Air pollution	Police services, public transportation
Litter	Solid waste disposal, police services
Noise pollution	Police services, zoning
Destruction of wildlife	Police services, park and recreation facilities, forestry maintenance, fish and game regulation
Destruction of scenic beauty	Park and recreation facilities, police services
Destruction of cultural heritage	Maintenance of museums and historic sites, police and services
Disease	Hospital and other health maintenance facilities, sanitation facilities, food-service regulation
Vehicular accidents	Police services, justice system

Besides direct incidental costs, Frechtling distinguishes secondary incidental costs. Additional visitors lead to new businesses or an extension of ones which in turn requires more employees and consequently more population. The latter imposes additional life-quality and fiscal costs on the community. Some of these costs for the additional residents are similar to those of additional visitors. Tourism demand is in many regions seasonal and provides seasonal job opportunities. There or country attracts labour that settles in and requires unemployment compensation and other income transfer programmes during off-peak seasons.

A number of benefits and costs of mass tourism have been dealt with above. In practice it is easy to compare both impacts of mass tourism. Some items, especially benefits, can be assessed without too many problems. There are more difficulties with the measurement of costs. Assessing the real value of many incidental costs is particularly difficult.

So far the discussion has dealt with the notion of mass tourism, timeless and spaceless. In reality mass tourism is taking place in a country or a region and in a specific period. Very often it is related to a huge tourism project. The research stages to be faced in comparing social costs and benefits are fivefold:

1 identification of social costs and social benefit items;

2 quantification of the cost and benefit items;

3 valuation or translating the costs and benefits into monetary terms;

4 calculation of the NPV (net present value) and/or IRR (internal revenue rate);

5 risk analysis

This brings up the question of social cost-benefit analysis. Of the five stages above, attention can be directed to the first: how to identify the costs and benefit items?

A scheme as set out in Table 8 can be used, distinguishing four levels of costs and benefits:

1 project level, whatever it may be;

2 unpaid level;

3 underpayment level;

4 side effects.

The unpaid level refers to (a) costs which are not taken into account by the paymaster of the project; and (b) benefits which do not accrue to the firm, organization or others who take the initiative. Only marginal costs and benefits should be considered. The underpayment level demands more specification. In many tourist regions unemployment is very high. The assessment of the items in using unemployed resources should be at opportunity costs. The employment of unemployed persons in a project brings zero opportunity costs and reduces to a large extent investment and operation costs. Very important is the spatial ' dimension of the project considered. A region does not take into account benefits which accrue to other regions; nor does it pay for costs financed by a higher level. Some items are intangible or incommensurable. In this case the NPV or IRR of the cost-benefit aria lysis should be completed with a qualitative table in which all items not expressed in monetary terms are mentioned.

Sustainable Alternatives to Mass Tourism

As one of history's oldest commercial enterprises, tourism has become the world's largest industry, surpassing both international oil and arms sales. On the demand side, this prominence has been caused by postwar affluence and increased leisure in developed countries and a marked decline in the relative cost of travel. On the supply side, the mutually beneficial confluence of airlines, tour operators, travel agents and hotel chains in conjunction with receptive governments, particularly in less developed countries (LDCs), has produced a vast worldwide network of vacation opportunities. Such LDCs, including islands, have been especially eager to reap the foreign exchange, investment, income, and employment promises of tourism as they restructure away from traditional colonial monocrops. As a result, at the turn of the twenty-first century, tourism has become the industry of choice for modernizing small-island LDCs and, in large part, the tropical island holiday and/ or cruise has become the vacation of choice of conventional mass tourism.

Today many strategically placed tropical islands enjoy burgeoning tour ism sectors, In fact, particularly for those constrained by extreme resource with tourism true than in the Caribbean, region where tourism represents a fourth of all export receipts. North America, Europe and, tourism diffused rapidly from the older destinations like Bermuda, Bahamas, Barbados and the US Virgins to the new growth leaders like Antigua, Aruba, British Virgins, Caymans, and St Martin/St Martin. Rapidly rising visitor densities resulted room a tripartite policy of aggressive promotion, aid-financed infrastructure, and foreign facility capital attracted by tax holidays. The common character of Caribbean small-island tourism has resembled a classic case of comparative advantage, with intense specialization towards mass hotel and cruise tourism to achieve high-volume, competitively priced product/ service in the international area. This 'mass' style is linked historically with the region's colonial monocrop staples (sugar, cotton) and postwar manufacturing (textiles, electronics). All three export industries share the same high-volume, thin-margin, low value-added structure.

After over a generation of entrenched tourism policy and growth, how er, the results in the Caribbean are mixed. Rising visitor densities among the highest in the world and associated affluence have caused intense crowding, pollution and utility breakdowns and produced marked alterations in fragile marine and terrestrial ecosystems. Particularly along delicate coastlines where large-scale infrastructure and resorts have been sited, pristine amenities have been irreversibly damaged by hotel and marina construction and heavy cruise traffic in the Caribbean as well as along intensely developed shorelines of popular Mediterranean and Pacific destinations. Added to a host of other economic distortions (inflation, Dutch disease), tourism has allegedly caused widespread cultural losses and disruptive occupation shifts and population substitutions that threaten the 'traditional cultural genius of the place'. These often unforeseen intrusions have challenged the long-term viability of contemporary mass insular tourism and spawned the arch for more compatible alternative styles.

There are, however, several problems linked to designing sustainable tour forms in islands. Like the amorphousness of 'authentic development' which is both an end product and a normative process sustainable or alternative tourism is difficult to define unambiguously except a vague catch-all in contrast to mass tourism, and even more difficult rationally to test. The literature is replete with supposed benefits in theory but there are few systematic impact studies that convincingly argue that alternative tourism is economically viable and culturally and environmentally benign. In fact, some authors suggest that ecotourism is 'just a new name for an old degradation' and that even soft-path tourism can ruin fragile soils, vegetation and marine life. Even whale and watching can damage species diversity:

Nests have been trampled, eggs destroyed, and brooding birds harried from their roosts by tourists hoping for a closer glimpse or more intimate photo of rare birds; whales have been disturbed both by the numbers and excessively. A recent review of nature, cultural, and adventure tourism similarly concludes: 'Many forms of alter native tourism create the selfsame set of problems as conventional tourism and often at a faster pace with more irreversible consequences'.

Such evidence suggests that there are structural propensities endemic to the practice of insular tourism which conflict with sustainability. First, there is the basic incompatibility between a large-scale consumption and waste intensive, open, throughput, highly dynamic international economy transposed upon a fragile, small-scale, static and relatively closed environmental system. A second involves the over growth thrusts of the capital-intensive travel, airline, hotel and cruise industries where all attempts are made to reduce fixed costs and enhance profitability by high-volume mass merchandising, often irrespective of insular carrying capacity. The third is the historical tendency in islands aggressively to overspecialize and rigidly promote exports despite the danger of overrun as a kind of 'quick-buck' adaptation to the boom-bust vagaries of the export cycle. The fourth involves tourism's pervasive nature and the uncertain 'spatial and temporal discontinuities between cause and effect. Such impacts, especially in closely coupled small-island systems, often breed unexpected externalities and make assessment and planning difficult.

Together over time these dynamic forces produce across the island world the familiar contours of Butler's resort cycle. With comparable cross sectional data. The destinations fall roughly into three broad stages. The first high-density group is populated exclusively by the traditionally mature Caribbean leaders: Aruba, Bahamas, Barbados, Bermuda, St Maarten and the US and British Virgins.

The second group of intermediate islands includes twenty transitional destinations at various stages between low-density and high-density status. 'This group comprises two subsets. The, first include the most rapidly growing Caribbean destinations such as Anguilla, Antigua, Cayman Islands and St Lucia. If also includes those Pacific areas favoured either by location and/or US political affiliation (i.e. Guam and the Northern Marianas Islands).

The second subset contains islands that have achieved international visibility but are growing at a slower pace. These include Caribbean areas like Montserrat, St Vincent, and Dominica, as well as several newly developing Pacific destinations: American Samoa, Cook Islands, Palau and French Polvnesia The final low-density, group of emerging tourist areas is populated exclusively by Pacific islands that vary in size and level of modernization..

As the resort model predicts and has been verified elsewhere (de Albuquerque and McElroy, 1992), along the S-curve of increasing tourist penetration there is, roughly speaking, a concomitant increase in environmental alteration. This is particularly true where mass tourism is aggressively promoted in fragile insular ecosystems. In addition to these cumulative natural disruptions, there are a number of associated commercial and institutional shifts peculiar to the maturing domestic and international linkages of the dynamic tourism industry.

These include rising general affluence, service occupational diffusion, an increase in infrastructure and facility scale, an expansion of external ownership and industry consolidation, increased visitor density and crowding, declining length of visitor stay, and the gradual substitution of man-made attractions (casinos, duty-free shopping) for lost natural amenities and experiences.

The implications of the resort cycle for sustainability are serious. The development of mass tourism, particularly as it is practised in the small-island Caribbean states has an inevitable and cumulative dynamic that progressively undermines the natural assets that form the long-term capital base of the economy. Just as the medium-density areas of today were the low-density newcomers of the 1960s and 1970s, so the high-density islands of today were the intermediate destinations of less than a generation ago.

Serious consideration is warranted to examine alternative tourism forms which will eventually be more compatible. Here we presents two Caribbean case studies drawn from Bermuda and Montserrat that highlight different approaches to arrest 'progress' along the resort life, cycle continuum.

Bermuda and Montserrat are small, tourist-dependent crown colonies that share a decidedly English rural but which differ measurably in population size (59,000 to 12,000) per capital income ($ 23, 000 to roughly $5000). According to data, Bermuda typifies the high-density mature destination with annual visitors (hotel and cruise) exceeding aver age daily densities approaching 150 visitors per sq km a hotel capacity close to 9000 beds.

Bermuda boasts an international airport, three cruiseship arbours with shopping complexes, and many large-scale, full-service international standard hotels. Lacking an international airport and any world lass resorts, Montserrat represents an intermediate, small-scale island with some 30,000 visitors, an average daily density of less than five visitors per sq. M, and hotel capacity of less than 500 beds.

Most of all, however, the two islands differ in tourism styles. Bermuda has followed its own unique path of upscale, luxury, high-density tourism while Montserrat has anchored its economy to a low-density, long-staying residential North American retirement community. Bermuda, riot surprisingly, also has a small but significant retirement community consisting mostly of Britons, Americans and Canadians. However, these resident expatriates have somehow never been factored into overall tourism policy, since they are viewed for all intents and purposes like all other permanent residents.

Retirement tourism has long been a successful strategy in industrial countries for rejuvenating rural backwaters and declining rustbelt communities. Less noticeable in the literature but increasingly significant in fact has been the emergence of scattered expatriate settlements in tropical islands across the mature Caribbean destinations like Bahamas, Bermuda, Caymans and US Virgins, as well as in Malta and Gozo. Greece and other Mediterranean islands. Montserrat's special character is twofold.

First, its retirement and long-vacation tourism was the result of conscious government policy and thus represents a legitimate case of deliberate alternative tourism in contrast to other more circumstantial variants sprouting up nearby through the play of free-market forces.

Second, the strategy has been successful. Before the disruption of Hurricane Hugo in late 1989, Montserrat was touted as one of the most highly desirable Edens of its kind.

Situated centrally in the Lesser Antilles between Antigua and Guadeloupe, the so-called Emerald Isle is rugged and lush, with black sand beaches, striking sea and mountain vistas, and few mineral resources besides the hot springs of the seismically active South Soufriere Hills, Its colonial history is dotted with a series of failed export (sugar, limes, long staple cotton) and a long-term propensity on the part of young to emigrate search of employment. Postwar restructuring was by tourism in general and especially the institution of a government-promoted real estate boom in North American retirement home construction.

This scheme transformed abandoned, mainly hilly agricultural tracts, primarily along the leeward coast north of the capital city of Plymouth, into a stronghold of well-manicured suburban 'residential' retirement vacation communities.

This initial takeoff was followed by secondary waves of infrastructure expansion, new hotels and local home construction, second-home building financed by remittances from Montserratians working abroad, and the establishment of an offshore US medical school. Today, the dominant export sectors of tourism, manufacturing and related construction account for half of all employment, while government absorbs about a third and agriculture/ fisheries less than 10 percent. Among its six close Eastern Caribbean neighbours, Montserrat enjoys one of the highest levels of per capita income and access to medical and educational services and one of the lowest rates of natural population increase.

In the late 1970s, visitor arrivals (stayover and cruise) doubled. This was followed by instability and stagnation during the world wide recession of the early 1980s. After the recovery in 1985, growth resumed until the disruptions caused by Hurricane Hugo in 1989. Provisional estimates since then indicate stayover tourists who arrive in small aircraft from nearby Antigua are again on the upswing. Over the entire period, it is estimated that visitor expenditure has more than quadrupled. Day visitors, who arrive primarily in small ships and windjammer cruises, have markedly increased in significance.

Montserrat's visitor profile is atypical for the Caribbean region which is heavily dependent on relatively short-staying Americans. In 1991, only 40 per cent of stayovers were from North America, with over a third made up of Caribbean nationals on business or returning emigrants on holiday, and the balance comprising long-staying Europeans (13 per cent British) and Latin Americans (10 per cent).

Compared to their Caribbean counterparts, Montserrat visitors are older and more affluent, frequently friend,' and relatives of resident retirees, and exhibit a greater propensity to repeat and a preference for the old world charm and pace and the intensive enjoyment of the natural amenities. Although the length of stay (hotels only) has declined somewhat since the late 1970s the long average stay, for all stayovers a Montserrat hallmark including those in second homes, with friends, and visiting family was approximately two weeks in the 1980s.

Despite strong recent growth, the pastoral environment has remained relatively unscarred by the evolution of a low-density, long-staying tourism style characterized by limited infrastructural intrusions, a small-scale accommodation structure, and the absence of ecology-altering mega resorts. Half of overnight visitors stay in private homes while a fourth stay in hotels and another fourth use villas and apartments. This preference pattern produces a low-key dispersed tourist plant that fits unobtrusively into Montserrat's variegated topography and reinforces its scenic land and seascape features and sense of unhurried tranquillity. Such modest accommodations plus the suburban retirement communities tend to be 'all of a piece with the main residential areas... the tourist appears to fit into the scheme of things'.

In addition to imprinting their low-impact footprints on the physical character of the island, resident North American retirees the so-called invisible base of Montserrat's tourism have contributed significant economic impacts. In a 1987 survey of long-term expatriates, we found that there were 287 mainly North American retirees in island residence for roughly 8.5 months per year comprising 200 households. They spent an average of $35 per day, comparable to the average expenditure of stayovers at the time. This spending was roughly split between basic consumption needs and capital maintenance items like housing and pool unkeep and gardening. In total, they contributed $2.6 million in gross tourist spending (287 X 255 days X $35) not captured in conventional visitor statistics.

This impact is significant on several counts. It represents more than 25 per cent of all conventional measured visitor expenditure for the same year ($9.4 million), and it approaches the estimated 1987 contribution of hotel tourists $3.1 million), villa/apartment visitors ($3.0 million), and private home guests ($2.9 million). From another viewpoint, the gross economic impact of one expatriate retiree spending $35 per day for 8.5 months ($8925 = $35 x 55 days) is roughly equivalent to the contribution of 17 stayover visitors remaining 2 weeks and spending $38 per capita per day during 1987 ($9044 = 17 X 14 X $38). Likewise, it is roughly equivalent to 300 cruise visitors averaging $30 per day in 1987. Though crude estimates, these striking orders of magnitude suggest both the economic potential of retirement tourism and also underline its promise as an effective low-density complement to more conventional tourism forms.

Although situated in the Atlantic, Bermuda resembles a Caribbean island in size, topography, colonial history and tourism dependence. Tourism began in the late 1800s when a monthly steamship service brought wealthy New Yorkers to' the English tropics'. Between world wars, 'heavy resort investment and celebrity visitors sparked international interest in the island as a beautiful and quaintly English destination for the well heeled, a carefully cultivated and marketed image which has endured. In the immediate postwar era, with the expansion of five new steamship lines and a modern airport, Bermuda was poised for a transition to an upscale variant of mass-market tourism.

Over the past forty years, total arrivals have risen tenfold. Since the mid 1960s steamship passengers have been replaced by a steadily increasing stream of cruiseship visitors which presently account for more than a quarter of total arrivals. Since reaching a peak in 1980 of close to half a million stayover visitors, this figure declined over 100,000 to about 37.5,000 in 1992. This sharp drop has had damaging consequences. It has been matched by parallel declines in hotel profits and bed capacity through the closure of major resorts, as well as sizeable cuts in hotel employment. As a result, although total visitor spending has risen over the past decade, it has not kept pace with inflation.

After over a generation of intensive development, Bermuda is now the most affluent destination in the region with the longest history of tourist experience and one of the highest cost-of-living and tourist penetration levels. The island exhibits all the characteristics associated with the mature high-density stage of the resort cycle. These traits include slow economic and population growth and flat or declining tourist arrivals, heavy, dependence on short-staying (90 per cent North American) visitors who are dominantly hotel guests (nearly 70 per cent), a large-scale hotel plant with nearly 70 per cent of all rooms in large (100+ room) hotels, high occupancy rates (60-70 per cent), expanding man-made attractions like, shopping complexes, and a share of one-day cruise visitors.

Despite forty years of tourist growth and its precarious positions at the peak of the resort cycle, Bermunda still remains noted for its British countryside quaintness, political stability, sophisticated and genuinely friendly populace and distinctive and maintained environment: pink sand beaches lush greenery, pastel-coloured homes, historical architecture, safety and order, and above all, its immaculately clean and uniquely trimmed landscape. As a result, Bermuda's image endures as a distinctive, quaint, upscale destination for sophisticated travellers seeking quality and charm. It is this same image that has served to attract wealthy retirees to Bermuda. Indeed, some of the declines in bed capacity that occurred in the late 1980s came about because some housekeeping cottages and apartments, were taken off the short-term rental market in favour of the longer term retiree rental market.

The reality and sustainability of this image is less fortuitous and more the result of conscious planning and community awareness. During the late 1970s and 1980s, increasing crowding, particularly from cruiseship trade, ;stimulated efforts to control visitor densities and protect the island's natural and cultural patrimony. A moratorium on new bedroom capacity was imposed and cruise traffic curtailed. Specific ordinances were enacted and ;strictly enforced to preserve special vistas, delicate natural areas and historical sites. Local materials and native vegetation were mandated for residential construction and landscaping. These planning initiatives had the widespread support of local residents who felt that Bermuda was suffering from visitor saturation and who viewed the island's pristine appearance as extremely important' not only for quality tourism but also for their own quality of life.

The implementation of this 'softer tourism path' coincided, however, with he worldwide economic instability and intensified destination competition characteristic of the past decade. The alarming decline in stayover visitors has suggested that Bermuda may be entering the stagnation and decline stage of the life cycle. This fear has spawned anew the policy debate over controls versus promotion, quality versus quantity. It has also sparked a host of visitor satisfaction surveys and an intense discussion of price-value issues. During the reassessment, several problems have surfaced that challenge the island's commitment to the recently adopted lower density tourism approach.

These include very high cost with labour at $10 per hour and utility rates triple US levels, some suspected erosion in service quality, inadequate resort amenities (hotel spas and fitness equipment, restaurant variety, etc.) and insufficient 'things to do' for vacationers. In response, recently some growth controls have been relaxed, tax incentives offered for hotel refurbishing, and discounts selectively designed for families with children. A public-private partnership has initiated a fresh promotional campaign that touts Bermuda's 'affordable quality'.

Other strategies include an innovative programme for cruiseship visits, the restoration of historical buildings as tourist facilities cultural reenactments and pageantry for visitor enjoyment. While the spirit of these policies clearly emphasizes achieving durable asset quality and is expanded length of stay in the longer run, decision making circles continue to be preoccupied in the short run with visitor numbers. In fact, provisional figures for 1993 suggest both stayover and cruise arrivals were significantly ahead of 1992 levels.

Contemporary trends expected to intensify over the next decade include an expanded demand for more pristine, natural and authentic cultural educational experiences by, an increasingly sophisticated clientele with more travel options available, and a more sharply competitive climate as both mature, intermediate, and emerging destinations vie for market share. Crowded high-cost islands may not fare favourably in such an aggressive environment. This suggests concern for the Caribbean region, abundant with relatively saturated destinations, with hotel rates among the highest in the world, and presently suffering a perceived decline in service quality. Clearly a more sustainable insular tourism will require a different approach from the traditional mass syndrome: rising scale, promotion and densities associated with declining visitor repeats, satisfaction, and asset and service quality fostering ever renewed rounds of more aggressive promotion to stave off the descent down the resort cycle.

8

Implications of Sustainable Tourism

In 1973, Robert Erbes commented that everything seems to suggest that developing countries look upon tourism consumption as manna from heaven that can provide a solution to all their foreign settlement difficulties. Although this statement was considered by some authors as a simplistic presumption it is, however, a useful introduction to the topic of tourism and development. Tourism has noticeably progressed to become a major economic activity and economic activity that has proved its vital and irreplaceable role world trade. However, tourism in the context of the national economy 'is not a unique devil'.

The ability of the national economy to benefit from tourism depends on the availability of investment to develop the necessary infrastructure and on its ability to supply the needs of tourists. etc. In general, small economies, are more likely to be dependent on imports, and the same is true of economics where tourism is not very well developed As suggested by some writers, 'there is no other international activity which involves such critical interplay among economic, political, environmental, and social elements as tourism'.

However, Young points out that the degree of acceptable reliance on tourism relates to the structure of the economy: Where there is high unemployment, a relatively unskilled labour force and few alternative sources of employment... then stimulation of the tourist industry may well be a correct course of action. The danger appears to be at the next stage of economic development, where unemployment and underemploy-ment have been reduced, the labour force is better educated and an infrastructure exists which might support other industries. Continuing dependence and emphasis on tourism may no longer be economically justifiable.

Economic Implications

Tourism stimulates the development of several sectors of the national economy. Tourism:

— creates new local requirements for equipment, food and other supplies fostering new industries and commercial activities and creating a new market for them,

— has a favourable impact upon employment in a country as it increases the opportunities available for work in accommodation, food industries, tour operations and travel agencies, government tourist offices, handicraft and souvenir trades, recreational, amusement, and entertainment activities, and various selling outlets,

— increases urbanization through the continuous growth of construction and renovation of tourist facilities. This implies creating and improving infrastructures and tourist superstructures, particularly in remote and depressed areas,

— helps to increase the state earnings of hard currency necessary for bridging or reducing whatever deficit there is in the balance of payments, and thus fosters the development of the national economy,

— is one of the most effective redistributive factors in international economic relations. To explain this, one has to admit that travel is a social activity arising from surplus income, Thus the flow of foreign travel is more significant from richer countries to the less privileged. A substantial portion of foreign travel is directed towards developing regions which are more attractive naturally as they are not yet spoiled by industrialization. Thus tourism redistributes capital between developed and developing countries, and

— activates the economic circuit in a country, thus accelerating the multiplier effect.

In contrast to the undeniable economic benefits that can accrue to the tourist destination, tourism also exacts a price from it. Such' a price is represented by investments in tourism infrastructures and superstructures, in the cost in foreign exchange of required imports, and other aspects such as distortion of the national value system, vandalism, congestion, increased crime, and the possible change or loss of the national architectural heritage and natural beauty.

In developing countries with good tourism potential, tourism may be adopted as an economic activity that could rationalize economic policy, especially through balanced growth brought about by new or additional business production cycles prompted by tourism expansion. Thus tourism can become the cause and the effect of rationalizing economic development, along with the economic production sectors of agriculture and industry.

Social Implications

Insofar as social development is concerned, tourism as a phenomenon represents an important leisure activity which has to be included in the state's national policy, in the interests of safeguarding its moral and health standards. Moreover, tourism is a factor of social solidarity and equilibrium.

The movement of tourists, whether domestic or international, across the different regions of the destination, makes it easier to bring about social homogeneity among the different ethnic, religious, urban and rural groupings. In addition, human contacts arising from tourism yield more social benefits than any other industry, in particular, developing new tastes and modern habits, and foresting cultural borrowings. However, strange habits, values, heterogeneous traditions and different mentalities may bring about a cultural shock which might lead to social problems.

Tourism's positive contribution to the economic, social, political and environmental advancement of developing countries is contingent upon the able implementation of' suitable scientific, technical and technological factors, as well as the appropriate deployment of available resources to maximize benefits and minimize disadvantages. This is nor an easy task given that developing countries usually lack adequate expertise. Such weakness could be surmounted by bilateral assistance from developed countries, as well as international cooperation through international organizations, namely WTO, ILO, the World Bank and Regional Development Banks. Both proponents and opponents of tourism as a tool of development in developing countries admit that tourism has made influential changes in the structure, value systems, traditions and behavioural patterns of many societies. The debate about whether these changes are good or bad is still unresolved, as the interests of society and the individual are not necessarily identical or even similar. Moreover, the varying conditions prevailing in different societies make generalizations difficult, if not impossible, to reach.

Environmental Implications

As rightly put by Pigram, 'tourism is, to a large degree, a resource-based activity, interacting with natural systems and with a capacity to initiate fat reaching changes on the environment' Therefore, management of environmental issues has become central to tourism planning in all destinations, developed and developing, and thus is a basic premise for sustainability. There is a long catalogue of environmental damage caused by various human activities, although tourism development projects are not the only offenders. Avoidance of such environmental damage in tourism must be given priority. Protected natural areas and national parks should be encouraged in environmentally sensitive areas.

In these areas, development should be prohibited or at least restrained. Unique cultural attractions such as the Giza Pyramids and the Sphinx in Egypt, Barubudur Temple in Central Java and Matsu Pichu in Peru should be properly protected and maintained as they are priceless examples of human heritage. A basic limitation, is the carrying capacity of these areas and attractions in relation to visitor use and the development of facilities. Tourism should be used as a medium to attain such conservation in order to maintain resource sustainability. Otherwise the environmental damage will adversely affect resource quality and tourists will avoid the destination.

Any alleged disregard for the environment by conventional tourism development typically yields expressions of outrage. Hong expresses this mood:

> Having ruined their own environment, having either used up or destroyed all that is natural, people from the advanced consumer societies are compelled to look for natural wildlife, cleaner air, lush greenery and golden beaches elsewhere. In other words, they look for other

environments to consume. Thus armed with their bags, tourists proceed to consume the environment in the countries of the third world that last 'unspoiled corner of earth',

Appendix

The World Ecotourism Summit

1. INTRODUCTION

This report contains the summaries of the debates held and conclusions reached at the World Ecotourism Summit and its preparatory process, as well as the Quebec Declaration on Ecotourism.

The World Ecotourism Summit, was held in Quebec City, Canada from 19 to 22 May, 2002. This was the principal event to mark 2002 as the International Year of Ecotourism.

The Summit was an initiative of the World Tourism Organisation (WTO) and the United Nations Environment Programme (UNEP). It was hosted by Tourisme Québec and the Canadian Tourism Commission. These four organisations were the partners responsible for the Summit.

The purpose of the Summit was to bring together governments, international agencies, NGOs, tourism enterprises, representatives of local and indigenous communities, academic institutions and individuals with an interest in ecotourism, and enable them to learn from each other and identify some agreed principles and priorities for the future development and management of ecotourism.

Main themes

UNEP and WTO, in consultation with other organizations and ecotourism stakeholders, had defined and adopted the following main discussion themes for the International Year of Ecotourism and for the Summit.

Theme A - Ecotourism policy and planning: the sustainability challenge

Sustainable ecotourism plans, policies and programs at international, national and local levels; integration of ecotourism policies into sustainable development plans and frameworks; land use planning; use of natural parks and protected areas; balance between development and conservation objectives in policies; development agency programs on ecotourism and their role in funding related pipeline investments; plans for human resource development in ecotourism.

Theme B - Regulation of ecotourism: institutional responsibilities and frameworks

Legislation, norms and other regulations for ecotourism activities; voluntary schemes and self regulation; certification, accreditation and ecolabels; international and inter-governmental guidelines, principles and codes; roles of different stakeholders in ensuring compliance with regulations or voluntary schemes.

Theme C - Product development, marketing and promotion of ecotourism: fostering sustainable products and consumers

Building sustainable ecotourism products; multistakeholder cooperation for product development especially in protected areas and biosphere reserves; market research, marketing techniques and promotional methods; information to tourists; ethical behaviour; environmental education for consumers; public-private sector relationships for marketing and promotion; co-operative marketing for small ecotourism operations.

Theme D - Monitoring costs and benefits of ecotourism: ensuring equitable distribution among all stakeholders

Measuring economic, ecological and social costs and benefits of ecotourism; contribution to conservation; assessing potential and actual environmental and socio-cultural impacts of ecotourism; taking precautionary measures at local, national, regional and international levels; integrating monitoring and evaluation procedures; research needs and adaptive management systems.

Cross-cutting themes

Throughout the discussions on the four themes the focus was on two main cross-cutting issues:

- The sustainability of ecotourism from the environmental, economic and socio-cultural points of view;
- Involvement and empowerment of local communities and indigenous people in the ecotourism development process, in management and monitoring of ecotourism activities, and in the sharing of benefits resulting from it.

The preparatory process for the Summit

During the latter half of 2001 and the first four months of 2002, 18 preparatory conferences were held. These conferences took place in all the regions of the world, either under the aegis of WTO or of UNEP (in association with The International Ecotourism Society). A list of the conferences can be found later, in the reports of the regional panels. The preparatory conferences provided an opportunity for all kinds of stakeholders in ecotourism to come together to present their experiences and discuss matters of local, regional or international concern. In total over 3,000 delegates attended the conferences and over 300 papers were presented at them.

The preparatory conferences addressed each of the four main themes of the Summit. The combined results of the conferences were summarised in four papers, one for each of the themes, which together formed a discussion paper circulated at the start of the Summit.

During April 2002, a web conference was held. This enabled any individual or body, at no cost, to participate in the debate about the four Summit themes. There were 948 registered participants in this conference.

Participants and presentations

A total of 1,169 delegates attended the World Ecotourism Summit, from 132 different countries. The range of delegates included:

— International agencies engaged in supporting conservation, tourism and sustainable development.

— National ministries of tourism, culture and the environment. In total 30 ministers of state attended the Summit.

— Non-governmental organisations working at an international or local level, representing conservation, indigenous communities, travellers and other interests.

— Private sector enterprises engaged directly or indirectly in ecotourism.

— Academics, consultants and other experts in the field of ecotourism.

Registered delegates were invited to submit statements relating to the Summit themes. A total of 180 statement proposals were received. From these, 120 were selected for presentation during the event, considering time limitations of the three-day programme. The selection was based on the relevance and originality of the contribution and on the need to achieve a representative balance of presentations from different types of organisation and parts of the world. In addition to the registered statements, participants had the opportunity to intervene freely throughout the debate sessions.

All statements, whether presented or not, which were received by the deadline were included in a CD-Rom, which was distributed to each delegate. This CD also included the reports from the preparatory conferences.

Structure of the Summit

Following introductory presentations from the partners, the Summit consisted of the following elements:

— A plenary session at which four panels reported on the preparatory conferences held, respectively, in Africa, Asia, the Americas and Europe.

— Four parallel working group sessions, covering the four main themes of the Summit.

— A ministerial forum, and two special forums covering the business perspective and development cooperation in ecotourism.

— A plenary session to receive and debate reports from the four thematic working groups.

— A final plenary session to receive and debate the draft Quebec Declaration on Ecotourism.

Summit outputs

The main output from the Summit is the Quebec Declaration on Ecotourism. This has been taken forward to the World Summit on Sustainable Development at Johannesburg, 2002, and has been widely circulated. The full text is included in this report.

2. REPORTS FROM THE REGIONAL PANELS

The opportunities presented by ecotourism and the need for its careful management are apparent in all regions of the world. Evidence from the preparatory conferences suggested that the fundamental principles and issues relating to the development of ecotourism are similar in all areas. However, it was also apparent that differences in resources, ecosystems, markets and socio-economic structures, mean that priorities and practicalities vary from region to region.

These similarities and differences were brought out during the reports of the regional panels at the Summit. During each panel session, short presentations were made by selected spokespersons on the preparatory conferences held in that region. In the main, these conferences had focused on the region in which the conference was held, but in a few cases the conferences covered types of destination (e.g. islands, deserts, Arctic lands) irrespective of continent.

Following the presentations on the preparatory conferences, the sessions were opened up to interventions from the floor and a discussion. At the end of each session, the key points that had arisen were identified by the rapporteurs.

Session on preparatory meetings held in Africa

Four reports were presented to the Summit on the preparatory meetings held in the following locations:

— Maputo, Mozambique, March 2001 - for all African states with an emphasis on planning and management

— Nairobi, Kenya, March 2002 - for East Africa

— Mahé, Seychelles, December 2001 - for Small Island Developing States (SIDS) and other Small Islands

— Algiers, Algeria, January 2002 - for Desert Areas

The presentations in this panel demonstrated that ecotourism is one of the main forms of tourism in which Africa has a comparative advantage.

Africa features extensive protected areas hosting a variety of ecosystems and traditional cultures that are major attractions for nature-oriented tourism. In many African countries, vast national and wildlife parks count for many forms of ecotourism activities.

Ecotourism seems the best way to prevent controversial effects and negative impacts on prevailing ecosystems, local communities and traditional cultures and to be a viable source of economic benefits for African countries, if developed and managed in a sustainable manner.

The specific circumstances and needs for different areas were separately identified.

Africa's international comparative advantage: National parks and protected areas

Ecotourism is a great opportunity for African countries and its parks, reserves and protected areas are an international level resource. Thus, many African countries can base their tourism development on exploiting their natural assets on the condition that the rules of sustainable development - the basis of ecotourism - are respected. Conservation of natural resources can become mainstream to socio-economic development in Africa. National parks and reserves in Africa should be considered as a basis for regional development, involving communities living within and adjacent to them. Given their strong international recognition, parks and reserves can be turned to sort of brands, providing advantage in tourism marketing and promotion.

Small islands and coastal zones

Particular attention must be focused on tourism development in small islands as development, even ecotourism development, can be at the origin of environmental and social problems - even before large number of tourist arrivals. This is the case of coastal zones in small islands where ecosystems, notably lagoons, are particularly vulnerable. Appropriate liquid and solid waste treatment systems must be put in place whenever any ecotourism activity is created.

Moreover, ecolabels are particularly important for small insular countries as shown in the example of the Seychelles. Ecolabels can be very useful for achieving landscaping and beautification objectives, such as by encouraging better use of gardens, and for stimulating environmental management, such as energy conservation, waste treatment plants and recycling systems.

Due to the natural and economic specificities of tourism in small islands it is not realistic to focus on ecotourism in the stricter sense. Rather, the broader concept of "sustainable tourism" is often a more effective policy position, though ecotourism plays an important role in further setting the standards for the protection of the natural and cultural environment.

The fragility of island ecosystems must be the cornerstone of any ecotourism plan and any action must respect the island's local, natural and cultural environments.

Desert areas

Desert areas represent comparative and even absolute advantages for Africa, which has the largest desert in the world. Deserts are also some of the largest conservation areas in the world. The seminar in Algiers concluded that there are great opportunities for ecotourism in desert areas - particularly for Africa because of its location near the large tourist generating markets of Europe. Desert areas represent complex ecotourism attractions, showcasing natural, geological, and archaeological features, nomad and other specific cultures and traditions. A special attention should be paid in ecotourism development and management in desert areas to the fragility of ecosystems, the extreme meteorological conditions, the presence of unique archaeological and geological remains, the scarcity of water resources and the difficulties of access.

Importance of trans-boundary cooperation

Many natural zones cross the political borders of several countries and this must be taken into account when developing ecotourism. Indeed, it is impossible to envisage diverging or even opposed development policies in zones shared by several

States where there is natural, human and social unity. In this case, trans-boundary cooperation is fundamental for all types of ecotourism development, which implies common policies between countries in the same region. This cooperation is particularly necessary in areas where wildlife crosses administrative and political borders.

The development and management of trans-boundary natural resources and parks has to become a central issue in Africa, recognizing the need to maintain ecological integrity and free movement of wildlife in certain territories that are divided by country frontiers.

The need to find commercial and financial solutions

The commercial viability of ecotourism initiatives is a recurring theme in the debates such as in the case studies presented in the preparatory seminars, specifically in Maputo. Participants emphasised the importance of strengthening small and medium enterprises and particularly micro enterprises to enable them to successfully engage with the tourism industry in Africa. The importance of identifying and demonstrating to funding sources the value of conservation and of ecotourism to national economies in Africa has to be recognised.

The need to reinforce capacity building

There is a lack of awareness of tourism among African local communities. Local communities need to appreciate the benefits and the demerits of tourism. It is important for governments to ensure that communities are trained to administer joint ventures, as without capacity building it is difficult to sustain an equitable approach to management. Capacity building is essential if local communities are to be real stakeholders in the development of ecotourism in Africa.

African necessity to focus on benefits for local people

Speakers and participants identified the need to generate local community benefits from Africa's natural heritage tourism as the critical issue. Ecotourism as a concept has most to offer in the African development context, linking to the rural economy to avoid leakages and maximise local economic benefit from tourism. In Africa, national parks, wildlife reserves and other protected areas have to play a significant role in encouraging local economic development by sourcing food and other locally produced resources.

Session on preparatory meetings held in Asia and Pacific

Five reports were presented to the Summit on the preparatory meetings held in the following locations:

— New Delhi, India, September 2001 - International NGO Workshop Tourism Towards 2002

— Gangtok, India, January 2002 - Conference for South Asia

— Maldives, February 2002 - Asia-Pacific Ministerial Conference on Sustainable Development of Ecotourism

— Chiang Mai, Thailand, March 2002 - Conference for Southeast Asia

— Fiji, April 2002 - Conference on Sustainable Development of Ecotourism in the South Pacific Islands

The papers and debates from the Session on Asia and the Pacific highlighted a number of issues and perspectives, as follows.

Need for baseline studies

The importance of baseline studies was highlighted, in order to provide a better knowledge on ground conditions, and changes over time. It was recommended that innovative approaches be examined, instead of reliance on government, particularly in under-resourced areas. Suggestions included involving volunteer organisations (e.g., those that provide programmes in which conservation and community development work is combined with educational, cultural exchange and tourist activities), or involving educational institutions (e.g., through PhD students).

Commoditisation in tourism

Particular mention was made of commoditisation in tourism in the region, in large part due to poverty. Commoditisation refers to the degradation of the intrinsic value of cultural items, beliefs, goods, and practices, and may even refer to treating a human being as a good for sale. This trivialisation of culture is demonstrated by the sale of culturally related trinkets, and even by people selling themselves (sexually) to visitors. Organisations developing or managing ecotourism are urged to focus on the improvement of basic human conditions.

Managing Impacts

A range of approaches were mentioned for managing impacts, from pricing and fees, to diversification of product offers (to alleviate crowding). However, a serious impact with no solutions offered, was that of global warming in the region.

The need to integrate a range of perspectives, with communications being key

In some Asia-Pacific destinations, ministries try to push their own agendas on other departments and vice versa (e.g., Tourism and Forestry). This achieves very little except resistance. There needs to be awareness and capacity building in government departments, to understand that ecotourism can be a force to assist both mandates.

It was observed by some participants that some NGOs always feel government actions are wrong, and governments tend to pay less attention to constant criticism. Other participants felt that NGOs have some valid perspectives whether in critique of governments or not, and that NGO comments deserve appropriate attention. It was also felt that some NGOs or governments actually undermine private business. The issue that emerged was: how to integrate the range of perspectives, and how to cooperate to mutually beneficial ends.

Improved communications are required. In particular, it was recommended that:

— governments should establish an open dialogue with local communities, private companies and NGOs;

— governments should develop transparent communication, consultation and decision making processes; and

— public-private partnerships should be seen as a key facilitating mechanism, particularly for informing and educating the travelling public about the consequences of their travels as well as their potential for beneficial action.

Challenges of implementing community participation

The challenge of how to implement sustainability through empowerment and participation was discussed, since local participation has an important role in preserving biodiversity.

Bottom-up participatory processes were recommended (e.g., as in Fiji, where the Fiji Ecotourism Association was formed, so that government and others could more easily communicate with an umbrella industry organisation).

Top-down participatory mechanisms were also recommended, as well as a mechanism for multi-sectoral involvement. It was suggested that communities should be consulted on a range of topics, from product development to elements of marketing.

It was acknowledged that time is required for awareness and capacity building, so that communities are able to participate effectively and make decisions.

Community control of local resources was said to be a key need in the Asia-Pacific region. It was suggested that communities should be involved in all levels of activity, including management.

Participatory management was said to be a key tool in ensuring participation in planning, decision-making and management. An example was given of Sri Lanka, where both poachers and policemen communicate together, and although it has taken five years (as well as time, patience, energy, and the efforts of the Eco-Development Committee), both parties now have confidence in the process, and poachers are using their locally-developed skills in a more sustainable way.

It was agreed that ecotourism is best developed to enhance and complement current community lifestyles and economic activities, rather than basing community economies solely or predominantly on ecotourism, or introducing a completely new activity. It was also frequently stated and agreed that communities should have control over ecotourism, including whether they wanted to have it at all, and if so how much, where, when and of what type.

Human resource development is required

It was recommended that there should be a bigger emphasis on training for local people. In the Asia-Pacific region there is a very great need to incorporate local indigenous peoples into any training programs. It was also felt that communities in general need to have awareness training or information related to ecotourism, and also to be made aware that they may have a choice about tourism or other activities.

A challenge related to this topic was how to develop mechanisms to ensure that revenues from ecotourism activities are invested in training (e.g., on-the-job training, management training, or sending workers to attend conferences).

Regulation and monitoring is required

Regulations can either have a positive role in facilitating movements of tourists and foreign exchange in SE Asia, or can be restrictive. It was suggested that very often poor planning has had adverse consequences and needs to be improved. Also, the lack of enforcement of current regulations is a problem.

Session on preparatory meetings held in The Americas

Six reports were presented to the Summit on the preparatory meetings held in the following locations:

— Cuiabá, Brazil, August 2001, for all American states

— Belize City, Belize, November 2001, for Mesoamerica

— Lima, Peru, February 2002, for the Andean region

— Oaxaca, Mexico, March 2002 - Oaxaca Declaration on Indigenous Tourism

— Buenos Aires, Argentina, April 2002 - First National Conference on Ecotourism.

The Americas are probably one of the regions in the world where ecotourism is developing fastest. There is also an increasing concern about the involvement of indigenous peoples and local communities both in the planning and development of ecotourism.

The preparatory conference reports showed clearly three main concerns about the development of ecotourism: the involvement of local communities; the need for certification schemes easily accessible to everybody regardless of their economic capacity; and much needed training at all levels. In general, there is consensus about the fact that ecotourism can and is contributing actively to nature conservation in the region, and also to a better quality of life for local people. It has also been recognised that it is very important to learn from past mistakes as well as successes.

Planning

One of the issues raised around planning was the specific problem of trans-boundary areas where there is a need for international regulations. Another important point was that very often not all available scientific information is used for planning.

A further concern was that it is important to have a diverse range of activities besides ecotourism such as agriculture, livestock, forest non-timber products, and others, thus avoiding over-dependence on ecotourism. Shifting from traditional sustainable use of resources (when these uses are sustainable, which is not always the case) to ecotourism is a high-risk strategy for local communities. Besides, in areas where ecotourism products mix with other kinds of tourism, it is agreed that there is a need to increase the sustainability of all tourism products.

Regulation and certification

A suitable approach regarding regulation is to follow a process leading from optional guidelines to obligatory regulations. Codes of conduct need to be established as well as procedures and all stakeholders should adopt these. The importance of ethics among operators, the community and consumers was also identified as one of the key issues.

Another important point raised was that regulation of ecotourism needs stakeholders sharing a similar concept of ecotourism.

It was agreed that there is a need for more transparency in certification processes and that these should relate both to environmental aspects as well as quality and participation of local communities. International certification systems are believed to be too expensive and it was suggested that local initiatives should be recognised by international systems. It was suggested that certification should occur at different levels that are more suited to specific regional and local conditions and allow community-based companies to take part in the process. There were proposals to establish incentives for certified companies. Finally it was recognised that in some areas there is a risk of a proliferation of eco-labels.

Participation of indigenous and local people

One of the main concerns was the lack of public participation in the process of planning for ecotourism in many places. It was stressed that local communities need to be the main actors and that they must take part not only in the planning process but also in the management of ecotourism products, which generally means also taking risks. A particularly sensitive issue was the concern among indigenous people about the fact that in some of their lands ecotourism development is being imposed by governments and private companies, without proper consultation and participation.

Capacity building and training

Capacity building and training were identified as key points in the proper development of ecotourism in the region. This included the need for capacity building of local communities, training and technical support. An important point raised was that training needs to be realistic, not creating too high expectations for local communities.

Policy makers were also identified as important targets for training and it was shown that they need to learn about ecotourism in the field. Very often policies are in the hands of people with very little practical experience in the subject. Another target much in need of education about ecotourism is the media in general, who very often cover ecotourism but without reflecting properly its real essence.

Marketing

A fairly common problem in the Americas is that marketing generally focuses in landscape, wildlife and cultural issues and does not put enough emphasis in social, environmental and sustainability aspects, which should be part of responsible marketing communications and very often can be of interest to potential visitors.

In recent years there has been a great development of communications within the region and the Internet has become an important tool for marketing, even for small companies and communities, as well as in remote areas where Cybercafés can be accessible. The Internet can fulfil its potential only if capacity-building and access to modern technology is provided in order to empower ecotourism stakeholders for the adequate use of this media.

Session on preparatory meetings held in Europe

Four reports were presented to the Summit on the preparatory meetings held in the following locations:

— St. Johann / Pongau and Werfenweng, Salzburg, Austria 12-15 September 2001 - for mountain areas, with an emphasis on European ecotourism

— Almaty, Kazakhstan, 17-18 October 2001 - for the transitional economies of the CIS countries, Mongolia and China

— Thessaloniki, Greece, 2-4 November 2001 - for European, Middle East and Mediterranean countries

— Hemavan, Sweden, April 2002 - for the Arctic countries, including North America and Asia as well as Europe

In addition, a paper was presented by the Minister of Tourism of Turkey.

Although the term 'ecotourism' is less frequently used in Europe than in other continents, the presentations showed that the principles and concepts associated with it are equally important here as elsewhere. Europe has many wilderness areas, yet in much of the continent attractive rural landscapes and biodiversity are dependent on traditional land management practices. There is increasing recognition within Europe of the important and mutually supporting relationship between tourism, agriculture, viable rural communities and the conservation of nature.

The preparatory conference reports demonstrated the contrasts to be found within Europe, in terms of landscapes, climate, culture and management priorities. The specific circumstances and needs of different areas were separately identified.

Mountains

Mountains are important locations for ecotourism. The report from the conference in Austria recognised the important linkages between the objectives of the International Year of Mountains and the International Year of Ecotourism, both declared for 2002 by the UN. Mountainous areas often display a particular cultural richness, economic fragility, a decline in traditional populations and activities, and sensitive biodiversity. Mountain communities can use ecotourism to address these issues. There is a close relationship between the needs and opportunities of ecotourism and sustainable activity tourism in mountains.

The Mediterranean

This area receives some of the largest volumes of tourist arrivals in the world, concentrated on the coastal belt. Yet, this is an area of rich biodiversity and also has immense cultural resources. The report from the conference in Greece identified the opportunity for ecotourism in the coastal hinterland and more remote inland areas, as a way of improving the image of Mediterranean destinations, diversifying the offer, reducing seasonality and bringing economic benefits to areas suffering depopulation. Careful planning will be essential.

The CIS countries

These countries have extensive natural areas including forests, wetlands, plains and mountains. Potential for ecotourism is considerable. However, as economies and societies in transition they have particular needs, especially in terms of the general services and infrastructure for tourism. Important issues include clarifying national objectives for ecotourism, stimulating and catering for the domestic market, filling knowledge gaps, easing visa restrictions and promoting cross-border cooperation.

The Arctic

This is a sensitive area with its own particular needs. The traditional values and practices of the indigenous peoples of the Arctic, in protecting and using natural resources, should be recognised, as should their rights over land and water. The report from the conference held in Sweden identified the need for certification programmes for ecotourism which take account of the particular circumstances of the Arctic. Appropriate codes of conduct for visitors and operators need to be applied. A restructuring of the cruise ship licensing system was called for, with local people having control over the use of their areas for ecotourism.

In addition to these priorities relating to specific areas or ecosystems, a number of general themes of particular importance in the European context can be identified from the presentations and the subsequent discussion.

Taking an integrated approach to destination planning

There is strong recognition in Europe of the need for a holistic approach to the planning and development of destinations for sustainable tourism, both in terms of providing a quality experience for visitors and addressing all the impacts of tourism. Ecotourism should be seen within this context. There should be concern about physical infrastructure, destination marketing and information services, linkages with other economic sectors, and relationships with other forms of tourism.

The important role of local authorities in supporting the development and management of sustainable tourism, including ecotourism, is well understood in Europe. This is helped by well-established local democratic structures, effective land use planning and development control processes. At the same time, the need to foster a participative approach at a local level, for example through engaging village communities, is recognised.

Addressing transport and other access issues

The use of transport to, and within, the destination was a key concern of the preparatory conference in Austria. Where possible, ecotourism should be based on forms of mobility which have low environmental impact. Discussion at the Summit widened the debate on access, with a call for more attention to be paid to facilitating access to rural and natural areas, including mountains, for example through networks of hiking trails.

Being concerned about demand and equity amongst users

Demand management was felt to be an important issue in the European context. Points made about this during the discussion included:

— avoiding discrimination and increasing access to ecotourism experiences for people with disabilities and disadvantages;

— promoting opportunities to domestic visitors, ensuring that they are not put off by high prices (e.g. in the CIS countries); and

— influencing larger tour operators as well as more specialist operators (e.g. in the Mediterranean).

Showing responsibility in promoting ecotourism in less developed countries

Europe is a source region for much global ecotourism. The responsibility of European governments and operators in encouraging more sustainable forms of ecotourism, and in providing technical advice and support in this field, is recognised.

3. REPORTS FROM THE THEMATIC WORKING GROUPS

The second full day of the Summit was devoted to four separate working groups on the four Summit themes.

Each working group meeting started with the presentation of a report from an expert, appointed by WTO and UNEP, which summarised the results of the preparatory conferences and served as discussion paper for the Summit concerning the theme in question.

A total of 71 presentations were made to the four working groups. These were restricted in time, to enable a range of topics to be covered and to give as many people as possible a chance to speak. Two presentations from the host country, Canada, were made during the first session of each group. The presentations were grouped into four sessions throughout the day, and after each one at least half an hour was allowed for interventions from the floor and for debate. In the closing session, the WTO/UNEP experts summed up the main points to be taken forward to the final day of the Summit, and these were further discussed and expanded by delegates during a final hour of debate.

On the third and final day, a report from each working group was made to a full plenary session of the Summit. This was followed by a discussion period which enabled all delegates to have a chance to make further points about each theme, and to comment on the conclusions of the working groups.

The four reports which follow set out the issues discussed and the key points and recommendations arising from the working groups, while also taking account of the points raised in the final plenary session.

These reports build on the summary reports of the preparatory conferences, adding to, illustrating and emphasising points made in them. A short resume of the key points arising from the preparatory conferences is given, before the points arising from the Summit are presented.

Many of the points made were repeated in more than one workshop. This is inevitable as most of the principles of ecotourism relate to all of the themes and each of the topics are interdependent. For example, ecotourism planning needs to take account of product development and regulation issues, and vice versa.

Working group - A

Ecotourism Policy and Planning

The sustainability challenge

Ecotourism is a complex activity, often seeking to meet a range of objectives, involving a variety of stakeholders and taking place in environmentally and economically fragile locations. It therefore needs careful planning. This working group was concerned with the frameworks, structures and processes of ecotourism planning and policy-making to maximise sustainability and local benefit.

There were eighteen presentations to the working group, which covered:

— National ecotourism planning, policy-making and strategy development - Botswana, Chile, Cote d'Ivoire, Haiti, Rwanda, France, Brazil, Senegal, Tanzania, the Mayan World.

— Ecotourism planning systems in federal and provincial parks - Canada

— A case study of ecosystem changes in tourist destinations - Nepal

— Guidelines to minimise negative impacts of ecotourism in vulnerable ecosystems (the Convention on Biological Diversity) or small islands (Seychelles)

— Integrated planning and management in rural areas - Greece, Chile

— Policies developed by origin countries for minimising tourism impacts in destinations - The Netherlands.

1. Issues Discussed

The main issues discussed were:

The best structures and tools for effective ecotourism planning, which relate to all objectives

— Planning for environmental conservation

— Planning for economic development

— Gaining social and cultural benefits

— Multi-stakeholder participation

The following specific issues arose throughout the debates:

The relationship between ecotourism and sustainable tourism

It was suggested that planning and policy development for sustainable tourism was the appropriate context for ecotourism planning, since ecotourism embraces the principles of sustainable tourism concerning the economic, social and environmental impacts of tourism. On the other hand, it was also suggested that there was merit in highlighting the particular characteristics of ecotourism, bringing positive benefits for conservation and communities and not simply avoiding negative impacts. It was recognised that ecotourism products may vary considerably, but that all should adhere to basic ecotourism principles.

Lack of appropriate infrastructure and services in destinations

In many destinations with ecotourism potential, it is felt that there is a lack of infrastructure (e.g., accommodation) and services (e.g., well-trained guides).

Foreign ownership or low levels of local jobs minimise local benefits

The issue of foreign ownership draining many of the benefits at the local level was raised. This is particularly the case with respect to infrastructure. In addition, the level and quality of jobs in which local people are employed is too often inadequate (e.g., in Senegal).

Ecotourism brand

The themes of the Summit are in many cases strongly interrelated. Within the Planning and Policy Development sessions, there were discussions about the desire to prevent the use of the word ecotourism by those who do not adhere to its principles, through some type of trademark or branding protection, although the difficulties in this were also acknowledged. This whole topic was the focus of considerable discussion in Session B, and reference to that section provides further insight.

Uncontrolled penetration of ecotourism activities into new areas

The penetration of ecotourism (or other forms of tourism) to remote areas can create management and monitoring problems. For example, in Egypt treks go to very remote areas of the country, which are mostly desert. The difficulty of monitoring tourism operations in remote areas enables the stealing of artefacts, fossils, etc.

2. Key points and Recommendations

A number of key points and recommendations arising from the working group were specifically related to conservation, economic development, social benefits and stakeholder participation. However, there were many points that cut across these issues and these are presented first.

Key crosscutting recommendations

Main recommendations from the preparatory conferences:

— Integrate ecotourism policies and planning across national boundaries

— Ensure national governments provide necessary leadership and guidance

— Create a planning framework for protected areas

— Formulate ecotourism plans jointly between public agencies, NGOs and other stakeholders, with a long term vision and clear goals

— Develop tools to assist in planning and management of ecotourism (e.g. appropriate land use planning and visitor management techniques)

— Provide adequate and appropriate funding for projects, protected areas and partnerships

— Involve governments, development agencies, NGOs, private businesses and others in building local capacity, to encourage participation and employment of local people

— Ensure careful consultation and participation of all stakeholders in planning and policy development processes.

Key points arising from the Summit:

Using transboundary management approaches

The need for trans-national policies was emphasised, related to many aspects of tourism, such as easier movement of peoples between regions, and cooperation with respect to shared ecosystem management.

Humans should be recognised and acknowledged as being a part of the ecosystem (as opposed to only using ecosystems). Transboundary movement possibilities should be built into plans and policies.

There was a recommendation that a world fund be established to enable appropriate ecotourism development particularly at the trans-national level, with the focus intended to be on enhancing cooperative activities between jurisdictions. However, no specific proposal was made on the nature and source of the fund.

It was proposed that global regions (e.g., the Caribbean) should come together for a range of planning and policy development functions (e.g., to highlight issues which have regional relevance).

Taking a collaborative approach to planning and policy development

There should be an overall national vision of how ecotourism can serve biodiversity, as well as how biodiversity can serve ecotourism. One of the biggest problems is lack of a sectoral planning perspective (e.g., the frequent divorce in dialogue between tourism agencies and environmental agencies). All agencies need to work together. It is recommended that lessons and failures be taken from such planning processes as Integrated Coastal Zone Management Studies, for integrating ecotourism planning. Integrated planning should be actively pursued, including collaboration with stakeholders.

Government must take a holistic perspective when developing sustainability strategies, which is both spatial and sectoral (e.g., as in Greece). Ecotourism planning should be conducted within the context of sustainable tourism planning, which in turn should relate to the wider context of planning for sustainable development. Ecotourism planning, actions and policies should be developed with the knowledge that they are likely to be applicable to other forms of tourism, and in all likelihood will be a force for positive change throughout tourism, considering the trends towards mainstreaming ecotourism values and principles. For example, in Tanzania, there are major policy reforms stimulated by the International Year of Ecotourism, which are focussing on poverty reduction through a range of sectoral perspectives such as developing economic opportunities and empowering communities through community participation.

Sectoral integration should be a foundation of all planning and policy development (not only in ecotourism). For example,

Chile's National Action Plan is based on an integrated approach, and has been done with the private sector, in a bottom-up manner. Another example is found in the Seychelles, where there are not only various topical themes within their National Environmental Management Plan (including tourism and aesthetics), but there are significant cross-cutting themes (education, awareness and advocacy; partnerships, public consultation and civil society participation; training and capacity-building; management; science, research and technology; monitoring and assessment; vulnerability and global climate change).

It was recommended that whatever the mechanisms, all decision-making be transparent, and also accountable.

Developing appropriate tools for planning and management

It was recommended that appropriate scale in ecotourism development be a part of planning considerations. For example, some destinations build in development controls ahead of time (e.g., Botswana has, as part of its planning framework, deliberately stipulated small-sizes for their ecolodges and camps, or temporary facility structures to enable them to be moved in the future).

There was a comment that in many areas, policies and regulations may exist, but are not implemented. While appropriate planning and policy development is one requirement, rigorous implementation is fundamental.

Planning systematically for protected areas

It was emphasised in debates that a protected area system must form a key part of planning and policy making for ecotourism, and that protected area managers be involved in planning initiatives (not only senior government officials).

A severe problem for protecting biodiversity and protected areas was felt to be the fragmentation of ecosystems. It was recommended that the issue of adequate size of protected areas be addressed in development and planning. It was suggested that a useful educational and management tool is the creation of maps to illustrate locations, threats, or other spatial variables, so indicating where it is most necessary to conserve biodiversity.

Committing adequate financial and other resources

Some countries lack the ability to mobilize the resources necessary to address significant ecotourism planning and policy development needs. Multilateral aid is required in the form of various types of assistance. One recommendation was that there be support for centres of development and dissemination of knowledge and cooperation; another was that there be a fund for trans-national ecotourism development.

The public may be encouraged to contribute funds. It was suggested that visitors and others should be able to donate funds to projects, and should receive some recognitions and benefits which reinforce the value of their donation. For example, the Coral Reef Action Network offers donors a range of educational reminders: stickers to heighten awareness, CD with a tool kit for customers, wall calendar, passport, poster, boaters' chart, quiz and similar items. These educate and keep donors involved with the project. In addition, they give donors guarantees that all their contributions will go to the chosen project.

It was suggested that some funding for education, in schools and elsewhere, be set aside from ecotourism revenues.

Capacity building

Training and capacity building is required for those professionals who are involved in planning and policy development. It is recommended that the WTO and other international institutions support or fund programs which train public officials who will be planning and developing policies, in order to build capacity within ministries and similar institutions (e.g., this could be through national level training institutions). This suggestion of appropriate training was also made for the personnel of park and protected area authorities.

At a more local level, it was suggested that the WTO and other institutions should continue to expand training programs, such as for local authorities, indigenous people and other stakeholders. Another suggestion was that a range of types of support be examined to develop capabilities locally, such as guiding skills.

It was recommended that tour operators also be involved in education and training.

Education and awareness-building is recommended as a significant tool for all players, from lodge owners and tour operators to local communities and young people. Suggestions included such innovative ideas as developing education caravans for community awareness building, or creating coursework for schools to better understand the concept of impact.

The views and perspectives of youth are a key influence on positive future directions. It is recommended that sustainable tourism education of young people be built into educational programs and ministry curricula in all countries.

It was recommended that the Internet be better used for information exchange. International agencies should collaborate to compile a database of information, which is web accessible, continually updated, and includes information on best practice for sustainable tourism and for ecotourism. It was suggested that qualified websites with useful information should be able to link to this site.

Building multi-stakeholder participation into policy and planning processes

Mechanisms should be developed to include a range of stakeholders in planning and policy development. It is always easier for governments to deal with umbrella organisations than with operators directly, thus developing industry organisations may assist. For example, Parks Canada and the Tourism Industry Association of Canada have developed an accord concerning heritage-based tourism, which is currently focussed on agreement about principles, which acknowledge shared stewardship in managing and protecting national heritage places.

Indigenous peoples' representatives (e.g., Shushwap Nation, in Canada) emphasised the need to build targeted participative mechanisms into planning and policy development. Since indigenous peoples tend not only to be the poorest members of society, but also to have land based economies and cultures (involving hunting, fishing and gathering), it is critical to involve them early in any processes.

Other suggestions for including stakeholder participation came from Tourism Quebec, who suggests that integrated management requires that there be government centres close and accessible to citizens (decentralised communications points).

It was also emphasised that past experience should be brought into the planning and policy development processes (e.g., South Africa) so that there is greater integration of ecotourism activities into the way of life of communities. It was recommended that the Global Code of Ethics developed by the WTO should be adopted by all stakeholders, to promote a balanced perspective in different forms of tourism development, including ecotourism.

It was also agreed that ecotourism should not be developed if consultation revealed that local communities did not want to have it.

Recommendations for Environmental Conservation

Main recommendations from the preparatory conferences:

— Conserve energy, water, and other resources, reduce waste and favour materials that are not imported.

— Plan more sustainable transport options.

— Promote awareness of conservation and biodiversity amongst local people and visitors.

— Use appropriate tools to identify limits to use and to manage impacts.

— Seek to influence demand as well as managing visitors who do come.

— Use economic tools, information and interpretation in visitor management.

Key points arising from the Summit:

Educating communities about biodiversity and conservation

It was felt that many local communities did not understand the value of biodiversity very well, and that education was needed. Visitors should also be educated about the value of biodiversity and that natural resources belong to local peoples and should not be removed by visitors (souveniring, biopiracy, or removal of fossils, etc.).

Managing impacts

Primarily, it is essential to ensure that ecotourism does not have negative impacts, and that operations adopt minimum impact practices and guidelines (e.g., in the St Laurent or Yukon areas of Canada). Other options are planning in the destination to exclude certain activities (e.g., in the Seychelles, where there are certain banned activities). In some locations, government regulations are required (e.g., to ensure that cruise ships adhere to minimum environmental standards where ships do not take voluntary action).

It is recommended that management decision-making be built into plans, together with other techniques (such as forecasting, environmental and social impact assessments or monitoring), to address potential problems or impacts as a preventative measure.

Managing visitors

Overall, it was recommended that an integrated approach is applied for the management of many variables, including supply and demand. Supply considerations, such as resources or culture, should be of primary concern, but management should also take full account of markets and demand.

Recommendations for Economic Development

Main recommendations from the preparatory conferences:

— Provide training, micro-credit and other assistance to small, medium and micro-enterprises.

— Provide incentives for enterprises to pursue sustainability

— Provide infrastructure, such as access and telecommunications, to assist communities in ecotourism development.

— Emphasise the role of governments as facilitators rather than operators.

— Place an emphasis on increasing retained economic value per visitor rather than expanding visitor volumes.

Key points arising from the Summit:

Providing government and other support for community level ecotourism

It was confirmed that the state should be a partner, not a developer of ecotourism operations.

In recognition that there is a spectrum of market interests, and a spectrum of tourism opportunities, there may be scope to link nature to cultural tourism and even to mass tourism (e.g., in Greece) particularly in areas where there are fewer pristine environments, in order to heighten the attraction of the destinations, and to generate community benefits.

Communities need a source of funds which can be linked to development. There may be opportunities to create community institutions and link them to forms of income generation; or to create Community Conservation Funds for donors, so ecotourism is viewed as a business by communities.

International assistance should be targeted more towards ecotourism projects. Assistance can be given in the form of finance, technology, training, information, mentorship, or in other ways. Loans might be given to countries, for example for training. Assistance could be targeted and conditional upon performance (e.g., demonstrating environmental protection). It is recommended that international agencies coordinate sources and conditions of assistance, and provide centralised and up to date information (e.g., on a website) for easy access by needy destinations.

Other forms of assistance may include staffing and human resources, and volunteer labour. This can provide a sense of ownership of the project by participants (e.g., in Senegal there are agreements between Parks and volunteers).

Recognising mutual benefits

Often, there are contributions which local communities bring to ecotourism or other developments, which are not viewed in terms of having conventional value (e.g., in Uganda, these might be spiritual, medicinal, or other information or cultural activities). It was felt that while ecotourism development can bring value to local communities, at the same time local communities can contribute valuable knowledge and information, practices, traditions, etc. to agencies, entrepreneurs, visitors, or others. In some cases, local people provide such information or knowledge without any recompense or benefit. It was recommended that such local contributions and sharing should be valued through financial or similar means. In this way there is likely to be more understanding that contributions are mutual, rather than the view that benefit flows are uni-directional to communities.

Exchanges of information can be of equal value to communities and to planners and policy makers. For example, imported technologies must be appropriate to the communities. However, indigenous technologies must also be acknowledged (such as India's Care and Share program), since traditional ecological and other knowledge and technologies will also have great value. For example, the Austrian Parliament has just called for a respect for the knowledge of indigenous peoples as a basis for sustainable development, and for indigenous land rights as a basis for human rights.

Recommendations for Social and Cultural Benefits

Main recommendations from the preparatory conferences:

— Use historic buildings and other heritage resources, thereby contributing to their protection.

— Involve communities in social and cultural programmes, to ensure local control, ownership and authenticity.

— Mount community awareness campaigns.

— Ensure that tour operators and other external companies are aware of their responsibilities towards communities.

Key points arising from the Summit:

Involving communities and ensuring local ownership

A number of areas have problems due to overpopulation (e.g., European coastal areas) while other areas (e.g., mountains) may suffer from depopulation. It was suggested that ecotourism may provide some benefits to both areas, by alleviating pressures on the coast, while attracting visitors (and development) to rural areas. For example, in Greece the planning process aims to link natural areas with cultural tourism and to link these to mass tourism destinations.

It is recommended that governments consider providing communities with land or resources which can enable them to act as partners in ecotourism operations. Botswana has allocated wildlife management areas to local communities for consumptive or non-consumptive use in tourism, so they can share in ecotourism benefits. An additional benefit is that this has led to decreased poaching.

Communities should have input to planning processes through, for example, local narratives and guides, wherein they provide information to visitors, plus develop their own self-esteem.

Communities should be involved and empowered, such that there is no ecotourism development where there is no desire for involvement in tourism. Opportunities should be sought to build on current economic and community activities rather than developing some totally new product.

Recommendations for multi-stakeholder participation

Main recommendations from the preparatory conferences:

— Build support for joint ventures into planning and policy initiatives

— Facilitate community-level joint ventures, such as co-management of protected areas

— Encourage strategic alliances between private businesses and local communities.

Key points arising from the Summit

Encouraging joint ventures

Origin-destination joint ventures were suggested. One innovative example is in the Netherlands, where there is increasing awareness by tourists or tour operators that they may be the source of problems when they visit other destinations. An outgoing tourism policy has been developed, and moves to link outgoing tourism with NGOs in receiving destinations.

It was emphasised by Tanzania that there needs to be strong involvement by the private sector in partnerships, not just governments or NGOs. The Tanzanian delegation to the Summit included a great many industry representatives as well as government representatives.

Overall, throughout the discussions on policy and planning, the points made at the preparatory conferences were reinforced, with the topics summarised above being the main focus of discussion. In addition, it was also said that the International Year of Ecotourism has already stimulated some of the actions and directions identified above.

Working Group - B

The regulation of ecotourism

Institutional responsibilities and frameworks.

The impacts of ecotourism on society and the environment can be positive and negative. The theme addressed by this working group was about providing the right regulatory frameworks and systems to ensure that products that are developed and marketed as ecotourism are beneficial and not harmful to environments and communities.

Nineteen presentations were made to the working group, covering:

— Examples of regulation and control of ecotourism - Quebec, Mexico, Japan and Seychelles.

— Certification systems - The experiences of existing and planned new certification schemes in Australia, Peru, and Costa Rica as well as the examples from the USA and Europe.

— International guidelines for ecotourism - Austria, Germany and Europarc.

— The need for quality control and for the identification of indicators - emphasised in two Canadian presentations.

— Specific methodologies and practical examples, from Uruguay, Indonesia, India and Korea.

— Ecotourism and ethics, presented by the representative of The Vatican.

1. Issues Discussed

The following were the main issues discussed by the working group.

Institutional frameworks

Legal frameworks and regulations are not always established for ecotourism only and very often are common to other kinds of tourism. The need to have specific legal frameworks and policies for ecotourism was stressed by different speakers, although in some cases it has proved difficult to have the same framework in different regions of a single country.

In some cases the work of individual countries is not enough to guarantee that ecotourism is properly developed. There were proposals in the Korean presentation to promote action for ecotourism development at the international level.

The need to develop ecotourism strategies at the national level through a consultation process was well demonstrated in the Seychelles.

Regulation of Ecotourism.

The role of the private sector in the establishment of regulations and in the certification process was discussed and different viewpoints were expressed. While some people felt that the private sector should take part in defining regulations, others considered that governments and NGOs should establish regulations in order to guarantee the preservation of natural and cultural resources.

Certification and labelling

These were issues that brought a number of questions and discussions. One of the points was whether certification should be just a voluntary process, or whether it should be an instrument to complement the regulation of ecotourism ventures. Another important point raised by different people concerned the components of certification schemes. Other aspects, beyond environmental issues, need to be taken into account and included.

The scale of certification met with a great deal of interest. How can certification schemes work at the local level and at the same time have international recognition? In relation to this, how to cover the cost of certification at the local level was a big concern in many areas and proposals were made to overcome this problem so that it can be made accessible to all sizes of business as well as to local communities. In Peru , for example, some communities receive technical and financial support from academic bodies, while in Australia, the cost of certification is proportional to the size of the business.

A final point discussed is the problem of the appearance of pseudo-eco-labels: too many labels are confusing and there was agreement that something should be done in this respect. A possible solution is the example of VISIT, a joint European initiative for the promotion of ecolabels and sustainable tourism development. VISIT has co-operated with 10 leading ecolabels in Europe and developed common basic standards for their criteria and verification procedures. These standards allow the identification of those ecolabels which guarantee a high environmental quality of their certified hotels, campsites, beaches or marinas. In 2004, VISIT will be established as a European accreditation body for ecolabels in tourism.

Sustainability indicators and monitoring

The need to monitor sustainability of ecotourism products was discussed and a number of approaches were presented. The difficulty of identifying indicators for social and cultural aspects was pointed out. Surveys to determine visitor satisfaction could be used to evaluate the quality of the visitor experience. At the same time, local people should be made aware of what was being done to the environment and how this would affect them.

A good example was the "European Charter for Sustainable Tourism in Protected Areas" which has proved to be a valuable tool for ensuring that tourism in protected areas is managed according to the principles of sustainable development.

Capacity building, training and education

This was considered a key issue for the sustainable development of ecotourism. Without adequate training and education of all stakeholders, from government to the private sector and consumers, in matters relating to regulation, certification and monitoring, it is impossible to progress towards sustainability in ecotourism. All players need to understand why some sort of regulation is necessary in many situations, why certification can help both the business and the environment, and finally why monitoring is essential to demonstrate that progress is being made towards sustainability.

Other issues

The impact of transport in relation to ecotourism was a key point in some of the discussions and suggestions were made on how to take it into account in ecotourism products and in certification schemes.

2. Key points and recommendations

Institutional frameworks

Main recommendations from the preparatory conferences:

— Ensure coordination between government ministries in the planning and regulation of ecotourism.

— Develop a framework of cooperation between public, private and non-governmental organisations.

— Ensure institutions understand the different dimensions of sustainable tourism and ecotourism.

Key points arising from the Summit:

There is a need to reach agreements between protected area management bodies, tourism departments or ministries as well as the tourism industry in general. A good example of this is the progress being made by the Canadian certification program. Good coordination among protected area managers and tourism departments is extremely important.

The development of legislative frameworks at the regional level should be supported, because they can positively influence sustainability issues, including the promotion of ecotourism and similar types of tourism harmonized with the environment. The recent establishment of quality and specifically ecotourism product rules in Québec, Canada, is a promising example in this field.

Incentives should be set up, such as lower taxes or public land concessions at lower rates, for ecotourism operators that promote environmentally-sensitive land use (e.g., the ones working on Crown land in British Columbia, Canada). At the same time, in Ontario, Canada, regulatory requirements ensure that resource stewardship agreements are established between the State and tour operators working within an area covered by the agreement, to preserve natural areas of high tourism value. This approach reserves the most pristine areas for ecotourism operations. The idea, in both examples, is to stimulate proper ecotourism in sensitive and valuable natural areas with a high potential.

Regulation of ecotourism

Main recommendations from the preparatory conferences:

— Move gradually from optional guidelines and simple codes of conduct towards obligatory regulations.

— Establish suitable legal frameworks underpinned by effective tools for regulating ecotourism.

— Develop guidelines and best practice information at all levels.

— Ensure protected areas are consulted and involved in regulatory procedures.

Key points arising from the Summit:

— Tourism operators, local government, and conservation departments should establish regulations. They should guarantee the protection of sensitive natural resources and cultural integrity.

— Legislation and regulations should be specific for ecotourism A good example was the case study of

Tourisme Quebec where a very specific legal framework is being established, clearly separating adventure tourism activities and ecotourism with an objective of avoiding a severe impact upon natural assets.

In some areas regulations need to be compulsory since in many countries voluntary regulations do not work and very often the public asks for minimum obligatory regulations, as it was presented in the example from Mexico.

Certain laws and regulations within protected areas should be extended beyond their frontiers.

Legally binding instruments for the implementation of sustainable ecotourism and avoidance of non-sustainable forms of tourism for sensitive areas should be established.

Strict regulations for ecotourism at an international level should be avoided, while guidelines are acceptable.

The potential negative impact of visitors should be taken into account from the beginning of the planning process. This can be realised through some measures such as reservation systems, routing in sensitive points, zoning within the site according to carrying capacity. The Bodogol Education Center, in Indonesia, has successfully put in place some of these preventive measures.

Certification

Main recommendations from the preparatory conferences:

— Provide guidelines on certification schemes for ecotourism.

— Avoid penalise very small scale enterprises and facilitate their access to certification schemes.

— Involve all stakeholders in developing and implementing certification processes.

— Ensure certification processes are transparent, understandable and updated.

Key points arising from the Summit:

Certification processes need to be global in concept, following international guidelines and recommendations, but local in application. An example of this is the need for ecolodge guidelines, which can always be adopted at the local level and can then be followed by some sort of international ecolodge certification.

Auditing teams must be independent and ideally should have representatives from different countries and proper training. They should also have different cultural backgrounds.

Certification should take into account social, economic and cultural aspects, besides the environmental ones. Most of the existing concepts for eco-labels, brands and certification systems have to be enlarged by social and cultural aspects to reach the aims of sustainable ecotourism.

NGOs should take part in the process of identifying certification schemes. In many cases NGOs have developed voluntary certification schemes which have afterwards been regulated and spread by governments.

International certification schemes must be multistakeholder. They should be promoted by international organizations including governments, academia, conservation NGOs, the private sector and with proper consultation with local and indigenous people. It was suggested that organizations such as WTO and UNEP could play a role in establishing an international framework for tourism certification systems and all existing certification schemes should be considered in this process.

Certification and accreditation should be industry driven

and paid for by the operators, as they can use it as a marketing tool and possibly marketing advantage over competitors, therefore it can be beneficial and profitable. The case of Australia is particularly interesting with well-established ecotourism and ecoguides certification programs.

In the case of very small businesses in developing countries, there should be technical and financial support through grant or loans or micro-credit systems to assist in making the necessary changes and to cover the costs of certification, either from strong NGOs, local government, academic bodies, larger profitable businesses or development agencies. There was agreement that environmental certification very often leads to economic benefits since energy, water and other resources are saved.

Easily accessible funding formulae to cover the cost of international certification schemes should be explored, so that small businesses can have access to them. Other funding and capacity building mechanisms should be identified and promoted for this purpose.

Ecotourism certifiers must be guided by social criteria geared to facilitating the integration of small businesses at preferential rates and through technical contributions or the promotion of collective certification alternatives.

Financially sound NGOs should shoulder the role of a certification body at a cost more affordable for local entrepreneurs.

Certification should provide powerful incentives and guidelines for responsible business practices.

A multistakeholder Sustainable Tourism Stewardship Council, such as the one being considered by Rainforest Alliance in coordination with a range of international organizations, could help local certification programs exchange information in a forum that allows for accreditation of certifiers, marketing and credibility.

The obligatory introduction of certification systems for ecotourism facilities and operations should be considered at least at regional and national levels, to guarantee that the quality provided is consistent with the principles of sustainability. This is the case of the national ecocertification scheme which will become compulsory in the near future in the Seychelles.

Capacity building, training and education

Key points arising from the Summit:

In the certification process, there is a need to train and educate all stakeholders, including the industry, operators and customers or consumers. This latter case is particularly important since the interest of consumers in true ecotourism will reward good products and punish examples of "greenwashing". A good example of consumer education is the brochure "Your Travel Choice Makes a Difference" from The International Ecotourism Society.

Certification programs should be promoted and explained to the public by both the tourism and the environmental authorities.

Education, transfer of know how, exchange and respect for local people must drive the development of ecotourism in all destinations. In the long term, customers will reward or punish ecotourism products according to their sustainability.

Demand from consumers and tour operators is a prerequisite for a certification system to work. Tourists must be informed of certification schemes and therefore, the promotion by government (by both the environment and tourist departments) is essential.

Monitoring and indicators

Main recommendations from the preparatory conferences:

— Include the economic, social and environmental impact of tourism in monitoring.

— Define targets to be achieved in a certain period of time.

— Establish continuous data collection, involving businesses and tourists.

— Ensure monitoring is a prerequisite of providing assistance to projects.

Key points arising from the Summit:

The issue of monitoring and indicators was central to the discussions of Working Group D, but the following specific points were raised within this working group.

The definition of sustainability indicators should not be left only to the private sector and should be the result of consensus among all stakeholders including local people, NGOs, government and protected area managers.

Sustainability indicators should be integrated with local planning.

Indicators must be identified at the local level and should take into account environmental, social and cultural factors.

New methods of evaluation of progress towards sustainability in ecotourism need to be identified, that are accessible to the local population both from the technical and economic point of view.

Other recommendations

It was suggested that World Ecotourism Sites should be

declared, where ecotourism would be promoted by the international community in order to guarantee the conservation of high value natural resources and the well being of local people.

Travellers should be made aware of their environmental impact due to transport and its effect on global warming when travelling to remote destinations. The impact of transport in ecotourism has not received enough attention.

Travellers should receive information on positive and relatively simple ways to compensate for their impact, such as taking part in reforestation projects in the areas visited.

The three pillars of sustainable development - public welfare, economy and environment - have to be effectively built into ecotourism.

The development and management of sustainable ecotourism should be promoted through not only the individual effort of a country but also through international cooperation.

Countries should develop national ecotourism strategies through a process of consultation in order to develop ecotourism in a sustainable manner.

Working group - C

PRODUCT DEVELOPMENT, MARKETING AND PROMOTION OF ECOTOURISM: Fostering sustainable products and consumers

Ecotourism will only bring benefits to conservation and communities if good quality, viable ecotourism products, which reflect market demand, are created and actively promoted. This working group was concerned with developing the right support structures, market knowledge, and attention to detail in product development, to enable this to happen.

The sixteen presentations at the working group covered:

Government policies and priorities for ecotourism development - Indonesia, Germany and Venezuela.

— The management and development of ecotourism in protected areas - Quebec (Canada), Sao Paulo (Brazil), Italy, University of Valencia (Spain), and UNESCO.

— The position of intergovernmental, non-governmental and media organizations in ecotourism development and marketing, and its relationship with communities and conservation - International Labour Organisation, Conservation International, Retour Foundation, National Geographic Society.

— Ecotourism initiatives by the private sector and partnership organisations - Earth Rhythms (Canada), Native Tourism Alliance (USA), PICE (Mexico), Casa Matsiguenka (Peru).

1. Issues Discussed

The working group concentrated its debates on creating the right context for ecotourism development as well as on practical development and marketing issues. Throughout, there was concern that the nature of products developed and the messages put across to visitors should reflect the need to bring economic, environmental and social benefits.

The report on the preparatory conferences identified a number of challenges for ecotourism product development and marketing. These were:

— The failure of too many products, through lack of profitability, often due to poor feasibility assessment and business planning.

— Difficulties faced by small enterprises and community-based products in reaching markets cost effectively.

— Inconsistency in the quality of the visitor experience and in environmental management of ecotourism products.

— The need and opportunity to gain more benefit from visitors to support conservation and local communities, for example through stimulating more spending per head and reducing leakages from the local area.

— A continuing lack of public awareness of ecotourism issues, with few people specifically seeking out sustainable ecotourism products.

— Participants in the working group were reminded of these challenges, which provided a context for the debates that followed.

In the light of these challenges, the report on the preparatory conferences identified five priorities:

— Creating the right structures for local communities, tourism enterprises, public bodies and NGOs to work together;

— Relating supply to demand, with a better knowledge of markets and how to reach them.

— Paying attention to all aspects of product quality, including design and management for sustainability as well as visitor satisfaction.

— Providing relevant support for communities and enterprises, which is locally delivered and tailored to the needs of communities and small enterprises.

— Strengthening the promotion of ecotourism messages and products, including promoting the concept of ecotourism as well as specific products.

This report takes each of these priority areas in turn and sets out the points and recommendations relating to them that emerged during the working group session.

2. Key and recommendations

Structures and relationships for product development and marketing

Main recommendations resulting from the preparatory conferences:

Address local community needs and opportunities.

— Recognise the key role of private sector businesses and strengthen their links with local communities.

— Strengthen networking between small enterprises and projects, so assisting market outreach and promoting common standards.

— Recognise protected areas as focal points for ecotourism products and marketing.

— Increase support from national and local government.

Key points arising from the Summit:

Recognising traditional values

Presentations at the working group emphasised that the principles of ecotourism are often enshrined in traditional values. Such values can influence the approach at a national level. For example, in Indonesia the national tourism policy is based on the principle of the 'Balance of Life' between exploitation and preservation of resources.

At a local level, many indigenous communities have values that are based on the stewardship of the earth's resources and hospitality towards visitors. These values must be respected. They provide a positive reason for assisting local communities to take their own decisions about the development and promotion of ecotourism and the way in which their natural resources and cultures are interpreted to visitors.

Building partnerships

The importance of establishing multi-stakeholder partnerships was underlined by many presentations and interventions. These can take various forms.

One way of assisting indigenous people to gain benefit from ecotourism is by helping them to form partnerships with organisations which can support and fund community projects, individual enterprises and joint ventures. An example is the North American Native Tourism Alliance.

Partnerships for ecotourism should be established between states, where appropriate. An example is the cooperation between Saharan states in a UNESCO pilot project, which is promoting cooperation in training, support for micro enterprises, and the identification and protection of natural and cultural resources.

More consideration should be given to involving tour operators, alongside communities and NGOs, in partnerships for successful ecotourism. An example is the project for the Development of Cultural and Ecotourism in the Mountainous Regions of Central Asia and the Himalayas. This even extends the partnership to tourists themselves - in one initiative, trekkers end their visit working with local people on social and conservation projects.

Linking conservation of biodiversity with direct economic benefits to local people

The role of ecotourism as a stimulus for the conservation of nature was strongly emphasised at the working group. This role is best played through providing a source of livelihood for local people which encourages and empowers them to preserve the biodiversity of their local area. The presentation by Conservation International (C.I.) confirmed the importance they place on ecotourism in their people-centred conservation approach, especially in the world's biodiversity hotspots, which contain millions of people living in poverty.

When challenged in debate about the effectiveness of ecotourism, C.I. cited numerous examples where it was generating significant conservation benefits. However, this requires ecotourism products to be based on integrated, participatory processes which take time to deliver results.

Strengthening the role of protected areas in ecotourism development

There was a specific recommendation that the key role of protected areas in the management and development of ecotourism should be recognised. In some cases they may require more resources to fulfil this role, although ecotourism may also provide a source of revenue.

It was recognised that protected area authorities need to work with local stakeholders on the development of ecotourism, and that appropriate structures should be established for this. Examples of parks working with local communities were provided by the approach of Parcs Québec in extending their network, and by the long-standing UNESCO Man and Biosphere model of evolving and adaptive management. In Italy, a national partnership for ecotourism has been established between the Federation of Parks, NGOs and private sector representatives.

A note of caution was sounded about the level of ecotourism activity to encourage actually within protected areas, rather than in surrounding locations, which may be more robust. There is a need for careful planning which reflects the resources and sensitivity of different areas and the type of designation. Further training and materials to improve the skills of protected area managers in ecotourism is required; an example presented at the workshop was the Toolkit for Sustainable Tourism in Wetlands.

Seeking a greater role for provincial and local authorities

There was a specific recommendation that provincial and local authorities should play a far more active role in ecotourism planning and support, providing a bridge between national policies and local communities. Such authorities often have responsibility for a range of services which affect ecotourism and also provide a long-lasting structure for developing, managing and supporting initiatives. However, more guidance should be given to local authorities on how to fulfil their role in ecotourism.

Understanding markets

Main recommendations from the preparatory conferences:

Use more market research.

— Take a broad view of the market, recognising different segments.

— Study current visitor flows and local market conditions before product development takes place.

Key points arising from the Summit:

Understanding visitor motivations and disseminating research results

A number of interventions pointed to the need for more market research to provide data on existing and potential visitor profiles and motivations for visiting natural areas. This research should not only take place within source markets. It is important to understand more about the kinds of people who are already responding to ecotourism products within destinations.

It was recognised that part of the answer is to ensure the better use of existing market research. There was a specific recommendation that the results of the WTO studies of seven source markets should be made accessible, to the extent possible and/or through the corresponding national tourism administrations, to small ecotourism projects and firms in less developed countries.

Recognising ecotourism as more than a niche market

It was pointed out at the working group session that ecotourism should not be equated only with a niche market but also with a set of principles, especially concerning benefits to conservation and local communities. There was general agreement that too narrow a view should not be taken in identifying the potential market for ecotourism. In a paper entitled 'Moving Ecotourism beyond its niche' the National Geographical Society presented research that suggested that a sizeable market in the USA would respond to concepts of supporting conservation and the well-being of local people in their travel choice.

A number of the case studies presented at the working group session were catering for a domestic as well as an international market, and not only for people with a specialist interest in nature. It was suggested that it is important not to isolate ecotourism from the mainstream of tourism. Examples were given of day visitors from coastal resorts coming to inland cultural or natural heritage sites. These may provide serious management challenges in some cases, but also a valuable source of income for ecotourism initiatives.

The presentations and debate pointed to the need for more, well informed, market segmentation, enabling products and promotional strategies to be adapted to different requirements.

Avoiding false expectations

There was a call for better market assessment and business planning for individual projects, taking account of location, resource constraints, current visitor flows and performance of comparable products. This should help to avoid false expectations and the development of ecotourism in areas where it is unlikely to be successful.

Key components of ecotourism products

Main recommendations from the preparatory conferences:

— Address quality, authenticity and security.

— Give top priority to effective interpretation of nature and culture.

— Design and manage service facilities, such as accommodation and catering, to maximise sustainability.

— Address destination issues, such as infrastructure and transport, as well as individual product issues.

— Relate ecotourism to sustainable activity tourism, where appropriate.

Key points arising from the Summit:

Underlining the importance of authenticity and creative interpretation

The need for authenticity in ecotourism projects was strongly endorsed. The advantages of creative interpretation and the use of local guides were emphasised. An imaginative example of participatory interpretation was provided by the Earth Rhythms project in Manitoba, Canada, which is all about enabling visitors to "Live the story with real people".

During the plenary discussion, attention was drawn to the value of involving environmentalists, anthropologists and other specialists to ensure the accuracy of interpretation and to add depth to it, while accepting the importance of effective, accessible presentation involving local people.

Facilitating design and management for sustainability

A fundamental point made at the Summit is that ecotourism projects should embrace all aspects of sustainability, in the way they are developed and operated. Ecotourism should give a lead towards more sustainable tourism generally.

A number of examples of excellent environmentally sensitive design, in terms of both aesthetics and technical factors, were presented at the workshop. It was apparent that a wealth of knowledge is available internationally on this subject. The recent publication on ecolodges by The International Ecotourism Society provides an example. It is recommended that priority should be given to disseminating good practice in this field.

Some concern was expressed about the cost of low impact construction but it was stressed that this need not be more expensive than traditional techniques and can bring significant savings in operational costs. It is recommended that evidence about this is put across clearly.

The importance of personal security is recognised. It was pointed out that tour operators promoting ecotourism often face high costs in meeting obligations in this respect, which have to be taken into account.

Addressing the issue of access to ecotourism destinations and experiences

A number of interventions suggested that the issue of access is too often ignored in ecotourism planning and development. Three aspects of this were raised.

First, in some locations there is a need to facilitate access, where communities may be isolated. It was recommended that there is a need to work more closely with transport operators in ecotourism development.

Secondly, there is considerable concern that ecotourism policies and products should promote the use of environmentally friendly transport options, both to and within the destination. In Germany, for example, the promotion of cycling and walking is of fundamental importance in policies towards sustainable tourism and ecotourism.

Thirdly, there is a need to avoid discrimination against people with disabilities or other disadvantages in terms of access to ecotourism experiences.

Technical support for communities and enterprises

Main recommendations from the preparatory conferences:

— Provide relevant local training, devised with local people and enterprises to encourage participation.

— Encourage people to look together at the local resource and at ecotourism projects elsewhere.

— Provide well-targeted, accessible financial assistance.

Key points arising from the Summit:

Giving priority to capacity building

Many presentations emphasised the importance of capacity building within local communities. For example, human resource development was seen as a priority requirement in Indonesia and Venezuela. It was emphasised that capacity building requires time and commitment. There was also a call for more financial assistance for training.

A particular point was made that, as well as supporting businesses, capacity building and specific training programmes in the field of ecotourism could be directed at young people at the start of their working life. An example of this was provided by the Sao Paulo Green Belt Biosphere Reserve and their establishment of eco-job training centres.

Helping ecotourism projects to learn from each other

It was agreed that a lot could be achieved by exchanging experiences between different projects. The value of the suggestion, arising from the preparatory conferences, of promoting twinning and multi-lateral links between projects, was illustrated in the presentations.

Raising the profile and knowledge of tourism within donor agencies, and the quality of applications to them

It was felt that donor agencies should take tourism more seriously. Many have no specific strategy for supporting tourism or particular skills or knowledge about ecotourism. This should be rectified.

However, the responsibility of applicants in seeking funding was also recognised. It was pointed out that projects seeking funding must have a well-prepared business plan.

Some delegates commented that there was not enough knowledge about the various sources of financial assistance, including international donor agencies, bilateral support programmes, and assistance available from NGOs. There was a specific recommendation that a database of information on this should be created and disseminated.

Structuring financial and technical assistance to the requirements of small businesses and local communities

There was considerable debate about appropriate forms of support for ecotourism projects.

A presentation at the workshop on the International Labour Organization's sustainable tourism project with indigenous communities in Bolivia, Ecuador and Peru set out a structured approach, with programmes of assistance at a micro level (for community-based enterprises), at a medium level (for clusters of tourism initiatives within community networks, and for local government), and at a macro level (to strengthen organisations, certification and marketing within states).

A clear message from delegates was that assistance should be in a form that can be accessed by small and micro businesses and local communities and one that is relevant to their needs. Specific recommendations were that:

— donor agencies should provide more schemes which channel assistance directly to enterprises and communities rather than through national governments;

— funding should be available in small packets, with a low minimum level, relevant to the size of small enterprises;

— there is a need for micro-credit schemes.

There was a call for the application of fiscal incentives as a tool to encourage tourism service providers to develop and manage their enterprises more sustainably.

A further specific recommendation was for the establishment of a network of ecotourism advisors or mentors as a readily available source of help for small ecotourism businesses.

Promoting ecotourism messages and products

Main recommendations from the preparatory conferences:

— Promote ecotourism as a concept, with an international awareness campaign.

— Grasp the significant opportunity presented by the Internet.

— Use a range of marketing techniques and partners.

— Provide comprehensive and educative information at all stages, before, during and after the visit.

— Create loyal ambassadors among tourists.

Key points arising from the Summit:

Raising public awareness of tourism impacts, ecotourism principles and actions to take

During the working group session, a number of comments were made on the importance to promote the actual concept of ecotourism, its ideals and values, rather than simply ecotourism products. However, there was a little concern that the word 'ecotourism' may actually be putting some people off. It was agreed that principles and goals are what is important; people should not get hung up on terminology.

The report on the preparatory conferences suggested that there should be a coordinated international campaign to promote ecotourism principles and concepts, but that this might not simply be a generic campaign; rather it should promote specific action that visitors could take. As an example of this, it was recommended that the process of visitors and tour operators making financial donations to local community projects or conservation causes should be more actively promoted, with a vision of this becoming the norm rather than the exception.

A strong recommendation was made in the presentation by the Retour Foundation, an NGO working with indigenous communities, that tourists should be provided with detailed information about the effect of their travelling.

Promoting mutual understanding of cultural differences and sensitivities

It was recommended that information for visitors should include how to respect the local culture of their hosts and the sensitivity of the local environment. At the same time, there was a recommendation that indigenous and local communities should be provided with information about the culture and expectations of their visitors.

Working effectively with tour operators and the media

The importance of tour operators was referred to on several occasions. There was a specific recommendation that priority should be given to involving and educating local incoming tour operators and agents within destinations. On the other hand, some delegates recommended that ecotourism principles should be promoted more heavily amongst international tour operators, including the larger companies.

The strong influence of media reports and travel guides, which can be both damaging and highly beneficial to ecotourism, was emphasised during the plenary session. It was recommended that travel writers should be introduced to genuine, interesting stories about real people and experiences, rather than bland details of product.

Using the Internet as a communication medium at all points in the tourism chain

There was widespread agreement about the importance of the Internet for promoting ecotourism products. One comment highlighted its value amongst the large market of independent travellers, where it can be used for exchange of information and testimonials amongst visitors and for providing information within destinations as well as prior to departure. A high priority should be given to helping small enterprises and community initiatives link to appropriate technology.

Raising confidence through branded products

Branding of ecotourism products was considered to offer more opportunities. An example was a proposal to establish a world-wide brand of ecolodges with strong conservation credentials.

Gaining support for ecotourism amongst future visitors

Discussion at the workshop echoed the need, expressed in the preparatory conferences, to promote the concept of ecotourism to children and young people, as a receptive audience and as the travellers of the future.

Finally, the results from many successful projects presented during the Summit reaffirmed the importance of delivering a quality experience, leading to word of mouth recommendation, as the best form of marketing. This will increase the volume of tourists who are committed to ecotourism principles, who become ambassadors for conservation, and who have a greater understanding of different cultures around the world.

Working group - D

Monitoring cost and benefits of ecotourism

Ensuring equitable distribution among all stakeholders

In many ecotourism strategies the aim is to reduce the costs of ecotourism and ensuring that a whole range of benefits are obtained for local communities, the environment, visitors and other stakeholders. However, unless there is a system for monitoring the impacts of ecotourism, then the success of new strategies and actions will not be known. This working group was concerned with effective processes for checking on impacts and improving the distribution of benefits.

Eighteen presentations were made to the working group, covering:

— The relationship between indigenous people and ecotourism - Quebec, Equations (India), U.S.A.

— Poverty and managing equitable distribution - South Africa, Sri Lanka, Ghana

— International guidelines for monitoring costs and benefits - UNCTAD, IBST (International Bureau of Social tourism), Australia, Canada

— World heritage protection - UNESCO, Indonesia, Uganda

— Monitoring small and medium enterprises - Ethiopia, Madagascar

— Public sector role - Balearics (Spain)

— Specific methodologies and national examples - Kenya, Brazil, Yugoslavia

— Social aspects and better access to ecotourism - IBST, Equations (India)

1. Issues Discussed

The following points were debated during the working group session.

New ecotourism cost/benefit evaluation methods that would highlight the social and economic benefits for local populations, as well as the limitations of the financial benefits generated compared to other forms of tourism, notably mass tourism.

Appropriate legal and institutional mechanisms to facilitate and make effective the systematic participation of local communities in the overall ecotourism process, including policy definition, planning, management and monitoring.

Financial and fiscal mechanisms to ensure that a significant proportion of the income generated from ecotourism remains with the local community or serves conservation purposes.

Methods to ensure the permanent control of impacts through the adaptation of carrying capacity methodologies to ecotourism development, including the definition of damage warning indicators and disturbance gauges for protected sites and other natural areas.

Distribution mechanisms to share the benefits of ecotourism development in order to reinvest a proportion of the revenues generated in protected areas.

Methods to assist understanding and measurement of social costs, benefits and change (i.e. changes in the behaviour and habits of the local population) so as to limit the negative consequences, to maximise social benefits for host communities and to improve attitudes, awareness and respect towards the protection of the environment.

Specific management and monitoring procedures for different types of ecotourism sites, (i.e. desert zones and islands), concerning such aspects as water and waste management, the management of scarce resources, and others.

Evaluation of appropriate price levels to ensure sufficient returns for firms, suitable redistribution in favour of local populations and that correspond to the purchasing power of tourism demand.

Ensuring that the principles of "polluter pays" and "user pays" will ensure genuine protection of the environment whilst guaranteeing ecotourism development.

The working group endeavoured to bring together development strategies aimed at differentiating ecotourism from traditional tourism and creating a real balance to achieve the desired equitable distribution between all the stakeholders.

As a result of the presentations and the debates during the working group session, guidelines and directions towards concrete solutions were devised. These solutions challenge traditional tourism development policies that, as was emphasised by the contributors, must not merely consider ecotourism as a priority but as a tourism development catalyst, thus providing a new approach to tourism development as a whole. This was particularly highlighted in the contributions by the delegates from Kenya, Brazil, India and Serbia.

2. Key Points and Recommendations

For this catalytic role of ecotourism to really be effective, it is necessary to consider recommendations relating to the main pillars of this topic, namely monitoring costs, monitoring benefits, and equitable distribution. Some global recommendations also emerged from the working group.

Monitoring costs of ecotourism

Main recommendations from the preparatory conferences:

— Determine the economic costs of providing suitable infrastructure, including energy and transport, resources such as water, and waste treatment.

— Use indicators such as site stress to monitor environmental costs.

— Consider factors such as the disturbance of traditional lifestyles in determining social costs.

— Take an integrated approach to determining costs, such as effect on employment in other sectors, such as agriculture.

— Research specific management and monitoring procedures for different types of ecotourism sites, e.g. deserts and islands.

— Research methods to ensure the permanent control of impacts, including damage warning indicators for protected sites and other natural areas.

Key points arising from the Summit:

The presentations showed that for ecoutourism to develop sustainably it needs direct as well as indirect support from the public sector at the national and local levels.

Recognising costs relating to environmental management

The conflict between protecting nature and ecotourism development induces extra costs which ecotourism operators must bear. In the case of Sri Lanka for example, with respect to wildlife, the problems associated with the protection of the elephants must be managed in such a way that the local population could also be able to live in total security, particularly the farmers. In this particular case specific planning guidelines must be drawn up, which include protection barriers, requiring very heavy investment. This need for large financial resources impedes the development of ecotourism and can rupture the sustainable development process in these destinations.

This situation can be particularly serious in mass tourism destinations as illustrated by the presentation on the Balearic Islands in which it was argued that there is a direct relationship between high tourist numbers and the attractiveness of the destination. In this case, there is a conflict between tourism development and economic development because of the extra costs on the environment, resulting in the deterioration of the tourism situation in these destinations.

Taking all development and operational costs into account, including training

Ecotourism itself engenders extra costs, notably in terms of funding training. This important point was much discussed during the sessions. Indeed, ecotourism often implies heavier equipment expenditure and more skilled personnel than are required in traditional tourism. Therefore, preliminary training funding programmes must be introduced, and this can harm the competitiveness of the ecotourism product in a very competitive market. As a result, the profitability of ecotourism projects may be deemed insufficient. Examples from France for instance show that quite often the financing of training must come from public funds, which implies that in certain developing countries, the financing of ecotourism training must be included in international cooperation programmes.

Considering the full costs of transition to ecotourism

The cost of protecting nature generally implies very high expenditure and can be the cause of usage conflict in economic terms but also in social terms. This is the case in India for example where, in some highly populated regions, ecotourism development replaces certain agricultural production activities that must be abandoned to safeguard the endowments of protected areas. In such cases, the creation of jobs for tour guides and wardens does not compensate for the jobs lost in the agricultural sector, and this can cause tension between the local population and ecotourism operators when the cost of reconversion of agricultural populations are not taken into account in public policies.

Monitoring benefits of ecotourism

Main recommendations from the preparatory conferences:

— Take account of local income benefits and tax receipts.

— Consider improvement in local employment, living conditions and social services.

— Measure the local population's satisfaction through surveys.

— Use tourism satellite accounting to show impacts on different sectors.

— Develop new evaluation methods to take account of wider benefits and costs

Key points arising from the Summit:

The discussions during the working group session showed that the benefits of ecotourism are not as obvious as might be first thought. These benefits can be the cause of problems and sometimes controversy.

Being realistic about financial benefits

The financial benefits, in terms of fiscal and parafiscal receipts, must be considered as particularly important for local populations. However, the examples presented during the sessions show that these benefits only become significant after many years. Case studies from Madagascar demonstrate that in the short term fiscal and parafiscal receipts generated by ecotourism activity are weak and cannot finance the environmental protection that is necessary for high quality tourism products. Furthermore, these examples show that these benefits are very difficult to distribute amongst public and private stakeholders.

Using ecotourism benefits to alleviate poverty

The benefits of ecotourism should be orientated principally towards the poorest local populations. This is the objective of the many programmes presented during the Summit such as those in South Africa, Ghana and Uganda. From this point of view, ecotourism is better adapted than traditional commercial tourism to achieve this objective. However, as the presentation from India emphasised, ecotourism is a type of tourism development that can harm the traditional activities of the poorer populations (i.e. agriculture). This means that the benefits of ecotourism are not always sufficient to provide a significant contribution to the problems of extreme poverty and even in certain cases it can harm the very means of subsistence of very poor rural populations. Therefore, the assertion that developing ecotourism is a good method of solving the problems of poverty in developing countries should be expressed with caution, spelling out the conditions for this to occur.

Emphasising the merits of ecotourism in benefiting small enterprises

The benefits in terms of liberalisation of international exchanges in the GATS agreement framework should facilitate access to tourism development for all countries including LCDs (Least Developed Countries). However, as the speaker from UNCTAD pointed out during the debates and during the presentations at the Summit, traditional tourism tends to mostly benefit large enterprises. This is not the case of ecotourism, which should therefore be favoured in commercial international negotiations. Furthermore, this was emphasised during the session on international cooperation, which clearly demonstrated that tourism was a privileged element of regional cooperation benefiting primarily small and medium size enterprises.

Taking full account of associated benefits

The presentations and debates showed that the balance between costs and benefits are not always obvious to justify ecotourism development in economic and social development polices. However, several new points were brought to the debates proving that the benefits of ecotourism are much more numerous and important if some major elements which are often forgotten or ignored are considered.

In particular, two very positive points concerning ecotourism were discussed after the presentations by the IBST (International Bureau of Social Tourism):

On the one hand, ecotourism benefits tourists by giving them the choice to enjoy a different type of tourism than traditional tourism. However, this benefit is only fully accountable if it is available to the whole population such as the young, the elderly and insofar as it is possible for the handicapped.

On the other hand, ecotourism favours the initiatives of non-profit organisations and cooperatives, which generally have important direct and indirect impacts, benefiting local and indigenous communities.

The equitable distribution of benefits amongst stakeholders

Main recommendations from the preparatory conferences:

— Establish financial and fiscal mechanisms to ensure that a significant proportion of income generated from ecotourism remains in the local community or serves conservation.

— Put in place distribution mechanisms which reinvest a proportion of the revenues generated in the protected areas.

— Consider the impact of price levels on the distribution of benefits.

Key points arising from the Summit:

It emerged from the presentations and debates that the principles of ecotourism are more of an aspiration than a reality for many countries, regions and local and indigenous populations, despite significant progress.

Equitable distribution is an aspiration for many stakeholders because there exist today a multitude of initiatives and ecotourism product development projects everywhere in the world. Nevertheless, a survey carried out in Australia showed that there are thousands of ecotourism schemes, which would suggest that the economic weight of ecotourism in world tourism is becoming increasingly important and could support the efforts to achieve a better distribution between all stakeholders of the benefits of tourism development.

The equitable distribution between all stakeholders is strengthened because of the prevalence of small and medium sized enterprises in the development of ecotourism. The example provided by Ethiopia, discussing the role of SMEs in the development of ecotourism, shows that the benefits of ecotourism can be turned from aspiration into reality if tourism development associated with ecotourism is sufficiently important.

The equitable distribution between all stakeholders will only become a significant reality when the benefits to be distributed are great enough. However, the contributions from the representatives of the poorest regions and countries emphasised that this is not the case everywhere in the world. One of the reasons put forward by UNCTAD is the lack of comparative studies to provide useful information on the successes and failures of different methods of equitable distribution amongst stakeholders. The aim would be to establish demonstration projects which would serve as references to ensure that the development of ecotourism will also provide real equitable distribution between all stakeholders.

Global recommendations

Main recommendations from the preparatory conferences:

— Ensure a constant monitoring of ecotourism activities to ensure they are meeting the required objectives.

— Determine distinct quantitative evaluation criteria or a range of standards, in cooperation with national and local authorities.

— Establish an evolutionary management system, including monitoring, based on public-private partnership.

Key points arising from the Summit:

The following overall conclusions were drawn from the presentations and the debates in the working group and were presented during the plenary session:

The existing ecotourism cost, benefit and impact evaluation methods, should be reviewed and new methods should be devised which would highlight the social and economic benefits for local populations and compare these with the costs, benefits and impacts of other forms of tourism and other economic alternatives.

Appropriate legal, political, institutional and funding mechanisms should be established in order to facilitate and make effective the participation of local communities in the overall ecotourism process, including definition, planning, management, monitoring and conflict resolution.

Indigenous communities and groups should be involved from the very beginning in the decision process about ecotourism including the assessment and monitoring of costs, benefits and impacts in particular with respect to their culture and traditions.

Financial and fiscal mechanisms should be implemented to ensure that a significant proportion of the income generated from ecotourism remains with the local community and is reinvested for environmental and cultural conservation purposes.

A permanent and consistent monitoring of ecotourism impacts should be implemented as an integral part of the overall management for protected sites and other natural areas, and therefore the existing approaches such as carrying capacity methodologies, damage warning indicators and other monitoring instruments should be adapted.

In addition, the participants in the working group proposed a recommendation to the plenary session of the World Ecotourism Summit to affirm the clear and inalienable rights of indigenous communities, in terms of international legal instruments, to self-determination and prior informed consent in ecotourism development.

4. REPORTS FROM THE SPECIAL FORUMS

On the final day of the Summit, two special forums were held in order to discuss the perspective of ecotourism businesses (Forum 1) and the issue of development cooperation (Forum 2). The results of these forums are presented in the pages which follow.

In addition, a Ministerial Forum was held. This forum enabled a wide range of countries to describe their policies and activities in the field of ecotourism. The majority of speakers were Ministers of Tourism or senior officials from the ministry of tourism in the respective countries, but some countries were represented by their environment ministry or their diplomatic representative in Canada.

The countries making interventions at the Ministerial Forum included

— Andorra
— Algeria
— Bangladesh
— Cambodia
— Cuba
— Cyprus
— Ecuador
— Egypt
— India
— Malawi
— Nigeria
— Pakistan
— Paraguay
— Philippines
— Romania
— Sri Lanka
— Uruguay

Each country representative explained the state of development of ecotourism in their country and the problems and challenges being faced. All of them reiterated their commitment to sustainability principles in tourism and set out the steps being taken to develop and promote ecotourism.

FORUM 1: THE ECOTOURISM BUSINESS PERSPECTIVE

This forum concerned the practical experiences and needs of private sector businesses operating in ecotourism. It centred on four presentations from enterprises based in the US Virgin Islands, Canada, Panama and India. There was also a considerable period for discussion with many points raised from the floor.

1 Issues Discussed

The need for government support for small ecotourism operators

Ecotourism operators often find themselves at a disadvantage because of specific government regulations. For example, in destination countries where business visas have a limited time before expiry, this may result in on-ground tour leaders or facilitators having to leave the country prematurely.

Other problems result from a lack of government action. One example is the lack of assistance for operators to develop new tours in destinations. This is a big problem for operators, since research and testing potential products on the ground may take some years, but once products are developed, other companies may replicate this new package, with no research costs. Developing new packages is becoming increasingly difficult.

Some problems occur when the ethics of the destination government are in conflict with the principles of ecotourism. Some ethically minded operators pull out of the destination, which ironically leaves the field (and their repeat clients and developmental groundwork) available to less ethically-oriented tour operators.

Problems of financing ecotourism operations

It was generally agreed that obtaining finance to initiate ecotourism operations is extremely difficult; it is often non-existent. Many operations are only possible by using personal savings or obtaining personal loans. The conventional banking sector is not currently helpful until after success is achieved, when assistance is least necessary.

Other costs concerns are related to proposed certification programs, which operators fear they will not be able to buy into; additionally, they do not have the time to engage in the often lengthy and difficult certification procedure.

Cost and lack of support for research and development

Operators agreed that it is difficult and expensive to research and develop new ecotourism packages in many destinations. Also, that when established, there are no mechanisms to prevent other operators from copying their packages.

Lack of integrated objectives

Some ecotourism operators started with worthy but limited motivations, such as a strong desire for environmental conservation or protection of endangered places or species. However, they discover that unless local jobs are created and operational profitability is an objective, the business will have difficulties or will fail, thus also failing to achieve the original objective. It was felt that entrepreneurs need to internalise the principles of sustainability in their business, and that if they emphasise only one or two perspectives, they will not achieve sustainability over the long term. Those businesses focusing on economic perspectives also need to integrate community and environmental perspectives; reciprocally, those businesses focusing on community benefits also need to consider environmental issues relating both to the community and their business. In this way, there is a greater likelihood that the business will be sustainable over the long term, whereas if other perspectives are not considered, long-term business viability is unlikely.

Environmental destruction

Operators expressed that poaching is an issue in a number of destinations, as well as slash-and-burn agriculture and other practices, which destroy forests and other habitats. These unsustainable land use practices are greatly affecting the quality of some destinations. Operators could improve environmental conditions at destinations by involving more local communities, bringing economic alternatives, and by this way providing incentives to preserve the environment; however, without government support it is difficult for them to tackle these problems alone.

2. CONCLUSIONS AND RECOMMENDATIONS

Separate policies are required for ecotourism, distinguishing it from mainstream tourism operations

Mechanisms should be developed to facilitate start-up funding for small tourism operations.

Governments or other agencies at the destinations should examine ways to provide assistance to ecotourism operations researching and introducing new packages. As an example, the Malaysia Tourism Commission has cost-shared advertising of new packages for a certain time period, which benefited both the operator and the destination.

It was recommended that NGOs should play a stronger role in providing up to date research information (destinations or markets) to operators.

Involve those who are part of a problem in the solution

It is recommended that all stakeholders should be involved in solving ecotourism-related problems, especially those who are part of a problem. For example, in India, there has been recent interaction between poachers, NGOs, forest officials, and the ecotourism facilitator.

Take an integrated approach

Ecotourism operators should take an integrated operational perspective from the outset. This will involve: protecting the environment that visitors wish to experience; providing local jobs so that the environment is not endangered by unsustainable local use (e.g., slash and burn agriculture); providing desired visitor interactions with local people; and focusing on business profitability to sustain the other objectives.

It was suggested that creative businesses can create profit streams within their operations through applying sustainability principles. For example, in Maho Bay Camps (US Virgin Islands), sustainable technologies contribute to cost savings as well as to guest satisfaction. Waste aluminium, glass and plastic is used in craft workshops and converted into products for sale, thus employing locals, providing guest entertainment, generating revenues, and removing waste from the island.

It is recommended that public-private partnerships be encouraged as a method of assisting business start-ups, as well as meeting joint objectives, involving business, government, NGOs, or development agencies.

Provide adequate remuneration to local employees at destinations

It was recommended that local people be paid significant wages by operators. This helps ensure ongoing reliability and quality performance, and acts as a model for others. For example, in India, slash and burn agriculture is reducing, unused cargo boats are being converted to viable house-boat operations, and poachers are being transformed into respected, well-paid employees.

The portion of total consumer package costs which destinations receive should be critically examined, since at present the average percentage is relatively low.

FORUM 2: DEVELOPMENT COOPERATION FOR ECOTOURISM

The development cooperation forum concentrated on the role of development agencies in providing financial and technical support for ecotourism.

Most of the speakers were representing international or bilaterial donor agencies or consultancies, including: GEF/ UNDP Small Grants Programme, SNV Netherlands, Swiss Association for International Cooperation, German Technical Cooperation Agency (GTZ), and the Inter-American Development Bank, besides the World Tourism Organization. The Minister of Tourism from Angola provided a recipient country perspective.

1. Issues Discueed

The need for international cooperation

The WTO and government representatives emphasised the crucial role of international cooperation in promoting a sustainable development of ecotourism, particularly in less developed countries.

The WTO, as the UNDP's executing agency for tourism development, is a catalyst for generating finance and can organise international cooperation. With its technical expertise

WTO can provide guidelines and solutions to achieve an appropriate balance between the economic development of tourism and sustainability. Thus WTO can facilitate the development of new types of international cooperation, motivating other agencies towards a common objective with public/private sector partnerships.

This need for regional cooperation on ecotourism projects, particularly in Africa, was pointed out by Angola's Minister of Tourism. An example of this kind of support was given through the RETOSA / SADEC tourism projects.

Speakers looked in turn at issues relating to bilateral, regional and international cooperation.

New objectives for international cooperation

There has been a notable change in the way development agencies are treating tourism projects. Whereas previously there was an emphasis on the quantity of tourism development and revenue generated, there is now greater concern for the quality of the end result and a range of social and environmental as well as purely economic objectives. The revision of tourism master plans has reflected this change of emphasis. This has led to a focus on the capacity of local communities to engage in, and benefit from, tourism.

A growing number of players

In the past development cooperation was mainly provided by a small number of international organisations dealing with states at a government level. Now there are many more agencies providing relevant assistance, including NGOs, regional organisations, bilateral aid schemes and private sector bodies. Some of these new forms of cooperation are particularly appropriate for ecotourism as they are often focused on generating self-help in communities (e.g. the approach of SNV Netherlands).

New structures and levels for cooperation

International cooperation itself has changed. Cooperation is now located in an inter-regional context and its focus is on decentralised programmes. This regional cooperation is well adapted to ecotourism. A new priority is given to training and capacity building, as key issues to strengthen ecotourism, and to providing support for indigenous organisations.

2. CONCLUSIONS AND RECOMMENDATIONS

Provide more support for capacity building

The recognition of the need to support capacity building, mentioned above, is important. A further focus on this in all assistance programmes should be encouraged.

Ensure that projects assisted are viable

Too frequently in the past assistance has been provided for ecotourism projects which may not be viable in the long term, after assistance has come to a end. More attention should be given to feasibility assessment.

Make sure that local communities are involved and benefiting

Development agencies should pay attention to organisational and participatory structures in recipient destinations. It is very important that there is local participation in programmes supported. A number of comments made stressed the importance of organisational strengthening and the role of local authorities.

Raise the profile of ecotourism within development agencies

In general, development agencies are still paying too little attention to ecotourism. They should be encouraged to develop strategies for their work in this sector. This should apply to individual agencies and collectively, as there is a need for more coordination between agencies in their work in this area.

Provide a range of levels of financial support

In the past financial assistance has tended to be provided in large amounts, relevant to larger scale projects. There is now a need for a full range of types and levels of assistance, including programmes suitable for very small enterprises and community-based initiatives, and for medium sized projects which are locally owned, yet with significant costs as well as local impacts.

5. PREPARING AND ADOPTING THE FINAL DECLARATION

The Summit closed with a final plenary session which addressed the text of the Quebec Declaration on Ecotourism.

An initial draft of the declaration had been circulated to delegates at the start of the Summit. All delegates were invited to submit written comments on the text, including specific recommendations for amendments, improvements and additions. A total of 160 written comments were received by the deadline at the end of the second full day of the Summit. WTO and UNEP also received verbal representation from a number of individuals and groups, including representatives of indigenous communities and of NGOs working with such communities. All these comments were carefully assessed by WTO and UNEP and taken into consideration in the preparation of a second draft.

The second draft of the declaration was circulated to delegates at the start of the third day. This draft formed the basis of the debate during the final plenary session. Many delegates made further comments and recommendations on it from the floor. These interventions were recorded. All of them were assessed and used by WTO and UNEP to produce a final text of the declaration on the day following the Summit.

Index